Ethnicity: anthropological constructions

Ethnicity has been a key concept in anthropology and sociology for many years yet people still seem uncertain as to its meaning, its relevance and its relationship to other concepts such as 'race' and nationalism. In *Ethnicity: Anthropological Constructions* the major anthropological and sociological approaches to ethnicity, covering much of the significant literature and the leading authors, are outlined clearly and concisely.

The term 'ethnicity' has been used to describe human social interaction, particularly in relation to groups that would previously have been described as 'tribes', and to minority migrant groups and their 'host' societies. Rather than simply outlining the situations in which ethnicity has been deemed to be important, this book constructs an intellectual history of the idea, examining how it has been fashioned by generations of anthropologists and sociologists.

Certain classic works are discussed and particular attention is paid to the considerable literature on ethnic minorities in Britain and the United States. Initially, much of this writing was driven by social concerns over immigration and the 'race problem' or 'colour bar'. Later writing reacts to these concerns in two ways: either by refocusing attention on the issue of nationalism and its relationship to the ethnicity of dominant groups, or by rejecting the concept of ethnicity altogether and replacing it with more ambiguous concepts such as 'locality' or 'identity'.

While ethnicity has become an over-used concept in the anthropological vocabulary, it is finding increasing use in public language and thought.

Marcus Banks is Lecturer in Social Anthropology, University of Oxford and Fellow of Wolfson College, Oxford.

Ethnicity: anthropological constructions

Marcus Banks

London and New York

First published 1996
by Routledge
11 New Fetter Lane, London EC4P 4EE

Simultaneously published in the USA and Canada
by Routledge
29 West 35th Street, New York, NY 10001

Typeset in Times by
Ponting–Green Publishing Services, Chesham, Bucks
Printed and bound in Great Britain by
Mackays of Chatham PLC, Chatham, Kent

British Library Cataloguing in Publication Data
A catalogue record for this book is available from the
British Library

Library of Congress Cataloguing in Publication Data
A catalogue record for this book has been requested

ISBN   0–415–07800–8 (hbk)
ISBN   0–415–07801–6 (pbk)

Contents

Acknowledgements

The circumstances that led to the writing of this book are outlined in Chapter 1. Here I wish to express my warm and profound thanks to a number of people who helped me along the way: to Sue Benson, Esther Goody and Caroline Humphrey who first introduced me to some of the key issues; to Chris Fuller, David Gellner, Graham McFarlane and Pete Wade for helpful discussions and for providing a number of key references; to Peter Rivière for showing me the piece on Rastafarians used in Chapter 6; and to Mike Morris, Librarian of the Tylor Library, Oxford, for cheerfully dealing with my many requests and for tracking down a number of sources. Two people nobly read the entire manuscript before publication: to Abner Cohen and Richard Jenkins I am more grateful than I can say. Monica Laptoiu and I co-authored the section on 'ethnic cleansing' in Chapter 6, but her contribution extends well beyond this in terms of helping me think through the issues. At Routledge, Heather Gibson and Margaret Conn were patient, helpful and supportive, for all of which I am grateful. Of course, while all those named above deserve credit for any strengths, any weaknesses or infelicities are my own. Finally, a debt must be acknowledged to Barrie Thomas, Anna Rayne and David Zeitlyn for providing constant support, encouragement and companionship during the times when I thought the book would never be finished. Anna also very nobly proof-read part of the finished text.

This book carries no formal dedication but I wrote it in memory and with hope. In memory of my sister, Merril, who began teaching in the East End of London when I was still a child, and who described to me from experience and observation many of the processes outlined in this book, though I had never heard of 'ethnicity' at the time. And in hope that the terrifying conflicts which are touched on in Chapter 6 and which so often invoke the language of 'ethnicity' can be addressed and resolved so that Merril's daughter Tessa Jane will know a world of less hostility and bigotry. The social sciences, anthropology among them, sometimes seem to have fanned as many conflicts as they have attempted to resolve. Within its narrow compass this book seeks to resolve little, except perhaps some academic confusions and cross-talk. But I hope it provides a starting point for anthropologists and others braver than I to attempt to dismantle the spurious ideological underpinnings of 'ethnic' conflict.

Oxford, June 1995

Chapter 1

Introduction: basic positions and the life of an idea

> Quite suddenly, with little comment or ceremony, ethnicity is an ubiquitous presence. Even a brief glance through titles of books and monographs over the past few years indicates a steadily accelerating acceptance and application of the terms 'ethnicity' and 'ethnic' to refer to what was before often subsumed under 'culture', 'cultural', or 'tribal'.
>
> (Ronald Cohen 1978: 379)

Despite Cohen's confident assertion it now seems clear, some fifteen years later, that he was describing a rather transient phenomenon. Certainly, books and monographs are still published that contain the key terms 'ethnicity' and 'ethnic' in their titles, but my impression is that they are less common than they were in the heyday of the 1970s. Anthropological interests have moved on since then and new topics and theoretical interests have seized the imagination. Ethnicity is not necessarily relevant to these new interests or, if it is, it has yet to be demonstrated.

Yet ethnicity continues to fascinate and perplex, particularly students of anthropology who sometimes feel bewildered by the vast and disjointed range of possible reading recommended to them. The purpose of this book is not to offer a startling or radical new interpretation of ethnicity, but to attempt to summarize and link much of the important work that has already been done. The linkage is not always easy. A number of disciplines have contributed to our understanding of ethnicity – anthropology, sociology and social geography are the major ones, but there have also been contributions from social psychology, sociobiology, social work and educational theory, and even literary studies. I could not possibly hope to cover all these disciplines and my major focus is therefore on anthropology and sociology.

The area I could perhaps have covered but didn't is sociobiology. Here there is only one author of real significance, Pierre Van den Berghe. Van den Berghe himself has provided a handy summary and overview of his work and the debate it has caused (1986), together with a significant book-length study (1981). Other contributions on the relationship between biology and ethnicity can be found in Kirkwood *et al.* (1983) and Chapman (1993a). It is always possible that such biological approaches will come to assume a position of dominance within anthropology, but for the moment they constitute a rather self-contained sub-field. The exception to this is the public, rather than the academic, discourse on ethnicity. I touch on this briefly at points through the book and have a more substantial discussion in Chapter 6.

WHY ANOTHER BOOK ON ETHNICITY?

Even within social anthropology the linkage between various approaches to the study of ethnicity is not always obvious. Even a cursory glance at the literature reveals that there are several authors – past and present – who have written in apparent ignorance of the work of other authors who claim to be writing about the same issue. One occasionally gets the sense that the wheel has been invented several times over. I will return to the issue of parallel strands of scholarship below, but first a brief account of my own motivation in writing this book.

As an undergraduate anthropology student in the 1970s I had learned about ethnicity from Sue Benson (author of *Ambiguous ethnicity* [1981]) and Esther Goody (among other things, the co-author of an article in the James Watson volume, *Between two cultures* [1977a]). They had taught me about Frederik Barth and from them and others I learned about the Manchester School's work in southern Africa (both discussed in Chapter 2), but I was also stimulated by their discussions of minority groups overseas or as ethnic enclaves within wider nation states. From Caroline Humphrey I learned about the Soviet Union and the 'nationality problem' (also discussed in Chapter 2).

Influenced by all three I went on to doctoral studies, originally concentrating on a migrant Gujarati religious group in Britain, although I later went to India and studied members of the same group there. Gradually, Frederik Barth and the Manchester School faded from my memory as I began to read studies of Asian and other minority migrant groups in Britain and to concentrate on the 'race and ethnic relations' literature (discussed in Chapter 3). I had no difficulty in describing at least part of my work as the study of 'ethnicity'; before I had finished my doctorate I attended a conference on 'Gujarati ethnicity' which was entirely concerned with overseas Gujaratis, there being not one paper on Gujaratis in Gujarat. I had not sat down to consider what the kind of 'ethnicity' I was now involved with had to do with the kind of 'ethnicity' that Barth was describing. Nor, it seemed, had any of the other participants at the Gujarati ethnicity symposium – certainly none of the papers referenced Barth.

In October 1987 I came to Oxford to take up a temporary post in anthropology, following the sudden death of one of the university's many distinguished anthropologists, Edwin Ardener. Shortly after I arrived, a one-day symposium on 'Ethnographic approaches to ethnicity' was organized by some of Edwin's former colleagues and students and, as his replacement and as one who listed 'ethnicity' as an interest, I was encouraged to attend. As the day wore on I became more and more ill at ease. I was reminded of an episode from my doctoral fieldwork in Britain when I had gone to attend an event organized by 'my' group but had mistakenly entered the wrong room where an entirely different Gujarati religious group was holding a meeting. It was at the start of my fieldwork and I knew few faces and had little grasp of Gujarati, but I struggled for an hour or more to make sense of what was going on before my mistake began to dawn on me. I was wondering if I should explain myself or simply slip out quietly when a member of 'my' group put his head round the door and rescued me. I had a similar feeling at the Oxford symposium. I recognized some of the words (particularly 'ethnicity') and had heard of some of the participants, but I couldn't seem to get a handle on what they were talking about. Undoubtedly, the fact that I was new to Oxford and its ways contributed to my feeling of being in the wrong place, but there was no one this time to rescue me.

It was when I encountered this third kind of 'ethnicity' at the Oxford symposium (discussed in Chapter 5) that I began to think that there might be some crossed wires somewhere. This book is an attempt to uncross those wires and to disentangle several strains of anthropological discourse on ethnicity. Even within the anthropological literature, I have chosen to discuss only a few works. For the most part these are the most popular and well-read works and therefore will be familiar – at least by title – to an undergraduate or new reader. This book is not, therefore, a comprehensive catalogue of everything anthropologists have had to say about ethnicity. It is instead an attempt to draw a basic ground plan which will allow readers, and particularly students new to the discipline, to place other texts with 'ethnicity' in the title (and – as I discuss in Chapter 5 – those without) that they may come across.

BASIC POSITIONS

Before I outline the approach that will govern the structure of this book, let us start with a selection of definitions and comments, culled from a wide spread of literature and written from a variety of theoretical approaches:

> Ethnicity may be evaluated almost entirely upon a biological basis or upon purely social characteristics. Negroes tend to be at the first extreme, since they are most physically variant of all the groups in the community, and the Irish at the other extreme since they are most like the native white stock.
>
> (Warner and Lunt 1942: 73)

> The term 'ethnicity' refers to strife between . . . ethnic groups, in the course of which people stress their identity and exclusiveness.
>
> (Abner Cohen 1969: 4)

> [Ethnic identity] is imperative, in that it cannot be disregarded and temporarily set aside by other definitions of the situation.
>
> (Barth 1969b: 17)

> [E]thnicity is a social identity characterized by fictive kinship.
>
> (Yelvington 1991: 168)

> The phenomenon of ethnicity is evidently much more complex than earlier analyses allowed.
>
> (Epstein 1978: 5)

> One senses a term still on the move.
>
> (Glazer and Moynihan 1975b: 1)

> [Ethnicity] is a term that half-heartedly aspires to describe phenomena that involve everybody, and that nevertheless has settled in the vocabulary as a marker of strangeness and unfamiliarity.
>
> (Chapman et al. 1989: 16)

> . . . it may be that 'ethnicity' is so vague, and so variously used,

a term that its definition can only be stipulative and arguments against its definition only sterile.

(Anthony Cohen 1985: 107)

In sum, ethnicity labels the visibility of that aspect of the identity formation process that is produced by and subordinated to nationalist programs and plans – plans intent on creating putative homogeneity out of heterogeneity through the appropriate processes of a transformist hegemony.

(B. Williams 1989: 439)

'Ethnicity' and 'race' are terms which cover many sins. Both terms suggest biological relationships between those identified with one or another group or classed together in one category; both terms suggest that there are social and sometimes cultural dimensions.

(Zenner 1985: 117)

. . . a collection of rather simplistic and obvious statements about boundaries, otherness, goals and achievements, being and identity, descent and classification, that has been constructed as much by the anthropologist as by the subject.

(this book, Chapter 7, p. 190)

These are eleven of literally dozens of quotations I could have used. They exemplify several of the difficulties I experienced in trying to write this book, and several of the issues raised in the following chapters. The first quotation is really only of historical interest, as it is possibly the first use of the word 'ethnicity' in the sense we understand it today (the *OED* makes reference to a rare earlier meaning of 'heathen superstition' from 1772). After the initial confidence of the first two or three quotations, it is startling how quickly and often the term comes to be doubted. By the 1980s it is not so much a term 'on the move', as Glazer and Moynihan describe, but a term under fire. The two penultimate quotations sound a slightly more positive note by seeking to understand ethnicity within the context of two other terms with which it has come to be associated – 'race' and nationalism. Chapters 3, 4 and 5 deal with these associations in more detail. The final quotation, taken from the last page of this book, is not so much a definition as a comment and not, I admit, a particularly illuminating one. I won't enlarge on it here, and it should be read in the context of the book as a whole (just as all the other quotations should, of course, be read in their own proper contexts).

I selected quotations that specifically talked of 'ethnicity' – the quality of being ethnic, not of the adjective ethnic itself. Is there any point in distinguishing sharply between 'ethnicity' and 'ethnic group', if we assume like many authors (for example, Abner Cohen 1969: 4; Chapman *et al.* 1989: 11) that the former is what the latter has or expresses? Certainly there are a number of earlier writings (for example, those of the early Manchester School discussed in Chapter 2) which make use of 'ethnic (group)' without feeling the need for an associated abstract noun, and, as we shall see in Chapter 6, it is the adjective and not the noun that has largely entered public discourse. There are also writings on ethnicity which make little or no reference to an associated adjective or which are dismissive of the whole concept of 'ethnic groups' (for example, Jenkins [1986]). It is not my intention in this book to cover the descriptive literature on 'ethnic groups', and although I am forced to use terms such as 'group', 'population' and even 'ethnic group' on occasion I am wary of the sociological reductionism involved. I do not think that ethnicity is simply a quality of groups, and for the most part I tend to treat it as an analytical tool, devised and used by academics.

THIS BOOK: STRUCTURE AND CONTENT

The book is organized into five main chapters, together with this introduction and a brief conclusion. In Chapter 2 I discuss some of the earliest and most influential writings on ethnicity. These writings conform most closely to the traditional anthropological paradigm of a European or American anthropologist travelling to a remote or exotic part of the world (that is, remote or exotic to the anthropologist) to study the people who live there. The exception to this pattern comes with a group of Soviet anthropologists whom I consider mostly for their contribution to theory rather than practice. The ethnographic focus in this chapter is broad, but concentrates mostly on Pakistan, the Soviet Union and south-central Africa. In Chapters 3 and 4 I turn to a consideration of a rather different literature, one that has been created as much by sociologists as anthropologists. The ethnographic focus here is on 'ethnic minorities' in the United States and Britain. These chapters introduce the subject of 'race' and its relationship to ethnicity.

In Chapter 5 I introduce another new theme – nationalism – and again examine its relationship to ethnicity. The ethnographic focus here is on the sub-national populations of Europe. Chapter 6 extends the discussion of the previous chapters by examining constructions of 'race', ethnicity and nationalism in everyday language and behaviour, away from the analytical constructions of academics. I present two case studies in this chapter: the first looks at the meanings and uses of the phrase 'ethnic cleansing' in press reports of the Bosnian conflict; the second outlines a dispute over multi-cultural education policy in Britain in the 1980s and again draws upon press reports. Finally, Chapter 7 offers some brief comments on thinking about ethnicity as an academic construct.

In a wide-ranging survey of literature such as this the material could be organized in a variety of ways. I could, for example, have taken the ethnography as my starting point and grouped my discussions around ethnographic focal points – either geographical (all the literature on Africa, followed by all the literature on Europe, and so on), or somehow topic focused (all the situations where there is ecological interdependency, followed by all the situations where there is economic competition, and so on). A second approach would be to group the literature according to the author's theoretical perspective – all the literature on primordiality, followed by all the literature on instrumentality, and so on.

What I have actually done is to group the literature by related clusters of authors, not ethnographic situations or ideas. In fact, as will become evident, this also serves to cluster ideas and ethnographic situations to some extent and this is partly my point. Authors influence each other, particularly when a dominant author tacitly or explicitly acts as the focal point of a 'school' of associated students and colleagues. Even when this is not the case, certain authors tend to exert a kind of gravitational force that attracts other authors who may agree or violently disagree.

By taking the scholars – anthropologists and sociologists for the most part – who have written about ethnicity (and who have also tended to share ideas, and work in similar ethnographic situations) as my main organizing principle, I hope to demonstrate that a number of wheels appear to have been independently invented, and conversely that there is no necessary coherence between all the positions on ethnicity that have been advanced. Occasionally as a scholar you read another author advancing a position quite familiar to you (for example, that nationalism was 'invented' in eighteenth-century Europe) and then citing an authority you have never heard of in support of this claim. Surely, you say to yourself, so-and-so would be a much more obvious reference. This is particularly apparent when you are reading across disciplinary boundaries, but even within your own discipline you can be surprised in this way. There are several reasons why A could come to cite B's work (A pulled B's book off the library shelf by chance, B is A's mother-in-law), but it also seems fair to assume that there could be some intellectual or institutional link between them (A was B's student, A and B were students under C or can trace a link back to founding ancestor X). It also seems fair to assume (indeed, I know this to be the case) that there are several authors who would never in any circumstance cite the work of a specific colleague, even if they are acquainted with it. The world of academia can be just as dirty as the world of politics.

In what follows I have tried to be as catholic as possible, discussing authors I consider intellectually thin (if influential) as well as those with something to say, discussing the work of those with whom I have intellectual, institutional or affective links, as well as those who are complete strangers to me. Doubtless those with a more distanced eye than mine will see biases in my scope, coverage and balance. All I can say is that as far as I am aware I have not excluded any author or group of authors out of maliciousness or in order deliberately to distort the picture I am presenting. My aim is to present the biography of an idea (if I may put it that way), and the life of that idea has been lived out through the work of a number of influential authors (and not in the lives of the people they have studied).

One result of this is that the book is rather short on examples and long on abstractions, all bread and no jam. Apart from a couple of brief and, I hope, original and interesting chunks of data in Chapter 6, my aim is simply to present a reasoned discussion of much of the substantial literature on ethnicity produced by anthropologists. The reader will quickly see that I have devoted more space to some ideas and their authors than others, and that I am clearly more sympathetic to some positions than others. It would be impossible to cover all the literature I have dealt with in some totally objective, even-handed way. It would also be unbearably dull for the reader, and be an exercise little more fruitful than reading a telephone directory or a library catalogue.

None the less, I have tried to concentrate single-mindedly on theoretical discussions of ethnicity and related subjects (such as 'race' and nationalism), with as few examples as possible. Some anthropologists would argue that this is impossible: theory and data are symbiotically linked and neither is worth much without the other.

I agree with this at one level, and would urge the reader to turn to the books that I refer to in order to see the theoretical issues discussed in their ethnographic context. I also sketch in as much of this context as I feel necessary in what follows. However, the problem with loading the text with too many examples or too full discussions of other people's field data is that the ideas become more and more embedded in local detail and variation until the focus of interest – ethnicity in this case – dissolves and is lost.

Between the covers of this book my interest is not in the 'actual' social conditions in which ethnicity is expressed, but in the theoretical framework of ethnicity that each author claims her or his data fleshes out. I want to pull each discussion out and hold it up for comparative scrutiny. It is entirely possible that by doing so 'ethnicity' will be seen to be a flimsy, ephemeral thing, of little substance or value. If so, then I don't believe that to be a fruitless project. For one thing, it ought to reassure the large number of students and more senior academics I have met who 'worry' about ethnicity: what is it? how to define it? which is the 'best' theory of it? and so on. It should also reassure anthropologists that a symbiosis of theory and data collection must continue. But it ought also to alert them to the fact that there are some well-worn tools in the intellectual tool-kit and that some of them, particularly ethnicity, are becoming blunt, either through over-use, or perhaps because they weren't very well fashioned in the first place.

So, this is not a book for reading. It is a book about reading, a book for consulting, a starting place before going on to read the original sources and, for the potential fieldworker, before going out to try to find ethnicity in the field.

TERMINOLOGY

In this work I have tried to tread a careful path, noting the cases in which a particular writer insists on the strict definition of some term, and yet recognizing that other writers (including myself on occasion) are happy to let the same term indicate a fairly broad semantic range. A good example of this would be the term 'ethnic identity', which one of the authors discussed in Chapter 2 spends most of his work defining and refining (Epstein 1978), and yet which I use in a more general sense of the feeling of belonging to some ethnically defined group (a feeling which may be subjective on the part of a particular individual, or my own shorthand way of referring to a position that a writer attributes to an individual). The term 'ethnicity' itself, as we have seen above, stubbornly resists definition and my own position, which I do not wish to stress too strongly, is that the term is of increasingly limited utility. For the course of this book, I use it simply as an identifying label to subsume the numerous literatures I am dealing with.

'Race' is a more problematic term, partly because of the emotiveness of both term and concept in contemporary popular discourse. I note in Chapter 3 that most social scientists are agreed that it lacks biological or scientific validity in human social contexts, but is none the less a powerful folk term. I try to restrict my use of it to mirror what other writers have said and trust that the particular context will give the word short-term salience. I use the term so frequently, however, that I shall breach normal convention and use it without quotation marks from here on.

In Chapters 3 and 4 I also use the terms 'black' and 'white' quite frequently. Again, these are to be understood as terms of sociological, not biological (or, for that matter, chromatic), categorization. Again, I use the terms without inverted commas and, like race, the reader should understand that they are provisional terms, much contested and highly misleading on occasions.

Chapter 2

Ethnicity unearthed

This chapter serves to introduce three significant approaches to the study of ethnicity, each of which in some sense 'discovered' ethnicity as a new approach. The chapter also touches more briefly upon a number of later approaches to similar or related ethnographic situations. The factor which unites all the works considered is that, by and large, the subjects of ethnographic enquiry are considered indigenous to the countries or regions where they were studied. In several cases, these ethnographic subjects would have been considered as members of 'tribes' by earlier generations of anthropologists and so this chapter also examines the shift from 'tribe' to 'ethnic group'.

There is, however, no strong set of linkages between the three major groups of authors I discuss (Frederik Barth and his colleagues, the members of the Manchester School and the Soviet ethnos theorists), despite the fact that all were working and publishing at around the same time. The work of each group, however, represents an attempt to break with earlier paradigms. Frederik Barth and his colleagues, and the Manchester School anthropologists, all sought ways out of the impasse that they felt structural-functional anthropology had led them to, while the Soviet ethnos theorists tried to side-step the macro-historical approach that had dominated Soviet ethnology.

BOUNDARY AND CONTENT – THE VIEW FROM NORWAY

The shift from 'tribe' to 'ethnic group' will be examined in more detail later in the chapter, in the section which deals with some of the earlier literature on rural-urban migration within Africa.

However, the Manchester School anthropologists who wrote most of the studies I will consider in that section initially had curiously little impact on mainstream social anthropology's discussions of ethnicity. Instead, it was a Norwegian anthropologist who, in 1969, published a book that was to form the backbone of much anthropological teaching on ethnicity through the 1970s and into the 1980s.

Frederik Barth's edited collection *Ethnic groups and boundaries* (1969a) was the outcome of a conference held in Oslo in 1967. The book contains seven short essays by Scandinavian anthropologists, each concerned with 'the social organization of culture difference', and analysing data from Norway, north-east Africa, Mexico, Pakistan and Laos. The chief impact, however, was made not so much by the studies themselves as by Barth's introductory essay.

Above all, Barth tried to show that ethnic groups are socially constructed (subject to environmental constraints) and that the content of the group – in terms of both 'culture' and personnel – has no a priori existence or stability. That is to say, it is not so much the group which endures as the *idea* of the group. Moreover, he claimed that the physical and ideological contents of the group should not be investigated in isolation – this would give a misleading impression and tend to confirm notions of stability and internal, bounded coherence. Instead, attention should be focused on the *boundaries* of the group.

Barth begins his introduction by outlining the main features that he thought characterized the identification of such groups in earlier anthropological literature – biologically self-perpetuating, bounded, sharing fundamental cultural values, forming a field of communication and interaction, conscious of a category identity which is recognized by others (Barth 1969a: 10–11) – and aims a criticism at the root of all such descriptions. These features, he feels, are assumed a priori and are implicitly assumed to be contingent upon external ecological factors which in turn are then reified by the group into internal cultural factors. Barth's main contribution is to urge a shift away from discussions of the content of ethnic identity through considerations of ethnic markers such as dress, food, language, and so on, towards a consideration of the boundaries that mark the limits of such contents. With regard to such boundaries he makes two salient points. First, that boundaries persist despite a flow of personnel and information across them (see, for example, Haaland's [1969] contribution to the volume); secondly – and as a corollary to the first – that such groups cannot exist in isolation but only in contrast to other such groups (see, for example, Siverts' contribution to the volume). That is, the boundary does not bound 'something' off from nothingness, but rather it distinguishes between two (or more) 'somethings' (Barth 1969a: 14–15).

Barth does not ignore the cultural content of the group, though he considers this to be of two types – diacritical markers such as dress and language, and 'value orientations' such as morality and other social norms (1969a: 14). But he argues that it is folly to try to typologize groups on the basis of lists of contents. Such lists are not finite in length and social actors will choose, or enumerate to visiting anthropologists, features which legitimate their location and status in any given situation. This idea of choice (or at least variation) in the expression of ethnic identity is one that is generally known as 'situational ethnicity' (see Okamura 1981) and one that is endorsed by several of the volume's contributors. We will see below that it is also an important feature (though not necessarily named as such) in the work of many anthropologists, particularly Clyde Mitchell. Looking more closely, however, it appears that Barth endorses this idea only in as much as it helps us to understand the *form* an ethnic identity may take. For Barth, ethnicity is a superordinate identity, one which transcends or is at least equivalent to all other identities (such as those based on gender, or status) and as such his position is closer to that usually known as primordialism – ethnicity as a permanent and essential condition: '[t]he constraints on a person's behaviour which spring from his ethnic identity . . . tend to be absolute' (1969a: 17).

As Barth's work has been very influential I wish to consider an actual example in some detail, drawn from his work in the mid-1950s among the Pathan population of western Pakistan and Afghanistan. The data relate to a large population spread out over a territory of some 180,000 km^2. This territory is ecologically diverse and straddles two nation states. Moreover, the Pathan population is in continuous contact with other, non-Pathan groups and is economically heterogeneous, including settled agriculturists and landlords, pastoral nomads, urban migrants and nomadic traders. While all Pathans may know some other Pathans – that is, there is a presumed network of intercommunication within the group – no local group knows all the other groups. The problem is simply stated: given that there are so many people, spread out over such a large area in such diversity, how can they all lay claim to the same ethnic identity? In addressing this problem Barth requires the reader to take much on trust, claiming as he does that 'Pathans constitute a large, highly self-aware ethnic group' (1969c: 117). He has clearly not tramped the length and breadth of the territory to verify his claim of shared identity and indeed gives some evidence to the contrary at the level of self-identification. For example, he reports that he could get the Southern Pathans only 'grudgingly to admit' that the Northern Swat Pathan could be considered as Pathan (1969b: 13).

In the Pathans' view, what serves to link the diverse groups is that they all share certain 'cultural traits' which they agree constitute some corpus of features necessary to considering oneself as Pathan. These features include patrilineal descent from a common ancestor, shared religion (Islam) and a vague category of Pathan custom, which includes use of a common language, a common oral literature and a set of attributes which revolve around masculinity – aggressiveness, autonomy, equality, and so forth (1969c: 119). However, this is the Pathano-centric view and Barth proposes his own observer-centric view. This consists of three arenas of activity: hospitality, holding councils of equals and the seclusion of women (1969c: 120–3). Both the Pathan view and the Barthian view, however, constitute a catalogue of features, the very approach to ethnicity that Barth claims to be rejecting. Moreover, all the features are shared with groups that interact with the Pathans causing the salience of Pathan ethnicity to seem extremely weak. In fact, the only principle of inclusion within the Pathan fold seems to be putative descent from the common ancestor.

Thus it is that Barth turns to examine the marginal areas on the frontiers of Pathan country in an attempt to investigate what takes place on the boundaries between the Pathan and other groups (an approach taken by many of the contributors to *Ethnic groups and boundaries*). In doing so Barth reifies a correlation between the physical boundaries of a population and the conceptual boundary of its ethnic identity.

At the southern extent of 'Pathan country', where Pathans are organized politically by lineage councils, they are faced with centralized Baluchi tribes, along a 'clearly demarcated territorial border'. The border is marked by knowledge and custom, not topology or ecology – it is an ethnic boundary, not a physical one (Barth 1969c: 123). According to Barth, the Baluchis are gradually moving northwards, encroaching on Pathan lands. At the same time, there is an intermittent flow of people from the Pathan group to the Baluchi group (but not vice versa) (1969c: 124). This flow seems to be mainly made up of adult males who reclassify themselves, rather than – for example – women who change identity on marriage.

Barth does not appear to link these two facts, stating them independently of each other and yet one could clearly assume some sort of linkage. According to Barth the Baluchi tribes are organized by a 'contract of political submission of commoners under chiefs and sub-chiefs . . . [which] freely allows for reorganisation and assimilation of personnel' (1969c: 124, citing Pehrson 1966). By contrast, the local Pathan political organization does not allow for the assimilation of personnel. Pathans can only be Pathans by descent, and thus assimilation can only be of clients, which is not necessarily desirable to would-be clients, nor, claims Barth, to the Pathans who would receive only a small surplus from client agriculturists in return for onerous political patronage. Thus the locally constituted Pathan ethnicity does not allow for personnel incorporation, while the locally constituted Baluchi ethnicity does.

Having identified the mechanism for incorporation, Barth turns his attention to the causes. These he identifies as the misplacement of persons owing to war, accident or crime (1969c: 124). That is to say, people who have become socially dislocated. But why should the proud Pathans 'choose' to become Baluchi? Barth says it is because they have already become alienated from their Pathan identity, or rather that their dislocation has placed them in a subordinate position to the rest of Pathan society, a position which is at odds with local Pathan values of equality and honour. The paradox can only be resolved by self-reassignment as Baluchi, the 'nearest' status to hand and one which does not impute shame to the position of being a client commoner. Thus Pathans are unwillingly or helplessly 'evicted' from Pathan ethnic identity but exercise agency in choosing to become Baluchi (1969c: 125).

One of the major criticisms of Barth's work with the Pathan (particularly his monograph, *Political leadership among the Swat Pathans* [1959]) has been of his transactionalist stress on free will and choice (see, for example, Asad 1972). In the original monograph a tension can be perceived between elements of choice, in, for example, the actions of landless labourers in 'choosing' a landlord, and elements of constraint – the caste system, for example. Here too, in the discussion of ethnic reassignment, we find individuals being constrained (by being squeezed out of Pathan-ness) and exercising choice (by becoming Baluchi). Such a description, however, serves to reify 'Pathan' and 'Baluchi' as primordial identities sharing equal but different positions in a non-stratified poly-ethnic system.

This 'poly-ethnic' society is Barth's version of earlier debates on the 'plural society' (see, for example, Furnival 1939 for a classic study, and M. G. Smith 1986 for a more recent assessment), a view which holds that while one group among several in a region may be numerically, politically or economically dominant, all the groups will 'share certain value orientations and scales, on the basis of which they can arrive at judgements of hierarchy' (Barth 1969b: 27). That is to say, stratification and hierarchy are consensual processes in which all parties – even those who appear to lose out by such processes – collude. It is a view shared by several of the contributors to *Ethnic groups and boundaries*, in particular Siverts (1969) and Izikowitz (1969).

In the Pathan/Baluchi case one could, however, advance an alternative explanation as to why Pathans become Baluchis. The Baluchi majority within which the displaced Pathan becomes incorporated is politically the stronger party – demonstrated by the process of northern land encroachment – and is thus in a position to categorize the incoming Pathan. That is to say, the displaced Pathan has no more choice about becoming Baluchi than he did at being evicted from the Pathan polity. He is labelled by the Baluchi majority and is too weak to resist. Barth states that 'large parts of some Baluch tribes acknowledge Pathan origin' (1969c: 124), but it is clear that they are powerless to assert it. This appears to be in the interests of the Baluchis for it would be politically dangerous for them to allow these once displaced persons to retain their original identity. Even if as individuals they are weak, there are strong Pathans to the north with whom they could identity and – at worst – for whom they could act as some kind of fifth column force. On the other hand, as Baluchi identity is not incompatible with inequality, and as the Baluchi tribes are presented by Barth as inherently expansionist, it makes sense to classify the incomers as Baluchi.

This interpretation does not necessarily invalidate Barth's, but it places a greater stress on political opportunism and very real factors of power and domination in place of Barth's more subjective (and certainly Pathano-centric) view of identities being exchanged in a free market-place of identity choice. In fact, of the contributors to *Ethnic groups and boundaries* only Harald Eidheim presents data that seem to challenge this approach (1969). In his study of the Coastal Lapps of northern Norway Eidheim presents a number of situations in which Lappish identity is clearly stigmatized, and in which Lapps are at pains to subdue or even efface their identity (by, for example, speaking Norwegian instead of Lappish, even when only other Lapps are present). Not unrelatedly, Eidheim is also the only one of the contributors who seeks to understand ethnic identity expression within the wider context of the state and national identity expression (though the issue is touched upon briefly by Siverts [1969]). This is an issue that will come increasingly to the fore in the following chapters.

Despite the criticisms above, Barth's work on ethnicity has an enduring place in anthropological thought. By breaking with the essentially colonialist paradigm of 'tribe' he paved the way for a whole generation of scholars to approach 'tribal' identities in a new light. His name will be mentioned frequently in the following chapters.

SOVIET ETHNOS THEORY

> In recent decades a minor revolution has taken place within Soviet Anthropology . . . its leader is Yulian Bromley . . . [and] it consists of making *ethno*graphy into the studies of *ethnos*-es, or, in current Western academic jargon, into the study of *ethnicity*.
>
> (Gellner 1988: 115; emphases in original)

Until his death in 1990 Yulian Bromley was perhaps one of the most well-known Soviet anthropologists outside the Union, and certainly one of the most powerful and influential within it, as Director of the Institute of Ethnography of the Soviet Academy of Sciences. Quite why Gellner names him as the leader of a 'revolution' (if only a minor one) and what the implications of this for Soviet anthropology were are questions that are beyond the scope of this book, though I shall return to them briefly at the end of this section.

During the 1970s and 1980s, however, Bromley and his colleagues developed a theory of ethnicity which demands our attention, not least because it throws up a number of important issues when contrasted with more familiar theories developed by western Euro-pean and American scholars (Bromley 1974, 1975, 1980, 1989). Curiously enough, the 'revolution' appears to have begun in 1969 – the year that Barth published *Ethnic groups and boundaries* – when Bromley delivered a paper in Leningrad entitled 'Ethnos and endogamy'. The paper was published the same year and led to a spirited debate (Gellner 1988: 129). Five years later, he published a paper in English that outlined the main content of ethnos theory (Bromley 1974).

The position on ethnicity taken by Bromley and his colleagues is one of the most strongly primordialist that I shall describe in this book. While not 'eternal' (Bromley 1974: 61) the expression of ethnicity is so strongly resilient that it persists through generations and through a variety of social forms. It must be remembered that Bromley and his colleagues are (or at least were at the time) committed to a Marxist interpretation of history. This view holds that all human societies pass historically through five social formations: primitive communism, slave-ownership, feudalism, capitalism, and finally socialism leading to communism. (In fact, the number and naming of the stages were constantly tinkered with by Soviet historians and philosophers, but the underlying idea of an inevitable social evolutionary progression remained in all the typologies.) As both Ernest Gellner and Tamara Dragadze have pointed out, Soviet anthropology did not undergo any equivalent of the western (and particularly British) conversion to structural-functionalism with its rejection of history and its insistence on synchronic analysis based on particularistic fieldwork data (Gellner 1975: 595–6; Dragadze 1975: 604); consequently, there is nothing strange to a Soviet anthropologist in considering vast spans of time and in making universalist statements. As a result, claims Dragadze, where the British anthropologist sees stasis and coherence, the Soviet anthropologist sees social phenomena as always in a state of flux, containing elements of the past and presages of the future (Dragadze 1980: 161).

Thus Bromley's theory of ethnicity proposes that a stable core of ethnicity – the ethnos or ethnikos – persists through all social formations. It is affected, however, by the prevailing economic and political environment of any formation and manifests itself as an 'ethnosocial organism': '[f]or instance, the Ukrainian "ethnikos" existed under feudalism as well as under capitalism and socialism (that is why we refer to the Ukrainians in application to the feudal, capitalist, and socialist epochs)' (Bromley 1974: 69). The term 'ethnos' is used in a general, abstract sense, while the term 'ethnikos' is taken to refer to a specific manifestation, though, as Bromley himself admits, there has been terminological confusion among his colleagues (1974: 71–2).

For Bromley, the problem is to define and establish the most typical intrinsic features of this stable core. He defines the ethnos as being 'a historically formed community of people characterized by common, relatively stable cultural features, certain distinctive psychological traits, and the consciousness of their unity as distinguished from other similar communities' (1974: 66). In a later publication he adds the criteria of common territory and ethnonym (recognized name for the group) (Bromley 1975: 11, cited by Dragadze 1980: 162).

Now this, it is clear, shares many features with Barth's list of features (given above); moreover, Bromley comes close to Barth by not simply working from the inside out – listing features – but by also observing the boundary that encloses these features: 'the notion itself [ethnos] . . . largely stems from the contraposition of one community to another' (1974: 58). That is to say, it is in ethnic interaction that ethnic identity is consolidated. Bromley then goes on to point out that this interaction must be long-lasting and not temporary – he gives the example of sports teams in different strips as interacting, self-defined groups, each with distinctive features and yet not constituting ethnic groups, for the duration of their team identity is strictly limited (1974: 58). As we shall see in the next two chapters, this issue of temporary versus permanent (or long-lasting) identity status becomes a problem when minority migrant groups are defined as ethnic groups. The actual origins of the ethnos are apparently unimportant – to possess it is simply an aspect of being human. Bromley warns against the fruitless quest of searching for such origins and assigning them importance: '[t]he point is that factors that have played an important part in giving rise to phenomena afterward usually retain their significance only as auxiliary forms' (1974: 67).

The prevailing economic environment does, however, affect the character of the ethnos, but it moulds it rather than breaking it or distorting it completely. Bromley's new term, ethnosocial organism, describes the interaction of the ethnos with the historical stage (or economic environment) (1974: 69–71). The ethnosocial organism is the core of ethnos lived out in a social organism – an historically located group of people – which is itself affected by other factors such as the physical and economic environments. These external factors are independent of the ethnos but affect it such that the salient characteristics by which the ethnos is recognized may change. We thus begin to come close to Barth – the boundary of the ethnos is always in place, but the contents or distinctive characteristics change.

Bromley demonstrates the strength of his discovery over other explanatory mechanisms, of which I shall discuss two: class and race. Both of these within western sociology act in a sense as competing theories to ethnicity – race because as an analytical category it preceded ethnicity; class because in its usual (western) Marxist understanding it is objective and scientific where ethnicity is woolly and attitudinal. In the next two chapters I shall explore some of the ways in which class and particularly race are contrasted with ethnicity in British and American theory.

Bromley actually devotes very little discussion to class, but it should be remembered that class stratification is a fundamental element of all state societies in Marxist thought. He does not claim that ethnoses can never be in conflict (although he offers little discussion on this) but if they are it is not a manifestation of class conflict (Dragadze 1980: 166). Ethnos and class are complementary, so that an ethno-social organism may be divided by class, while the core of ethnos remains constant. The study of class is a 'horizontal' analysis while the study of ethnos is a 'vertical' analysis. Moreover, members of the same class within a multi-ethnic society may be members of different ethnoses and yet still come together in class solidarity (Dragadze 1980: 166).

On race Bromley is more forthright. He dismisses a correlation of ethnos with 'race' ('race' in this context being understood to mean the expression of phenotypical difference) and points out that in cases of migration (that is, internal migration, within the USSR), the people who move do not take on the characteristics of the people they come to live among, even if they have changed their economic system in the process (for example, by giving up pastoralism to become agriculturists) (Bromley 1974: 60). One hypothesis would be that this is because they have certain physical features (skin colour, hair type, facial features, and so forth) which mark them off from the people they have come to live among. Bromley notes that this is very often the actor's view – that is, we don't look like them so we don't behave like them – but he disputes that matters are clear cut in every case: 'racial characteristics, though plainly apparent, cannot serve as a sufficient basis for distinguishing ethnic communities' (1974: 63). In fact, Bromley's argument is curiously weak at this point; in the next two chapters we will see that the perception of physical difference frequently serves to mark ethnic boundaries. What he does is claim that even (Soviet) physical anthropologists cannot agree on the basis for the significance of phenotypical variation and that any local account will hardly be of a scientific character (1974: 61–2). That is to say, while physical difference may be observable, one cannot predict what the local interpretation of that difference will be.

Instead of physical difference, Bromley proposes that it is activity that sets people apart and he quotes Lenin: '[a]ll history is made up of the actions of individuals' (1974: 63). As we shall see in the next section and in the next chapter, activity or action is also a key element in other people's theories. (For example, early writing on race concentrated heavily on perceptions of visible difference; the rise of a strongly instrumentalist theory of ethnicity in the United States brought about a shift in emphasis to what people *do*, not simply who they are or how they look.)

What then of the content of the ethnos at any particular historically located moment? The ethnos is seen by the Soviets as morally neutral. It neither helps nor hinders the transformation of a society into a smoothly functioning socialist society. As we shall see in Chapter 5, several authors believe there to be areas of broad if not total overlap between theories of ethnicity and theories of nationalism (or between ethnicity and nationalism as social phenomena). This, however, was not an option for the Soviet anthropologists of the 1970s. The assertion of any form of proto-national identity (as Georgians or Latvians, for example) which threatened the security of the Union was taboo, and by being taboo did not exist. Therefore, it is not surprising that ethnic identity or the characteristics of the ethnos tends to manifest itself in the Soviet view in terms of overt cultural forms – language, dances, folklore, costume, and such like (Bromley 1975, cited in Gellner 1983: 57, footnote). While overt, these forms must also be integrated: 'ethnos is not a mere sum of "features" and "common characteristics" but an integral system which is conscious of its integrity' (Bromley 1974: 66). Thus does Bromley save himself from over-naïve positivism: first, by asserting that the content of the ethnos is affected (though not radically disrupted) by the prevailing economic environment; secondly, by pointing out that all 'features' will be integrated and that to list them one by one is to destroy the significance they have by virtue of being parts of a whole.

The significance of Bromley's ethnos theory has two components. First, although still paying lip service to Marxist notions of social evolutionism, it marked the emergence in Soviet anthropology of a movement towards synchronic analysis based upon fieldwork investigations (Gellner 1988: 118). This was in marked contrast to the previous emphasis in the discipline on archaic societies, 'primitive' pre-state societies and abstract, broad generalizations (Gellner 1988: 116–25). Two short articles in English in the same volume as Bromley's main position paper give some idea of the (largely survey-based) fieldwork approach that developed in opposition to the previously dominant approach (Arutjunjan 1974; Vasiljeva *et al.* 1974).

Secondly, it was an attempt to tackle an obvious problem within the Soviet Union head on. We will see in the next chapter that early writing on migrant 'ethnic groups' in America tended to assume that, after an initial period of transition and possibly disorientation, members of these 'ethnic groups' would gradually shed their ethnic distinctiveness and 'Americanize' or assimilate – the so-called melting pot hypothesis. A later literature proclaimed that this had not in fact happened, and sought instead to explain the persistence of ethnic identity. So too in the Soviet Union. After the Revolution it was assumed that ethnic or cultural distinctiveness would wither in the face of rational socialist planning and be replaced by a 'Soviet super-ethnicity' (Shanin 1989: 418). Under Stalin, discussion of the subject was prohibited (Shanin 1989: 412–13), but by the 1960s it was clear that, despite the ideology of the Revolution, despite intensive Russification programmes, despite the forced movement and acculturation of native peoples and national minorities under Stalin, groups within the Soviet Union still persisted in retaining their Georgian-ness or their Buryat-ness or whatever. In the more liberal political climate under Brezhnev, Bromley and his colleagues felt able to explore this cultural landscape which was, as Gellner notes, 'conspicuously important . . . of practical use . . . [and] comparatively unperilous [politically]' (Gellner 1988: 121). Bromley in fact sought to make a virtue of a necessity.

How can ethnos theory be made into a virtue? Dragadze claims that it helped to extricate Soviet anthropologists from a 'trap' they had set for themselves (or rather, had set for them) – that of the system of five-plus historical stages (Dragadze 1980: 163). According to this evolutionary theory, societies dissolve and re-form as they pass through the stages and, as their formations are held to be dependent upon the stage they are in (feudalism, capitalism), it is therefore difficult to explain continuities that are observed. Moreover, different socialist societies (say) may behave differently, even though they all share the same economic base, which hinders horizontal comparison. Ethnos theory provides a bridging mechanism, by positing a stable core which runs through all the historical stages any society will undergo. It therefore acts as a tool for diachronic analysis. It is important to remember that in this analysis the ethnos – the core of ethnicity – is morally neutral. The ethnic or core identity of a group does not hinder it advancing through the historical stages, even though the current economic environment of the group – feudalism, for example – may be reprehensible.

But there was also a shadowy concept lurking behind ethnos theory and its application that was not fully explored in the discussions of the 1970s. Under Stalin, the claims of any constituent parts of the Soviet Union to political independence were ruthlessly suppressed. Notionally, the autonomous republics of the Union represented a rough mapping of territory to major groupings of people, such that Georgians lived in Georgia, Armenians lived in Armenia, and so on. The standard Russian term to describe such 'ethnic' identity, *natsional'nost'*, is often translated into English as 'nationality' but this is not held to imply anything about an individual's relationship to the state (which is an aspect of citizenship – *grazhdanstvo*) (Shanin 1989: 409–10). As we shall see in Chapter 5, one of the crucial analytical distinctions made by most authors between nationalism and ethnicity hinges on the relationship to the state. But although, as some authors have pointed out (for example, Eriksen 1993: 119), many of the 'nations' of the Soviet Union did not demand independence, this did not mean that they were not frequently regarded as a threat to the Union (see Szynkiewicz 1990). The mass deportation and scattering of the Crimean Tartars under Stalin is perhaps the most notorious example of the reaction to this 'threat' (Akiner 1983: 87–93; Sheehy and Nahaylo 1980), but even without such drastic measures, the ethnic 'effectiveness' of a population could be reduced administratively. Caroline Humphrey notes that the Buryat-Mongolian ASSR (Autonomous Soviet Socialist Republic) was established in 1923 and included most of the territory within the Soviet Union inhabited by the Buryats (a non-European Buddhist group living in the east of the Union bordering China and Mongolia). In 1937, however, the boundaries of the Republic were substantially cut back leaving the Buryats outnumbered by (ethnic) Russians in all the administrative divisions they now found themselves within (Humphrey 1983: 24).

The 'nationalities problem' is only hinted at in Bromley's 1974 article, though it is more to the fore in a later paper which otherwise covers much of the same ground (Bromley and Kozlov 1989; see also Shanin 1989; Szynkiewicz 1990). By then 'ethnic' unrest was manifesting itself throughout the Soviet Union, as the Baltic Republics of Estonia, Lithuania and Latvia demanded independence, and as disputes over territory – such as that over Nagorno-Karabakh in Azerbaijan – grew bloody. It is not at all clear that ethnicity – the manifestation of the primordial ethnos – is to blame for this unrest (which foreshadowed the break-up of the Soviet Union itself), although this has been a consistent assumption of western journalists (see, for example, *Observer* 3.9.89). The issue of the relationship between theories of ethnicity and theories of nationalism forms the main focus of Chapter 5; in Chapter 6 I address popular understandings of ethnicity and the confusion between the level of description and the level of analysis or explanation.

For the moment, however, the case of Soviet ethnos theory stands as an important example of a theory of primordial ethnicity. Furthermore, even in the essentially emasculated discussions which must avoid references to antagonistic proto-nationalism and adhere more or less firmly to a Marxist orthodoxy, Bromley and his colleagues predispose us to seek a situational view of ethnicity. They give us a theory of ethnicity which, despite its claims of a primordial core of identity, recognizes the importance of specific historical, economic and – although they play this down – political factors in shaping the expression of ethnic identity. In this the Soviet ethnos theorists share ground with the Manchester School theorists, discussed below, as well as with several of the authors discussed in the next three chapters, a territory which Barth – as pointed out above – does not really enter.

'TRIBALISM' AND ETHNICITY – THE MANCHESTER SCHOOL

For the British anthropology student the study of the peoples of Africa has long formed a part of the syllabus. Much has been written concerning the relationship between the development of British social anthropology and British colonialism, particularly in Africa (see, for example, Asad 1973), but the role of one particular group of anthropologists working in Africa during and after the colonial period has not received as much attention as it might. In immediate post-war African anthropology we can detect two distinct strains of interest. On the one hand, we have the Oxford and Cambridge anthropologists such as Evans-Pritchard, Meyer Fortes and Jack Goody, who were concerned with the 'traditional' social organization of African tribes. On the other, we have members of the Manchester School who were concerned with the changes brought about by urbanization and colonialism, and with the building of the industrialized, urbanized nation states of post-colonial Africa.

The Rhodes-Livingstone Institute was established in Northern Rhodesia (now Zambia) in 1938 as a social and economic research institute. It was staffed by many Oxford-trained anthropologists, several of whom went on to academic careers in Britain, most famously at Manchester University. These older members of the Manchester School, and many of their students, conducted field research all over the world, but are most well known today for the studies that rested on research conducted in southern, central and western Africa (see Brown 1973 for further details). Of their many studies, covering topics as diverse as land tenure, nutrition, urbanization and legal systems, what concerns me here are those produced by a number of anthropologists who were interested in the changes brought about in indigenous social organization by interaction with whites and with other indigenous groups.

These anthropologists are of interest for two reasons: first, they – unlike some of their contemporaries – saw the presence of white colonialists as a crucial factor to be included in any account of indigenous peoples; secondly, they are responsible – perhaps more than any other anthropologists – for bringing about the terminological shift I have already mentioned, from 'tribe' to 'ethnic group'. The first point places the Manchester School authors clearly on one side of a divide that runs through the literature discussed in this book – whether or not an author explicitly recognizes and explores the relationship between the 'ethnic group' under consideration and the state (in this case, the colonial state); the second point I shall discuss in more detail below.

Of the several authors I might consider in this section I shall confine myself to just four: Abner Cohen, A. L. Epstein, Philip Mayer and J. Clyde Mitchell, together with their teacher and mentor Max Gluckman. The reader should be aware from the outset that in many ways the Manchester School did not constitute a school at all, in the sense of there being a group of scholars who worked together and shared a common theoretical orientation. In fact, in the words of Clyde Mitchell, 'seen from the inside, it was a seething contradiction. And perhaps the only thing we had in common was that Max

[Gluckman] was our teacher, and that meant that we wrote ethnography rich in actual cases' (personal communication to Richard Werbner and cited in R. Werbner 1984: 158). Werbner goes on to note that this 'seething contradiction' has allowed subsequent researchers of varied theoretical dispositions to extract from the School's work material which interests them or is relevant to their own researches. Indeed, by concentrating on the School's writings on ethnicity, I am being similarly selective; the reader who wishes to learn more about the School's writings and activities as a whole should consult Brown (1973), Gluckman (n.d.), Kuper (1983 [Chapter 6], Van Teeffelen (1978) or R. Werbner (1984).

My study starts with a brief look at three works which do not mention 'ethnicity' at all: Max Gluckman's *Analysis of a social situation in modern Zululand* (1958 but first published in 1940), Clyde Mitchell's *The Kalela dance* (1956) and Philip Mayer's *Townsmen or tribesmen* (1971 but first published in 1961). All three works are important for the present study, however, in that they allow us to see the development of the ideas that would later be explicitly acknowledged as ideas about ethnicity (for example, Epstein 1978: 1–3).

The first essay in Gluckman's work ('The social organization of modern Zululand') describes a single day in January 1938 on which the author attended the opening of a new bridge and a session at the local district magistrate's court. The bridge opening took the form of a short ceremony, during which speeches were made and refreshments served. Gluckman describes the proceedings in a detailed manner, noting who sat where, who offered tea to whom, and so on; the description is followed by a lengthy analysis.

Gluckman's main concern is to understand the actions, motivations and perceptions of the Zulus and Europeans present and to offer these particular observations as exemplary of the wider pattern of black–white relations in Northern Zululand as a whole. He discusses the possibility that, for analytical purposes at least, the Zulus and Europeans can be considered as a 'community'. 'That Zulu and Europeans could co-operate in the celebration at the bridge shows that they form together a community with specific modes of behaviour to one another. Only by insisting on this point can one begin to understand the behaviour of the people as I have described it' (1958: 9). He then goes on to describe exactly what these relations consist of, pointing out frequently that the relationship is not equal, as the Europeans are dominant (for example, Gluckman 1958: 12–13). In seeking to understand Zulu society as it was in the 1930s through an understanding of both white and black groups, we can see Gluckman as moving towards two concepts that later become central to the study of ethnicity: context and boundary maintenance.

The importance of context (sometimes known as situationalism) is seen by Gluckman as meaning that the particular relations between the two groups in question are influenced by the situation in which they find themselves in contact at any particular moment – 'the association of certain Zulu with Europeans and their values and beliefs, creates groups within the Zulu which in certain situations cross the separation of interests of Africans and Whites, but emphasise the difference between them' (Gluckman 1958: 21). Thus, in a language with which we are familiar today but which Gluckman does not employ, we might say that there is no monolithic and homogenous Zulu (or European) identity or ethnicity, but rather a number of identities are manifest depending upon the situation. By focusing especially upon the whites and the situations where they interact with or distance themselves from the Zulus, Gluckman is making points about the identity or ethnicity of the dominant group (albeit in a numerical minority) that will largely be ignored for the next fifty years (see Chapman *et al.* 1989: 18–19).

In making these points he is also sketching the outlines of what Barth was later to call 'boundary maintenance' (Barth 1969b: 15ff): 'Black and White are two categories which must not mix, like castes in India, or the categories of men and women in many communities. On the other hand, though a son is distinct from his father, he in turn becomes a father' (Gluckman 1958: 12). The key term here is 'categories' – Gluckman is not talking about two groups of people (when he does, he calls them 'groups' and names them as Zulu and European, not black and white); and in this he is more subtle than Lloyd Warner and his race-as-caste hypothesis discussed in the next chapter. What Gluckman is raising is the possibility that individuals have concepts of identity categories, both of themselves and of others, which implies the possibility of exchanging one identity for another (a point he discusses in actual fact – Gluckman 1958: 12). He also goes on to note that, although this possibility exists, the 'boundary' (using Barth's term, not Gluckman's) is patrolled by the Europeans – 'the maintenance of this separation is a dominant value' (1958: 12).

Although he talks in terms of the material and cultural differences between the two groups ('differences of colour and race, of language, beliefs, knowledge, traditions, and material possessions' as well, most importantly, as differences 'in their interrelationships in the social structure of the South African community of which Zululand is a part' [Gluckman 1958: 13]) – in short, the listing of 'contents' which Barth deplores (Barth 1969b: 12) – he goes on to state that '[t]hese differences are also, in the co-operation of the two groups, balanced by customs of communication' (Gluckman 1958: 13). That is to say, the two groups are well aware of these differences and yet need, on certain occasions, to co-operate. Gluckman may well be criticized for taking a consensual view of black–white relations in Zulu society, a criticism which as I noted above has also been made of Barth's analysis of the Swat Pathan (Adam Kuper among others claims to see the influence of Gluckman on Barth; see Kuper 1983: 143, 166), and in some measure this may well be justified, though throughout *Analysis of a social situation in modern Zululand* he makes reference to European political and economic domination of the Zulu.

Based on fieldwork conducted some 12–13 years after Gluckman was working in Zululand, Clyde Mitchell's *The Kalela dance* (1956) follows many of Gluckman's themes, particularly the changing identity of southern African 'tribesmen' under colonial rule. Indeed, the themes of 'tribalism' and 'detribalization and retribalization' are central to many of the Manchester School monographs of this period. In this comparatively short, but much cited work, Mitchell follows a similar pattern to Gluckman. A short descriptive sequence describing the form and content of a 'popular "tribal" dance on the Copperbelt of Northern Rhodesia' [present-day Zambia] (1956: 1) is followed by a lengthy analysis. This type of presentation – the 'social situation' or the 'extended case study' – became the hallmark of Manchester School ethnography.

As Mitchell describes it, the dance is performed on Sundays and public holidays by specialized teams of dancers, each of whom has a particular role in the dance. Although from only one 'tribe' (Bisa) the team wears European dress and the songs, though sung in Bemba, are not as one might predict (according to Mitchell 1956: 9) songs describing the beauties of the Bisa homeland or the activities of the rural Bisa there. Instead, the songs lampoon both the urban situations and the personalities (such as 'the smart modern [but black] miss, who uses powder and paint' [Mitchell 1956: 6]) who are found there, as well as making caricatures of the other 'tribal' groups who are to be found on the Copperbelt (such as the Lamba and their 'preoccupation with adultery' [1956: 7]). There is thus, according to Mitchell, 'an apparent paradox. The dance is clearly a tribal dance in which tribal differences are emphasised but the language and idiom of the songs and the dress of the dancers are drawn from an urban existence which tends to submerge tribal differences' (1956: 9). This paradox can only be resolved if we consider the possibility that the 'tribalism' of the Copperbelt expressed in the Kalela dance songs is about something other than the idea of 'tribe' that Barth sought to criticize.

Mitchell mentions that some consider 'tribalism' to be dying out (1956: 30) but that there are exceptions of which the performance of the Kalela dance is one. In this and other works of the period 'tribalism' refers to the apparent persistence of 'tribal' identities among African migrants in towns of European creation, such as the mining towns of the Copperbelt. 'Tribalism' was problematic for European administrators and anthropologists alike. If Africans had left their homelands and appeared to all intents and purposes to have severed their connections with their rural origins, what benefit could possibly be obtained by maintaining such identities? For the administrators the problem was one of controlling a large black urban population which could be treated as homogenous in some contexts (labour relations, for example), and yet which manifested numerous differences of 'custom' and exhibited internal cleavages. The anthropologists, who had absorbed the ideas of Tönnies and Durkheim, were predisposed to see a sharp difference in mentality between rural and urban dwellers. 'Tribalism', which was essentially a 'rural' feature, thus made no sense in towns and other urban locales where a different set of rules for social organization and intercourse was supposed to operate. As we will see in the next chapter, there is a direct parallel between this and the worrying persistence of ethnicity among European migrants to the United States in the early years of this century.

Mitchell, Gluckman and others of the Manchester School were pioneering in discovering that the 'tribalism' of the towns had little, if anything, to do with being a member of a 'tribe' in a rural area. On this point they were largely united, while they were divided as to what it actually *did* mean. In the *Kalela dance* Mitchell advances his own hypothesis that 'tribalism' 'remains essentially a category of interaction in casual social intercourse' (1956: 42). He tested this by administering a questionnaire to over 300 African students, asking them to envisage hypothetical situations in which they might find themselves in contact with members of certain named 'tribes' – for example, would they marry someone from the so-and-so tribe?, would they share a meal with him?, would they allow him to live close to their home village?, and so on. The answers demonstrated the degree of familiarity urban migrants had with their fellow migrants from elsewhere – or what Mitchell calls 'tribal distance' (1956: 22).

The essence of his argument is that in an urban migrant situation where a lot of people from a variety of backgrounds must interact, if only briefly, actors use 'tribal' labels to distinguish broad population bands from one another. These are used to construct what Epstein calls 'cognitive maps' of the urban landscape (Epstein 1978: 11). One urban migrant from one part of the country may have only a limited knowledge, or no knowledge at all, of the language, dress, customs, political system, and so on, of a workmate from a completely different part of the country and may therefore not know how to behave appropriately with him or her and in a way that will not cause offence (or, contrarily, may be wishing to find some behaviour that will be offensive). The migrant could learn, of course, but this would involve learning the appropriate customs or codes for a huge variety of other groups. Instead, the migrant has a small number of categories, each bearing a tribal name, into which she or he lumps anyone who appears to have roughly the right kind of diacritical markers (language, dress, and so on). 'The main point that emerges from the experiment is that the more distant a group of peoples is from one another, both socially and geographically, the greater the tendency to regard them as an undifferentiated category and to place them under a general rubric such as "Bemba", "Ngoni", "Lozi", etc. In this way, from the point of view of the African on the Copperbelt all tribes other than those from his particular home area tend to be reduced into three or four categories bearing the label of those tribes who, at the coming of the Europeans, were the more powerful and dominant in the region' (Mitchell 1956: 28).

While Mitchell's point about classification and tribal distance is an interesting one and the underlying mechanisms are well described it leaves unanswered the question of quite why the Copperbelt workers should behave in this way. The hints are that such behaviour acts as a psychological stabilizing mechanism for 'tribesmen' who have been uprooted from a face-to-face network of kinship and other links in their rural communities and dropped into the impersonal and alien urban setting (Mitchell 1956: 44). As we shall see, this assessment formed the basis of a disagreement between Epstein (whose own findings on the Copperbelt were largely in accordance with Mitchell's – see Epstein 1958) and Abner Cohen.

Before moving on to discuss Abner Cohen, mention should be made of Philip Mayer and his study of two groups of rural Xhosa moving into the town of East London in Cape Province, South Africa (1971). Mayer notes that, while the Copperbelt studies of Epstein, Mitchell and others were concerned with inter-'tribal' interaction and the consequent rise of a certain kind of 'tribalism', East London's migrant population in the 1950s was made up of members of a single 'tribe' (the Xhosa) who exhibited a number of cleavages into discrete groups (Mayer 1971: vii–viii). Those still living in the rural homeland are divided into 'Red' Xhosa who are traditionalists and anti-colonial and 'School' Xhosa who are mission educated and have adopted western ways in matters of dress, literacy, and so on; within the town there is a distinction between 'tribesmen' who live in the town but are not of it, by virtue of the persistence of their ties to the rural homeland, and 'townsmen' who have fully adapted to life in the towns. An incoming migrant, therefore, will bring with him or her one of two identities and, once in East London, will take on one of a further two identities.

There are numerous points to be made about Mayer's work but I wish to discuss only one here – the matter of choice. Mayer claims that, because the East London migrants come from a single 'tribe', the Xhosa, they share a number of common features, as well as those that divide them (into 'Red' and 'School' and into 'townsmen' and 'tribesmen'). Thus, he argues, the situationalism of Mitchell and Epstein needs to be modified (1971: ix): a Xhosa cannot claim another tribal identity than that with which she or he was born, neither is there any need to make the categorical judgements that Mitchell describes. Instead, a Xhosa in East London 'can choose between Red, School, or "townsmen's" patterns' (1971: ix). These choices are made in the realms of leisure and free time rather than the workplace, where the Xhosa tend simply to choose appropriate 'urban' behaviour by Mayer's account.

There is no need here to go into the reasons that a migrant chooses to develop one identity rather than another, though it is related to the strength of their kin and friendship networks (Mayer 1971: 288ff; see also Mitchell 1969). The point is that the Xhosa identities are not fixed and enduring, not brought intact from the rural areas and doggedly maintained; instead, 'as the possibilities of transferring allegiance from one reference group [i.e. 'Red', 'School', 'towns-man'] to another are considerable, a man's choices have a particular significance: they show whether or not he intends to remain within his original social category' (Mayer 1971: ix). Thus Mayer seems to have found an example of what Gluckman could only hypothesize for the black and white categories of Zululand. In doing so he draws closer to Barth, who is after all arguing that ethnic identities do not 'naturally' persist, but need to be maintained.

Mayer, however, retains some of the older thinking on 'tribal' difference. Thus while he asserts that identities can be shifted within a single 'tribal' group (though in fact he acknowledges that he has lumped the 'Xhosa proper' together with a number of other, Xhosa-speaking 'tribes or sub-tribes' – 1971: 3), he believes this would not be possible in a situation such as the urban developments of the Copperbelt where 'the social categories . . . are ethnic, birth-determined ones' (1971: ix). That is, he appears to be espousing a belief in primordial ethnic identities (as both Barth on some occasions and, more especially, the Soviets do) at one level – identities which cannot be transgressed – while allowing for bound-ary crossing (as we would now call it) at a lower level. In the next chapter we will see that a similar problem has taxed many writers on minority migrant groups, with some opting to maintain a distinction between 'race' (fixed, birth-ascribed) and 'ethnic' (fluid, culturally constructed) identities.

I now move forward to consider one of the classic studies of what we might call the Manchester School's middle period: Abner Cohen's *Custom and politics in urban Africa* (1969). The work is a study of Hausa traders in the southern Nigerian city of Ibadan and the way in which manipulation of ethnic identity allows them to control long distance trade in kola nuts and cattle. It shows many of the preoccupations of the earlier studies considered: in particular, the problem of 'tribalism', the new conditions brought about by urban-ism, and relations between the group under study and the state structure within which it is embedded. The fieldwork for the study was conducted in the early 1960s and yet the few short years between Cohen's study and those of Gluckman, Mitchell and Mayer had seen many changes. On the one hand, the independence of many African nations was now a fact (Nigeria finally achieving independence in 1960), even if many more would have to wait years and even decades. On the other, the term 'ethnicity' had come into vogue and Cohen uses it extensively, mentioning specifically that he has taken the term from North American sociology (1969: 3; see also Glazer and Moynihan, 'Ethnicity seems to be a new term' [1975b: 1]). By contrast, Gluckman, in *Analysis of a social situation in modern Zululand* (1958), uses neither 'ethnicity' nor 'ethnic' as analytical terms, and Mitchell and Mayer use only 'ethnic' in compounds such as 'ethnic group' and 'ethnic distinctiveness'.

Cohen's main thesis is that ethnicity is instrumental; that is, there are reasons for a group asserting and maintaining an ethnic identity and these reasons are economic and political rather than psychological. The Hausa he is studying are migrants from the north of the country, but he is quick to point out that there is no monolithic category of 'Hausa-ness' or Hausa identity that would encompass all Hausa everywhere. For example, other Hausa in the south of the country, who are not involved in trade but work as seasonal labourers, do not form strong and highly organized communities as those in Ibadan do (Cohen 1969: 15). Nor is there anything special about Ibadan (a Yoruba-dominated city) which would encourage the development of such tightly organized communities – western Ibo migrants who have settled there have accommodated themselves to the Yoruba majority, living in ethnically mixed settlements where their children speak Yoruba and maintaining only a very weak and ineffective 'tribal organization' (1969: 187–8).

Hausa ethnic solidarity in Ibadan is manifested in a number of ways. They live in an effective ghetto (the quarter of Sabo in the north-west of the city), they speak their own language, they are involved in certain economic activities and they are members of a particular Muslim Brotherhood which in certain ritual and doctrinal particularities distinguishes it from the Islam of the Yoruba. Though exclusive to the local temporal and spatial circumstances, none of these diacritical markers is in any way primordial or fixed (Cohen criticizes the French anthropologist Jean Rouch who assumed that the strong 'tribal' organizations he found among Hausa immigrants further south, in Ghana, were somehow a result of their 'tribal traditional culture' [1969: 14–15]). Indeed, membership of the Tijaniyya order, the Muslim Brotherhood to which the Hausa belonged in the early 1960s, was relatively recent: introduced from the north in the early 1950s, 85 per cent of Hausa men had joined the order in the two years 1951–2 (Cohen 1969: 150). Moreover, a new migrant arriving in Ibadan has to 'learn' how to be Hausa, or 'retribalize' as Cohen puts it (1969: 29): 'Hausa culture in Sabo is in many ways a new culture and a Hausa newcomer from the North has to learn it and adjust to it. He will not become "one of us" simply because he comes from Hausaland and speaks Hausa' (1969: 49). More radically, Cohen goes on to state that 'Hausa' is a generic label that may be adopted by 'non-Hausa' in Sabo, provided they can speak Hausa, can name a place of origin in Hausaland, are Muslim and have no external features (such as facial scarification) that would link them to another 'tribe' (1969: 49). In this, then, Cohen is drawing very close to Barth in his discussion of how Pathan may 'become' Baluchi.

So far we have seen *how* Ibadan Hausa ethnicity is constructed which then leaves us with the question of *why* this is the case. It is at this juncture that Cohen explicitly rejects the quasi-psychological explanations of Mitchell and Mayer. 'Tribalism [meaning, in this context, ethnicity] *is* a live political and economic issue and is not just a method of categorization to help the African migrant to deal with the bewildering complexity of urban society or to regulate for him such "domestic" matters as marriage, friendship, burial, and mutual help' (1969: 193). Cohen instead proposes the notion of 'political ethnicity' (1969: 27; see also 3–4, 198ff); that is, ethnicity not so much as a form of identity as ethnicity as a strategy for corporate action.

Cohen identifies two, linked, sets of causes that have brought about the strong ethnicity of the Hausa in Ibadan. First, there are the internal causes which revolve around the need to maintain a monopoly of the kola nut and cattle trades. Hausa traders in Ibadan send kola nuts (which are chewed as a stimulant and much used throughout West Africa) to Hausa traders in the north. The nuts, which are more heavily in demand in the north than in the south, are only grown in the south (1969: 131). Conversely, the trade in cattle is from origin and production in the north to consumption in the south (cattle were at risk from tsetse fly in the south at this time). For a variety of technical reasons to do with the production and storage of the two commodities the organization of their trade is a complex business requiring a high degree of trust, co-operation and credit facilities, hence the Ibadan Hausa come together as they control their end of the two trades.

Secondly, there are the external causes. Cohen notes that in the colonial period of indirect rule small ethnic groups, such as the Ibadan Hausa, were granted a degree of autonomy and developed corporate political and economic interests (1969: 24). In particular, Sabo – the Hausa quarter of Ibadan – was officially recognized as a 'tribal area' and dealt directly with the colonial authorities over matters such as land access (1969: 13). As indirect rule began to falter in the run-up to independence and as Nigerian national politics became more and more developed, this autonomy for the Ibadan Hausa began to be eroded. Simultaneously, the Yoruba, who had previously been non-Islamic in contrast to the well-Islamicized Hausa, became Islamicized very rapidly (1969:13). Thus two distinctive features of the Ibadan Hausa – their territorial and religious exclusiveness – were challenged. While there was little the Hausa could do to retain their control over Sabo, they quickly changed the course of their religious adherence becoming, almost *en masse*, members of the Tijaniyya order.

Thus, the response of the Hausa 'at the time when politics came' (to use the evocative Hausa phrase cited by Cohen 1969: 12) was to 'retribalize' (1969: 1–3, 29); that is, they focused and defined their ethnic identity as a response to an external threat. 'Retribalization', says Cohen, 'is a process by which a group from one ethnic category, whose members are involved in a struggle for power and privilege with the members of a group from another ethnic category, within the framework of a *formal* political system, manipulate some customs, values, myths, symbols, and ceremonials from their cultural tradition in order to articulate an *informal* political organization which is used as a weapon in that struggle' (1969: 2; emphases in original).

Why did the Ibadan Hausa do this? Not because they have a strong 'tribal' tradition which reasserts itself willy-nilly. They did it to maintain control of the kola nut and cattle trades. As mentioned, both trades rely on careful organization and a high degree of mutual trust between partners; if the Ibadan Hausa became increasingly indistinguishable from the Ibadan Yoruba, what would prevent Yoruba from beginning to infiltrate the trade? As Cohen says: 'Hausa identity and Hausa ethnic exclusiveness in Ibadan are the expressions not so much of a particularly strong "tribalistic" sentiment as of vested economic interests' (1969: 14).

There is much more that could be said about *Custom and politics in urban Africa*, but the main point should now be clear: political ethnicity is goal-directed ethnicity, formed by internal organization and stimulated by external pressures, and held not for its own sake but to defend an economic or political interest. For Cohen, such ethnicity needs to be built upon some pre-existing form of cultural identity (in this case, the customs of the Hausa 'tribe') rather than be conjured up out of thin air, but will only come into being when the conditions are right, rather than being a 'natural' phenomenon. There is little discussion of what the Ibadan Hausa themselves think about their identity – Cohen's overtly anti-psychological stance prevents this (see Cohen 1974a: xff for a later and bolder statement of this). Instead, Cohen refers to ethnicity as a 'sociological term', to be distinguished from the 'native term' 'tribalism' (1969: 4). Ethnicity, then, is something that the analyst uses as a tool to describe and understand processes of which those involved may have no clear grasp (for example, the pious Hausa might be surprised or even offended to be told that his commitment to the Tijaniyya order was 'merely' a building block in the construction of his ethnic consciousness).

This apparent divergence between the analyst's and the actors' perceptions of the actors' behaviour and the motivations for it should be familiar ground for a student of anthropology, found at the nub, for example, of discussions about emic and etic approaches. It is explored more fully with relation to ethnicity in Chapter 5, but a further refinement of the problem is found in the next work I wish to discuss: A. L. Epstein's *Ethos and identity* (1978). In the book's first essay, 'Exploring ethnic identity', Epstein goes back over much of the work that he and Clyde Mitchell did on the Copperbelt in the 1950s and teases out from it the fact that: '"tribalism" [the term Epstein and Mitchell were then using for ethnicity] has to be looked at in two aspects: one, socio-centrically or "objectively", as a system of social categories; and two, egocentrically or "sub-jectively"' (Epstein 1978: 38). This is not the same as saying there is an analyst's viewpoint and an actor's viewpoint; rather, Epstein is saying that the actor her- or himself may have two viewpoints: an 'external' socially given one and an 'internal' (basically psycho-logical) sense of identity.

There are many types of identity that an individual may carry, but Epstein endorses the view that ethnic identity is a 'terminal identity, one that embraces and integrates a whole series of statuses, roles, and lesser identities' (Epstein 1978: 101). Epstein's concept of identity draws on the writings of a number of psychologists and post-Freudian psychoanalysts, but in particular on the work of Erik Erikson who argued that an individual's development of identity was a life-long process and as much influenced by external, social factors as it was by internal psychological ones (Epstein 1978: 7). This influence leads Epstein to endorse the idea of 'cognitive maps' developed by Mitchell (Epstein 1978: 11) and to reject the 'political' or 'instrumental' theory of ethnicity as advanced by Glazer and Moynihan (discussed in the next chapter) and Abner Cohen (Epstein 1978: 93–4).

Epstein concedes that the Ibadan Hausa can be seen to be acting as an 'interest group' and using their ethnicity to defend an economic field of action, but argues that there are two weaknesses: first, Cohen does not define what is meant by an 'interest group'; secondly, while this analysis holds true for the particular situation Cohen encountered it cannot explain all expressions of ethnicity or ethnic identity to be found in the modern world. The two criticisms are tied together to some extent as Cohen would need to show his instrumental theory to be universally applicable or at least more widely applicable than just the case study of the Ibadan Hausa in order for the concept of 'ethnic interest group' to be self-explanatory and unproblematic. Indeed, Cohen discusses ethnic interest groups in fairly general terms at some points (for example, Abner Cohen 1969: 194) implying that political or instrumental ethnicity is the only kind there is; he also implies that there will be a conjunction of ethnic interests with incipient class interests, at least in post-colonial states such as Nigeria (Cohen 1969: 194). As we saw in the earlier discussion of the Soviet ethnos theorists there are some who hold that class and ethnicity are fundamentally opposed categories – a point I shall also return to in the next two chapters.

Epstein's second criticism – that there are situations in which ethnicity is active but does not seem to have any 'aim' – is the more cogent and he brings in Frederik Barth in support (Epstein 1978: 96–7), claiming that in the situations of 'relative stability' with which Barth and his colleagues concerned themselves there was no particular 'need' (in economic or political terms) for ethnicity to assert itself (1978: 96). Moreover, if – as Barth claims – the content of a group's ethnic identity is fluid and shifting and yet the presence of an ethnic identity persists, one can assume that it will persist both in times of economic or political 'need' as well as in times of 'relative stability'. Yet my comments on the case of the Pathan above were intended to demonstrate that there were perhaps political imbalances between, for example, Pathan and Baluchi; furthermore, Barth has been criticized for not taking long-term historical factors into account in his analysis of the Swat valley (Meeker 1980), which carries with it the implication that Barth has merely asserted but not demonstrated the continued existence of an ethnic identity.

Epstein's alternative model of ethnicity is rather less easy to pin down with a label and harder too to summarize. Although he levels explicit and – to my mind – rather ill-tempered criticism of Cohen's avowedly anti-psychological stance (see, for example, Epstein 1978: 94, fn. 52), he is less than clear as to why an ethnic identity rather than a class identity or a gender identity or some other identity should be so important. To some extent he is as much a victim of his fieldwork and research as Cohen, finding or assuming an ethnic identity to be of paramount analytical interest in the three situations he discusses in the book ('retribalization' on the Copperbelt, the crystallization of identity among the Tolai of New Guinea, and the reworking of Jewish identities in New York). Conversely, the insights he takes from Erikson and others are vague and weakly descriptive rather than strongly analytical; for example, Erikson's concept of a 'pseudo-species' – 'throughout human history groups of various kinds have emerged and bound their members in loyalty by developing, within a territorial framework, their own body of custom, mythology and rite, and history' (Epstein 1978: 109) – appears in Epstein's account of it to be so vague and generalizing as to be of no value at all.

Moreover, as Epstein notes, his own case studies concern groups in the process of radical change that seems to be characterized by the opening up of new political and economic opportunities (this is particularly so in the case of the Tolai). Finally, there is an argument that history, in the form of the development of anthropological theory, has overtaken Epstein. First, far more sophisticated explorations of the frontier between anthropology and psychology have characterized what has come to be known as cognitive anthropology (although it is true that none that I know of examines issues of ethnic identity). Secondly, anthropological explorations of personal identity have seen a marked increase in the (as yet) unrelated fields of moral personhood and 'community' studies (the latter characterized by the work of Anthony Cohen and his colleagues, who will be discussed at length in Chapter 5). Thirdly, the development of an anthropological interest in nationalism (stimulated almost single-handedly, it seems, by Benedict Anderson's *Imagined communities* [1983]) has put instrumental ethnicity far to the forefront.

In retrospect, it seems that the value of *Ethos and identity* lies in the additional material and insights brought to bear on the Copperbelt situation of the 1950s and in the warnings against an oversimplistic and narrowly synchronic interpretation of the political and economic factors that might motivate the expression of an ethnic identity at certain times and in certain places.

OTHER VOICES

As we shall see in Chapter 4, the focus of British studies on ethnicity has shifted in the last two decades or so to an exploration of the ethnicity of newly migrated groups. For North American sociology this has consistently been the case. None the less, studies of ethnicity among long-settled groups continue to appear and in this final section I shall consider some of them briefly.

One of the most important strands raised in the literature in recent years has consisted of a number of solutions to the 'primordiality versus instrumentality' debate. This debate, aspects of which we have already seen above in the contrast between the work of Abner Cohen and A. L. Epstein, revolves around the reasons for the existence of ethnicity. At its most extreme, the primordialist position would hold that ethnicity is an innate aspect of human identity. It is a given, requiring description rather than explanation. At the other end of the scale, the instrumentalist position (known sometimes as the 'circumstantialist' approach [Volkman 1984: 152]) would hold that ethnicity is an artefact, created by individuals or groups to bring together a group of people for some common purpose. Another way of putting it would be to say that primordialist ethnicity simply is, it has no purpose (beyond a psychological one of giving individuals a sense of identity as members of a group), while instrumentalist ethnicity is motivated, it comes into being for a purpose and its continued existence is tied to that purpose.

Before moving on to consider some possible resolutions to this debate, let us consider the two positions more fully. Of the literature already dealt with in this chapter, it should be clear that the Soviet ethnographers are the most clearly primordial, followed closely by Epstein, and Barth to some extent. On the instrumentalist side, Abner Cohen is perhaps the most obvious. Participants in the debate usually cite Harold Isaacs, an American political scientist, as advancing the most strongly primordialist view, particularly in his paper 'Basic group identity: the idols of the tribe' (1975).

Taking his cue from Edward Shils, as later commentators have observed (for example, Blu 1980: 220), Isaacs states that 'basic group identity consists of the ready-made set of endowments and identifications which every individual shares with others from the moment of birth by chance of the family into which he is born at that given time in that given place' (Isaacs 1975: 31). These 'endowments and identifications' consist of the child's body, exhibiting a particular phenotype, and the history, language, religion and overall 'value system' of the child's parents. Isaacs' approach to these 'endowments' is straightforward and unquestioning; at the grand, pan-human level on which he sustains most of his discussion, he considers 'the child' to have an unproblematic place in the society into which it is born and ignores much anthropological evidence which demonstrates that the moral or social existence of an individual (as opposed to his or her biological existence) needs to be constantly reforged in many societies – reforged through rituals (including rituals surrounding birth), through manipulation of genealogies, through certain acts (through bearing or fathering children oneself), and so on.

However, several later authors have sought to build upon Isaacs' somewhat vague position. For example, Karen Blu comments that many who have cited Isaacs have misunderstood his use of the term 'primordial', thinking that he believes there to be immutable and enduring identities, whereas he is in fact using the term as a native category; that is, those who subscribe to an ethnic identity *consider* it to be immutable and enduring even if objectively it can be shown to be a fairly recent invention or transformation (Blu 1980: 220). She goes on to endorse Isaacs' position (as she restates it) and states that it is ethnic identity or self-perception that should concern the analyst, over and above 'external' explanations of ethnicity (1980: 2, 228). Though she does not cite him, she seems to share a strong affinity with A. L. Epstein, although her approach is less influenced (if at all) by psychological borrowings from Erikson (though she does cite him in other contexts) and other social psychologists and more by the ethnosociology of David Schneider. Blu, like Epstein, clearly comes down on the 'primordialist' side of the debate, but, following her reading of Isaacs, she is concerned with the sense in which Native Americans, blacks and whites in Robeson County, North Carolina, see their ethnic identities as being deep-rooted and linked to their sense of their own history and to folk conceptions of biology.

In undertaking her study of the Lumbee Indians of Robeson County she encountered the problematic and – one suspects – unusual situation of a group of people who had an ethnic boundary (in Barth's sense) but no apparent 'contents' which were contained by that boundary. As the opening sentence of her book states: 'How do a group of people who are legally designated "free persons of color" and who have Indian ancestry but no records of treaties, reservations, an Indian language, or peculiarly "Indian" customs become accepted socially and legally as Indians?' (Blu 1980: 1). Moreover, and paradoxically, this group has continually accepted in-migration of blacks, whites and other Native Americans, and has a reputation (among themselves and others) for constant factionalism – in other words, a combination of elements that would seem to render any attempt to assert an ethnic identity stillborn.

Blu, while not denying that there were at times certain economic and political advantages to be gained by the Lumbees asserting an ethnic identity (a nod in the direction of the instrumentalist position), is convinced that the Lumbees' basic group identity is strong enough to overcome any factors that might at other times mitigate against the expression of this identity (Blu 1980: 2) and spends most of the book detailing the findings of her ethno-historical research. She shows how the Lumbees gradually organized themselves politic-ally, seeking to change their official designation from 'mulatto' to 'Indian' and then through a variety of 'Indian' names (1980: 42–65, 77–90).

As she describes it, one gets the sense that the Lumbee Indians have individually and collectively been pursuing a strategy whereby every twist and turn (for example, through their various changes of name) have followed a well-defined path with clearly signposted forks and junctions periodically. In the course of a discussion of identity choices that the Lumbee Indians *could* have made, Blu notes that we have no way of knowing how people now dead perceived their choices, but adds that '[a]ll we have are accounts of the way they behaved. Judging from these, they have single-mindedly claimed to be autochthonous and have struggled for legal status reflecting that claim' (1980: 184). Thus Blu's concept of 'basic group identity' is shot through with a sense of instrumentality. The aim of the Lumbees' collective action is not merely some material, economic or political achievement, however. Rather, their aim in Blu's opinion is to express that basic group identity, for its own sake.

On the instrumentalist side of the debate we find, as we have seen, Abner Cohen's work on Hausa traders, which is often cited as the classic work of this type. Also often cited in this category are Glazer and Moynihan, and Paul Brass. Interestingly, none is an anthropo-logist; Brass is a political scientist, while Glazer and Moynihan hold professorships in education and government respectively. In accordance with many political scientists, and in sharp contrast to interpretative anthropologists such as Blu, they favour clearly defined, objective definitions of ethnicity and ethnic groups. Brass, for example, states in his study of language politics in north India that he has deliberately left 'the notion of identity' out of his definition of ethnicity, and goes on to say '[a]n ethnic group is a group which is objectively distinct' (Brass 1974: 8). His 'instrumentality' consists of documenting the advantages which ethnic groups in India (by which he means a whole range of caste, religious and linguistic groups) gain by asserting their corporate identity (that is, a commonality of language, religion, or – more recently – region) in order to win concessions from the state.

Glazer and Moynihan, whose 1975 collection of essays, *Ethnicity: theory and experience*, is often cited, contribute an introductory essay to the volume which is overwhelmingly instrumental in tone (Glazer and Moynihan 1975b). Their adoption of this stance rests on the fact that they consider the phenomenon of ethnicity to be (a) a social fact (and not an abstract conceptual tool of the analyst); and (b) a relatively recent phenomenon. The two are interdependent: 'We are suggesting that a new word ['ethnicity'] reflects a new reality' (Glazer and Moynihan 1975b: 5). It is because the world has changed through processes of nation building and modernization that expressions of ethnic conflict have intensified and changed their character. They cite, for example, the case of Northern Ireland: in the (unspecified) past there existed religious conflict, 'based on issues such as free and public practice of a religion'; today, by contrast, the conflict is based on 'the issue of which group shall gain benefits or hold power of a wholly secular sort' (1975b: 7).

This view of ethnicity as a product of the modern world (a view similar to that adopted by Benedict Anderson with relation to nationalism [Anderson 1983]) means that they can pay no more than lip service to the primordialist position. They include Isaacs' essay in the collection, and state: 'We must modify the bald assertion that ethnicity becomes a *means* of advancing interests – which it does – by insisting that it is not *only* a means of advancing interests' (Glazer and Moynihan 1975b: 19; emphases in original). However, they then go on to 'shy away from' a notion of primordiality, partly because it implies a rigidity and fixedness of identity, which they feel not to be borne out 'in a world of rapid change and shifting identity'. As most of the contributors to *Ethnicity: theory and experience* are political scientists who have almost a disciplinary duty to highlight arenas of political competition, it is no surprise that most of the contributions to the volume share Glazer and Moynihan's instrumentalist stance. I shall consider the volume in more detail in the next chapter. For the moment, let me conclude with some recent theories that have attempted to transcend the instrumentalist/ primordialist debate.

The majority of these writings begin by acknowledging the intellectual limitations of earlier theories and particularly their apparent determination to distil some form of pure, abstract, essence of ethnicity which could then be analysed. In contrast, these more recent theories have sought either to add theoretical vigour from another source, or to insist that the specific context of ethnic manifestations is vital to any analysis. Thomas Eriksen, for example, in a recent article claims to have achieved a new, synthetic theory, by blending insights from previous studies of ethnicity with Wittgenstein's idea of 'language games' (Eriksen 1991). Although rejecting a narrowly instrumentalist position in his analysis of ethnicity in Trinidad and Mauritius, he is no more sympathetic to a primordial position. His reading of Wittgenstein leads him to see that the 'goals' identified by the instrumentalists as the motivating factor for ethnic organization and consciousness are not necessarily unproblematic or uncontested. How, when and where do people learn to value the things they take to be important and worth striving for? How do they know that others share these values? For Eriksen, the values that one strives after are established through cultural negotiations in the family and among close friends; these are private arenas in which individuals learn to see the personal worth of the consensual positions they are encouraged to adopt. Only once shared meanings have been established in this way are they taken into 'the unitary language-game of institutional politics' (Eriksen 1991: 139). Eriksen claims that his analysis allows him to transcend the gap between the individual and the (ethnic) group, between the psychology of individual identity and the sociology of group action by focusing instead on contexts of interaction (1991: 131; disappointingly this original perspective is not explored in these terms in his later book-length study of ethnicity [Eriksen 1993]).

Using a very different language and from a very different theoretical stance, Brackette Williams also acknowledges that the goals towards which ethnic groups in nation states are striving may not be monolithic (B. Williams 1989). Along with other recent authors, she notes that the term 'ethnicity' has acquired ever more confusing layers of meaning. This is not, however, solely the result of woolly or confused thinking on the part of academics such as anthropologists (which some, such as Blu, would see as good reason for abandoning the term altogether – see Blu 1980: 226–7). Rather, it is because ethnicity is so important in the modern world, and particularly in the 'race to nation[hood]', that it has become a crucially contested term. She notes that the term 'ethnicity' has become increasingly attractive, not only to academics such as anthropologists, but to politicians and ordinary citizens (B. Williams 1989: 402). Thus, like other key terms and ideas such as 'democracy', it is the ambiguity of what ethnicity means and implies that invests it with such power.

Ethnicity is a 'lightning rod' in Williams' phrase (1989: 401) that attracts all those who have a vested interest in promoting or defining the interests of one group as against another. Developing an argument of Ronald Cohen's (1978), Williams notes that ethnic groups in a society do not exist as isomorphs, each structurally similar. Instead, there are overlapping sets, groupings which encompass other groupings. The relationship between these groupings is defined, not by their relative power or status in comparison to one another, but by their position within the state: '[t]he concept of ethnicity, whether defined in terms of nested segments or horizontal interest groups, is most useful when used as a label for a dimension of the identity formation process in a single political unit, most specifically the nation-state' (B. Williams 1989: 421).

Williams agrees with the instrumentalists that there is competition between groups, but this is less over resources and more over defining whose voice will become the voice of the state or, failing that, whose voice will accord with the tenor of the state. The competition between groups is a competition over defining the rules of the game of nation-building. Unsuccessful groups, those that are marginalized and disadvantaged, are those that are perceived not to have made any contribution to the building of the nation. Of course, there is no objective criterion of what counts as a useful contribution in these cases (just as for Eriksen there is no objective criterion of what counts as a resource to be competed over). Rather, it is the politically dominant groups that set the agenda and the subordinate groups compete among themselves to show that they have lived up to that agenda. As a consequence, 'ethnic' is a label that is given to the groups that fail to make the grade and which are denied a place in nationalist rhetoric by the ruling élite, who refuse to acknowledge their own ethnicity (B. Williams 1989: 426).

I will return to Williams' work again at the end of Chapter 5 where I discuss the relationship between ethnicity and nationalism. She is clear, however, that ethnicity can only be understood in relation to the state and to questions of nationhood (1989: 416). Although strongly critical of the simplistic instrumentality of, for example, Abner Cohen – the 'resource competition model' as she calls it (1989: 412) – she is none the less instrumentalist in her overall thrust, even if – like Eriksen – she appreciates the difficulties of defining goals.

G. Carter Bentley, on the basis of fieldwork conducted in the Philippines, is also anxious to transcend the instrumentalist/ primordialist dichotomy (Bentley 1987). Like Eriksen, Bentley is also concerned about the link between private, individual identity and public, corporate identity and critical of earlier theorists who have focused narrowly on one or the other. He cites Epstein (1978) as an example of an individualistic focus, and Nagata (1974) as an example of a large-scale group focus (Bentley 1987: 49); one could also cite political scientists such as Glazer and Moynihan who have, by focusing at the level of the state and the nation, tended to deal with homogenized group identities.

Bentley's solution, like Eriksen's, is to import an additional theoretical strand to twin with existing conceptualizations of ethnicity. The addition is what has generally come to be called practice or praxis theory (see Ortner 1984 for further details) and Bentley draws in particular on Pierre Bourdieu's *Outline of a theory of practice* (1977). He identifies the complex of unconscious habitual action and behaviour towards the world that Bourdieu calls 'habitus' as the locus of ethnic identification. It is through a shared experience of the world that members of a group identify themselves as having a common identity. Bentley dismisses instrumentality – people are living out an unconscious pattern of life, not acting in a rational, goal-oriented fashion (1987: 28). Similarly, there is nothing primordial about their ethnic identity as the common reading of Isaacs would imply. Although habitus is unconscious it can change, particularly from generation to generation. Habitus changes when the 'objective conditions' of life change, that is, when material and economic conditions change. As people strive to accommodate their understanding of the world and their position in it in changed circumstances, they generate a new habitus, one which may make more sense to their children than to themselves.

Bentley notes that ethnic movements often appear to be 'attempts by ethnic juniors to precociously assume (or usurp) leadership positions' (1987: 43), but that this is less an attempt by the young to gain access to the resources that the parental generation controls (a classically instrumentalist position) and more a result of inter-generational differences of habitus. Ethnic revitalization movements begin as *individuals* try to resolve personal identity problems (brought about through the world moving on and consequent shifts in habitus); Bentley cites the cases of the Sinhalese Buddhist leader Anagarika Dharmapala (see Obeyasekere 1975) and American black leaders such as Malcolm X (1987: 46–7).

Bourdieu's theory of practice and the role of habitus has much in common with the position of the Soviet ethnos theorists, discussed earlier, when applied to issues of ethnicity (although Bentley makes no reference to Soviet ethnos theory). This, of course, is not surprising – Bourdieu is commonly labelled a structural marxist. But as developed by Bentley, the theory is more subtle than the Soviet position. Where the Soviets would tend to see ethnicity or ethnic identity as a primordial and stable 'core' of identity, remoulded only slightly in its manifestation in any particular 'ethno-social organism', the habitus is dynamic, constantly changing, constantly feeding an unconscious and deep-rooted structural pattern to the individual and yet being changed in a kind of feedback process as the individual meets changes in the economic and political environment. For Bentley, therefore, the content of an ethnic identity is as important as the boundary around it (contrary to Barth and more extreme versions of Barth's position). Praxis theory holds that it is experience of the world that creates that content; it is not arbitrary, but tied crucially to material and economic conditions (1987: 35–6).

Kevin Yelvington, in a comment on Bentley's article, points out a number of flaws in the argument, many of which have the dispiriting effect (for the student of ethnicity) of negating Bentley's attempts to advance the debate, by returning to earlier, well-trodden paths (Yelvington 1991). For example, he implies that Bentley has gone too far in advocating the importance of the content of an ethnic identity and has consequently ignored one of Barth's crucial observations concerning ethnic boundaries – that 'the activity of "ethnic others"' is as important for the definition of an ethnic identity as any attempts by a group's members to define their own identity

(Yelvington 1991: 158). He goes on to cite the case of the Lue of Thailand who, despite having a sense of being an 'ethnic entity', are unwilling or unable to define this except by reference to others, according to their ethnographer, Michael Moerman (1974). They are 'semantically required' to contrast themselves with those who they are not (Yelvington 1991: 163–4). Yelvington is also critical of the use of Bourdieu's notion of habitus; while helpful for Bentley's theory, it can only be so because it is effectively a black box – its workings are mysterious, its contents vague and it seems at times to be a repository for Bourdieu to hide an ill-defined theory of psychological motivation (see also Jenkins 1992: 74–84).

There are many further examples of recent related literature I could cite. As noted in Chapter 1, the stream of books and articles on ethnicity, while diminished from the 1970s heyday, shows no signs of drying up completely. According to the Social Science Citation Index, over 350 articles in the last ten years alone have cited Barth's *Ethnic groups and boundaries* (a figure which, of course, excludes books, articles in books, theses and articles in journals not covered by the SSCI). While many of these citations are but passing references, an obligatory nod in the direction of an 'idol of the tribe', a few are serious attempts to develop Barth's work and take it in new directions (for example, Jenkins 1994; Tambs-Lyche 1980; Wallman 1978, 1986).

Instead of trying to cover further literature in this field, let me summarize the ideas that have been raised so far. The theories dealt with in this chapter have largely oscillated between a number of polar extremes: the individual versus the group; the contents of an ethnic identity versus its boundary; the primordial gut feeling of an identity versus its instrumental expression; ethnicity as an all-inclusive general theory versus ethnicity as a limited approach to particular problems. In fact, this last pair of polar opposites to some extent encompasses the rest. While most authors, when espousing one position or another, usually cite their position's polar opposite and distance themselves from it (for example, Glazer and Moynihan [1975b], discussed above), some authors, no matter what their position on the instrumentality versus primordial, or individual versus group etc. debates, are determined either to propose or imply a general theory of ethnicity which will hold good in all situations. This would be true of Epstein (1978), for example.

Other authors, particularly those writing more recently, are critical of this stance. Brackette Williams, while at first criticizing Ronald

Cohen's theory for leaving certain manifestations of ethnicity uncovered (B. Williams 1989: 417), goes on to criticize it again for trying to find ethnicity in situations where the concept is not – in Williams' eyes – helpful or relevant (1989: 418). Meanwhile, Karen Blu, already discussed above, seeks to narrow dramatically the range of social contexts in which ethnicity might be a salient feature. She adopts a somewhat extreme position by arguing that 'the term ethnicity should be dropped altogether as a cross-culturally useful analytic term . . . [and] restricted to describing and analysing what it does best, namely, an important form of social differentiation in the United States' (Blu 1980: 227).

Some of the authors discussed in this chapter have been cognizant of others and have attempted to deal seriously with each others' position. Others, such as the Soviets, have worked largely in isolation, and have been ignored by others. For the student of ethnicity it seems advantageous to construct some kind of typology, some way of pigeon-holing different theories and authors (for example, political scientists of the 1970s tended to favour a contents-defined, instrumentalist, group-level general theory of ethnicity). I am wary of doing so explicitly, however, though I recognize that I have done so implicitly by the way I have chosen to contrast one theory with another and through the general structure of this book.

Instead I would ask the reader to make her or his decisions about the literature they read based on a knowledge of the context in which that literature lies. As we saw in the case of the Soviet ethnos theorists, academic theories do not simply drop out of the sky ready-formed; they are as much the products of the historical and political contexts in which they arise as any of the data that these theories strive to make sense of. The next two chapters, which deal with theories that arose in response to large-scale international migration, should make this point abundantly clear.

Chapter 3

Ethnicity and race in the United States

By and large, the literature I considered in the previous chapter was written by academics who developed their theories of ethnicity in relation to data gathered from the observation of non-western people who had been domiciled in the same region or nation state for several generations. By contrast, the literature I wish to consider in this chapter and the next was produced (for the most part) by a different set of Euro-American academics who have developed their theories of ethnicity in relation to data gathered from the observation of non-western and other people who have recently migrated to the academics' home countries. 'Recently' in this context means within the last five hundred years; 'migrated' here covers all forms of migration, from the forced migration of slavery to the voluntary migration of economic betterment.

This apparently trivial difference – the geographical location of the group studied – conceals a division between the two groups of academics. For a start, the two academic groups rarely overlap in disciplinary interest: those who study the ethnicity of groups outside the academics' own country tend to be anthropologists, with a few political scientists; those who study the ethnicity of groups within the academics' country tend to be sociologists, with a few anthropologists, social geographers and social psychologists. Secondly, the issues that are deemed to be of importance vary between the two groups. The anthropologists tend to focus on subjective perceptions of identity within the group studied and on relations between the group and other similar groups; the sociologists tend to focus on objective or external group characteristics and on relations between the group and the political context in which it is located.

Are we then to assume that there are (at least) two kinds of ethnicity? Disciplinary boundaries aside (and, of course, there are anthropologists who study minority migrant groups and sociologists who study groups overseas), the answer to the question depends largely on the approach taken. Those who subscribe to the real existence of ethnicity as an innate component of identity should, in general, assume it to be homogenous, similar in essence (if not in form) no matter what the context. This – the position supported by the Soviet ethnos theorists – is simply a manifestation of the general principle of the psychic unity of mankind that underpins much western social science. Those who see ethnicity as a political tool, developed by the groups and individuals who manifest it, might also subscribe to this view, though perhaps arguing that the variations of form are of greater sociological significance. Only those who see ethnicity as no more than a theory developed by social scientists could really argue that there are as many kinds of ethnicity as there are people who write about it.

I will return to the issue of one or many ethnicities at the end of the next chapter, but before going on to consider the relevant literature for the United States I wish to concentrate on a word that is frequently invoked by the sociologists and others who look at minority migrant groups – race. For analytical purposes I consider it helpful to distinguish initially between (theories of) race and (theories of) ethnicity, but to do so cuts against the grain of some traditions (particularly some branches of British sociology though it is mirrored in many branches of American sociology and anthropology) and I should explain myself a little further.

THEORIES OF RACE

In the United States and, to a lesser extent, in Britain and Europe, there is an elision of social problems and sociological problems. Social problems are those that society at large, particularly its vocal representatives in the form of politicians and journalists, identify as being of importance and demanding of solutions. Such problems vary from society to society and through time: currently in Euro-America one could cite drug abuse, child abuse and – crucially – race relations and immigration as being foremost among internally or society-defined social problems. Conversely, sociological problems need have no bearing upon the perceived problems of any particular society and can be abstract in the extreme: the nature of human agency, the classification of kinship systems, and so forth. Occasionally, however, social problems and sociological problems converge, particularly so when sociological (or anthropological) field research is conducted in response to social problems. It is here that many studies of race and ethnicity are located, for theories and topics of study frequently mirror the given conditions and 'folk theories' of particular societies at particular times.

Some social scientists blur the distinction between theories of race and ethnicity (as, for example, in the title of Rex and Mason's edited collection of essays, *Theories of race and ethnic relations* [1986]), and use a single catch-all term – 'race-and-ethnicity' – to indicate the broad field with which they are concerned. Others seek to encompass one category within the other: currently, several authors are claiming that, properly understood, ethnicity subsumes race. Still other social scientists seek to deny the validity of either or both, claiming that another analytical category (usually class) is sufficient.

There is also, to some extent, a division of labour between anthropologists and sociologists, with anthropologists concentrating on theories of ethnicity and sociologists concentrating on theories of race; Sue Benson has argued that anthropologists feel more comfortable with 'softer' theories of ethnicity and have concentrated on apolitical discussions of classification and boundary maintenance, while avoiding the realities of racism and socioeconomic disadvantage (Benson in press). While I believe there to be some truth in Benson's position, one cannot lightly dismiss *all* anthropological theories of ethnicity as attempts to evade unpleasant political truths. Instead, one should be seeking theoretical and data-led distinctions between the two. For example, many of the cases discussed in the previous chapter (as well as those in Chapter 5) concern the interaction of groups which have been settled in a region for many generations, where the power relationships between them are not predicated upon the facts of migration, and which exhibit few if any phenotypical differences. By contrast, a standard ethnography of race relations, such as Little (1947) (discussed in the next chapter), would be concerned with the relations between a minority, migrant and typically black or dark-skinned group and the majority, domiciled and typically white 'host' population.

Karen Blu, already mentioned in the previous chapter, provides a synthetic account that is more in line with current thinking in anthropology. In her study of blacks, whites and Native Americans in North Carolina, she acknowledges that 'race consciousness is pervasive in Robeson County' (Blu 1980: 22) but avoids letting herself be lured by the obvious and taken-for-granted implications that this might entail. Indeed, it is through her use of an ethnicity paradigm that she gets behind the stereotypes of American race relations. In effect, she subsumes a race relations perspective within a theory of ethnicity. She notes that in American folk or everyday usage the terms 'race' and 'ethnic' have separate if overlapping meanings, 'race' being a term used when the biological characteristics of an individual are being considered, 'ethnic' being a term used when the cultural characteristics of an individual as a member of a group are being considered (1980: 204). It is the issue of groupness that is most important: 'ethnics' as Blu calls them share, in American usage, something cultural in common – a common background, a set of ancestors, a religion, and even a race (1980: 204–5). Thus for Blu race and ethnicity are separate categories in analytical terms because they are separate categories in American folk terminology. Unfortunately, many of the authors discussed in this chapter and the next, especially the earlier non-anthropological authors, did not particularly concern themselves with such folk terminology and did not document it. Blu's assessment of the terms may hold true at a greater historical depth and in a broader geographical range, but it is very difficult to assess. Certainly this is an appropriate point for me to state that in what follows I do not consider the issue of *racism* directly, though I do touch on it in Chapter 6.

So what are these 'theories of race'? Most modern sociologists are anxious to point out that the term race has only spurious biological or scientific significance when applied to human populations, but that it is none the less a popular concept (for example, Rex 1986: 18–19), while others defiantly state that regardless of biological definitions race is of interest to sociologists only as a sociological problem (for example, Cashmore and Troyna 1983: 10). Michael Banton, mirroring the opinion of Blu, cited above, states that not only is there a 'folk concept' of race, but there is also a folk concept of 'race relations' and that the academic sub-discipline should allow itself to be guided by the folk concept (Banton 1979: 137). The problem or limitation with these and many other statements is that the authors have usually decided that their prime focus of interest will be Britain and/or America (a limitation shared by Blu), where of course the English term 'race' and its derivatives exist in popular discourse. Cognate terms may not exist in other languages (and hence in other cultural discourses) and so terms such as 'volk' in Africaans and German present special problems (see Cashmore and Troyna 1983:

28 who note this but then continue to treat it as a synonym for 'race' anyway). What we get is a partial overlap between analytical sociological terms which are intended to be universally applicable and everyday or folk terms which are bounded by their cultural and historical context. While most, if not all, authors writing on race are aware of this, there is always the danger that either they will not be specific about which level of discourse they are using at any one moment (thus confusing the reader), or they will themselves move unconsciously between the two, or assume the overlap to be complete and total (thus confusing themselves).

As to actual theories of race, most are more usefully considered as theories of race relations and most writers here seek to differentiate them from theories of ethnicity. Earlier, nineteenth-century writers had theories of race in the sense that they wanted to explain differences in supposed racial origin – that is, biological differences. This is not the place to discuss what has come to be known as 'scientific' racism; Cashmore and Troyna (1983: 19–31) provide a brief overview, while Stocking (1968) and Banton (1987) provide a more detailed historical analysis.

For many sociologists ethnicity is a straightforward and unproblematic phenomenon and is to do with cultural differences felt at group level, while race is usually seen to be some kind of cultural construction or folk notion based on physical difference. 'Ethnicity', here, is often just a synonym for 'country of origin', while 'race' is apparently a larger-order category, used to define whole blocks of humanity. For example, William Petersen *et al.* note that 'many American writers now distinguish "racial" from "ethnic" minorities, the former being Negroes, Asians, and other "nonwhites", the latter the European nationalities' (Petersen *et al.* 1980: 6). Interestingly, they see the lead for this coming from the English language itself: 'English . . . has shown a trend toward what would be a useful distinction, reserving "race" for mankind's major biological divisions and using another designation for smaller groupings within it' (1980: 6).

Unsatisfied with this rather simplistic division (which is anyway inaccurate as far as the idea of 'major biological divisions' goes), others have attempted a more theoretically rigorous assessment. Take, for example, Cashmore and Troyna's view that ethnicity is a subjective feeling of oneness or unity that a racial group may feel in certain contexts (Cashmore and Troyna 1983: 12, 162). Or Banton's view that ethnicity describes a positive, insider's desire for inclusion, while race describes a negative, outsider's desire for exclusion (Banton 1977: 136). John Rex's view that conflict is more important than phenotype is, in his own eyes at least, one of the most radical (Rex 1986: 20). Rex, like many other authors, argues that race relations are fundamentally relations of inequality and that therefore any attempt to subsume them wholly within the field of ethnicity is inappropriate. This is because he assumes from his sociological perspective that theories of ethnicity are only about 'group differences' rather than 'discrimination and oppression' (1986: 19). Thus attempts such as Blu's to subsume race within theories of ethnicity are flawed.

Instead, in 1970 Rex argued that a 'race relations situation' was one where groups could be clearly distinguished in some way (through physical appearance *or* culture), where there was difference *and* inequality between groups, and where there was some kind of theory (often of a biological nature) that explained this inequality (Rex 1970: 30). Given that such a 'race relations situation' could include a number of cases that one would not normally consider to contain a 'racial' element (for example, class conflict within an otherwise apparently homogenous ethnic group), Rex later conceded that physical difference between groups (which he now called quasi-groups to indicate that this was an external, sociological term of analysis) was perhaps more important than he had at first thought. 'None the less', he adds, 'it is useful perhaps to distinguish within situations of conflict between those marked by physical and those marked by biological differences' (Rex 1986: 21).

Thus, at the risk of oversimplifying greatly, we can say that sociological theories of race, *on the whole*, define and are in turn defined by situations where phenotypically dissimilar groups are in some sort of long-term unequal power and/or economic relationship and where the dominant group justifies its position through some kind of legitimating ideology. In addition, we might note that sociologists of race (together with political scientists, and in contrast to anthropologists and social psychologists) are as much, if not more, concerned with apparently objective, externally defined criteria of difference and inequality as they are with subjective feelings of difference on the part of members of such groups, or with relativist concerns beloved of anthropologists that such categories may not be cross-culturally relevant.

As should be evident to any student of social science, previous research tends to dictate the course of future research, so that counter-current attempts such as Rex's to argue that there are (or were) certain class relations at specific moments in the history of capitalism that could profitably be analysed within a context of race relations theory (Rex 1986: 21) tend, on the whole, to be ignored. We saw at the end of the last chapter how more recent anthropological theories of ethnicity have tended to refine earlier theories, often by adding an extra theoretical ingredient (praxis theory, nationalist ideology, language games). So too, theories of race – and anthropological theories of ethnicity in situations sociologists might call 'race relations situations' – have tended to be cumulative in development, however much individual authors might vehemently proclaim their originality, or their refutation of all previous work. In order to reach an understanding of recent anthropological work on the ethnicity of minority migrant groups, we must therefore consider some earlier research on such groups. In the remainder of this chapter I consider the relevant literature for the United States. In the next chapter I turn to an examination of the literature on Britain.

RACE AND ETHNICITY IN THE UNITED STATES

The literature on race and ethnicity concerning the United States alone is voluminous and a comprehensive survey is well beyond the scope of this chapter. We can impose a rough and ready order upon it, however, by dividing it into two groups: literature that is largely descriptive (and often survey based), and literature that is more analytical and contains theoretical insights into ethnicity. The first group is by far the larger and I shall refer to it less often in what follows. The works in this group tend to describe the pattern of race or ethnic relations in some area of the United States, either in general terms or – especially during the heyday in the 1960s and 1970s – with reference to some particular issue, such as education, or housing, or political representation. The particular topic investigated is often suggested by some perceived social problem in the United States at the time. These works rarely make any innovative state-ments about the nature of race or ethnicity as terms in the soci-ological discourse and tend to take a positivist or commonsense view of their subject of enquiry. The same attitude prevails when defining the population units to be studied, especially when individuals are selected for a questionnaire survey, as the following quotation reveals: 'In general, it was not difficult to define a minority population by relying upon the commonly accepted local definitions, crude and simple as this method may seem. That is, "Negroes" were all persons so regarded by themselves and by other persons who clearly were themselves Negro. "Jews" were persons who regarded themselves as Jewish and were so regarded by others' (R. Williams *et al.* 1964: 11).

The second and smaller group of works, while often relying on field data gathered by the author, are more concerned with situating the observations within a wider context of theory and research. The authors' own observations are extrapolated outwards, sometimes profitably, sometimes naïvely, but always in an attempt to further theory. For example, in a paper on 'unhyphenated' white American ethnicity, published some twenty years after the book from which the above quotation came, Stanley Lieberson says: 'In short, when examining the racial and ethnic groups found in a given society, there is a tendency to take for granted their existence. In point of fact, a given racial or ethnic group does not go back to the origins of the human species . . . ethnic groups are under continuous flux in terms of their birth' (Lieberson 1985b: 160–1).

At the turn of the twentieth century academic attitudes to race and ethnicity were probably even less sophisticated than those of Williams, cited above. While Williams does at least consider both the insiders' and the outsiders' perceptions of race or ethnicity (even if he does not apparently consider that there could be any mismatch), the majority of early twentieth-century American writings on race assumed that there were two 'races' – the white and the black. What we would now consider to be categories were at the time assumed to be clearly differentiated population groups (defined, of course, largely by white academics). The groups were not only differentiated; relations between them were assumed to be problematic, and many works throughout the first half of the century (and beyond) sought to investigate the 'race problem'; Michael Banton has pointed out that in such works it is rarely, if ever, clear what – or more specifically whose – the problem is (Banton 1983: 61).

However, the nature of the 'problem' – as well as whose problem it is – is even more complex for those interested in ethnicity. As Banton (1983) demonstrates, an understanding of contemporary processes of race relations cannot be properly understood without an understanding of eighteenth- and particularly nineteenth-century thought on race. In the particular context of the United States, however, there are two discourses – one on race and one on ethnicity, the latter only really appearing at the start of the twentieth century.

Both discourses have academic as well as popular manifestations, and both are shot through with implicit or explicit reference to each other. Throughout the century a wide variety of academic (and popular) authors have attempted to deal with one to the exclusion of the other, largely as a result of the perception that the 'problems' attached to each are self-contained and independent. But even then, many such authors, especially those concerned exclusively with ethnicity, seem to feel a need to explain why they are not considering the other side of what is perhaps the same coin. We will see in the next chapter that a similar problem pervades the writing on 'race-and-ethnicity' in Britain, but this does not make the task of separating the two discourses (at least for analytical purposes) any easier. Banton's injunction to let the popular discourse guide academic study (Banton 1979: 137) is one solution to this problem – as Karen Blu's work demonstrates – but it is not necessarily advice that is helpful in allowing us to read earlier writings on the subject.

Most sociological writing from the first half of the twentieth century adhered to a positivistic para-scientific paradigm which upheld academic objectivity. Without doubt, these texts were informed by popular discourse on race and ethnicity, but this was a largely unconscious influence. It would therefore require a great deal of careful background research, much of it biographical, to establish which particular aspects of popular discourse influenced which particular writings, and why. For analytical purposes, therefore, I shall deal initially in this chapter with two major issues and their associated literature, before going on to look at more recent attempts to transcend the divide between (theories of) race and (theories of) ethnicity. The race issue I wish to deal with is the so-called 'Negro problem'; the ethnicity issue is raised by the controversy over the 'melting pot'.

BLACK AND WHITE IN AMERICA

In the early part of the century, the 'Negro problem' (as it was called by both black and white writers) was one of the dominant social issues in the USA, although it is by no means clear whose problem it was, nor even quite *what* the problem was (see also Banton 1987: 100). Certainly, the common perception was that the abolition of slavery in 1865 had brought very little positive change in relations between black and white. In the southern states rampant discrimination continued unchecked, while in the supposedly more liberal northern states blacks were rapidly forming a new underclass. Studies conducted by academics in the northern states often focused on the issue of whether race or class was the predominant factor in black disenfranchisement (an issue we will meet again when we turn to consider the literature on Britain). That is, were northern blacks an underclass because of their skin colour and some kind of innate racial prejudice among non-blacks (a position akin, as it were, to the primordial theories of ethnicity discussed in the previous chapter)? Or did the historical structures of slavery mean that black attempts to enter the economy and politics of the nation were sufficiently delayed that all the best jobs, opportunities and positions of power had been taken by non-blacks who were not prepared to relinquish them?

Many studies of northern US black life-chances in the first half of this century owe something to the pioneering work of the sociologist Robert Park and his colleagues at the University of Chicago in the 1920s and 1930s. Known as the Chicago School, they developed a form of analysis known as social ecology, which had a major influence on American sociology and also on social or human geography (see, for example, Clarke *et al.* 1984; Jackson and Smith 1981; Peach *et al.* 1981). Perhaps because of his pioneering work and his voluminous output, Park has fallen in and out of favour with sociologists over the last few decades. In particular, controversy has been generated around the issue of whether he understood American blacks to be another American ethnic group, and therefore to be viewed with the same analytical tools, or whether he understood them to be an analytically distinct category. Banton, for example, sees Park as endorsing the former position and applauds him for it (Banton 1987: 92); Philpott also sees Park as endorsing the position but castigates him for it (cited in Lal 1990: 5); while Barbara Ballis Lal, in a major survey of Park's work, claims that a 'careful reading of his books and essays' reveals him not to endorse such a position at all (Lal 1990: 5–6).

It is clear that over the course of almost half a century of writing Park's position on various issues must have shifted and we should not be surprised that apparently contradictory statements can be found within his work. What is more interesting within the context of the present work is that one of the key issues of this chapter and the next – the relationship between (theories of) race and (theories of) ethnicity – is very much a real issue within sociology and anthropology, and that Park's work has been used to endorse or reject various formulations of this relationship.

In their pioneering work, *The city* (1967 [1925]), Park, Burgess and McKenzie outlined their idea of an ecological model by asserting that the city is 'the natural habitat of civilized man' (Park *et al.* 1967: 2) in the same way that plant and animal species had their natural habitat. There was, however, deemed to be development among the different kinds of people who inhabited this environment, which led to their now classic typology of the zoning of the city. As each group – say, businessmen or industrial workers – outgrew their city zones, they moved on to other zones, leaving their original zones ripe for colonization by a new group. In fact, this picture is something of a distortion, dictated partly by the broader research interests guiding the present book. In Burgess's chapter on 'The growth of the city' (the book consists of a series of singly authored articles) the agency for change seems to be assigned less to groups or even individuals, but rather to the physical environment of the city itself. Using explicit organic analogies (mobility is '[l]ike the pulse of the community' [Park *et al.* 1967: 59], urban growth can be considered analogous to 'processes of metabolism in the body' [Park *et al.* 1967: 53]), Burgess attempts to categorize and even quantify the growth and organization of the city (Park *et al.* 1967: 61). Likewise, McKenzie's chapter on urban ecology ('The ecological approach') grants agency to the ecological mechanisms at work, rather than to human beings; he says, for example, that attempts by 'reformers' to keep young people in rural areas and prevent them migrating to cities are doomed to failure because they go against 'the general principles of the ecological order' (Park *et al.* 1967: 71).

The city is really a set of programmatic statements, outlining an anthropologically influenced new approach to urban sociology (Park *et al.* 1967: 3). It has little to say about race or 'the Negro problem' and it must be admitted that what is said seems as ecologically deterministic as the comments above. For example, Park in a chapter on 'Juvenile delinquency' notes that '[t]he mere movement of the population from one part of the country to another . . . is a disturbing influence [that contributes to the disorganization of modern society]' and he gives the migration of 'the Negroes' from the southern states northwards as an example (Park *et al.* 1967: 108). He also notes that the 'enormous amount of delinquency, juvenile and adult, that exists today in Negro communities in northern cities is due in part, though not entirely, to the fact that migrants are not able to accommodate

themselves at once to a new and relatively strange environment'
(Park *et al.* 1967: 108). This view of the city as a strange and hostile
place, which bewilders and confuses the (presumably) rural migrant,
is one that we encountered in the last chapter and is obviously of a
piece with both the organic analogy employed (dysfunction of the
metabolism) and the characterization of the 'zone in transition' (the
area of the city immediately surrounding the central business
district) as the '"bad lands" with their submerged regions of
poverty, degradation, disease, and their underworlds of crime and
vice' (Park *et al.* 1967: 55). Needless to say, this is the zone within
which the 'Black Belt' of Chicago is located.

I am not trying to say that the area immediately around the Chicago
central business zone was without poverty and deprivation; what I
am trying to point out is that Park and his colleagues were clearly
torn by a dilemma imposed by their use of the ecological model: the
city was 'man's' natural habitat, yet its ecology seemed dysfunctional. The presence of so many migrants and ethnic groups in
the dysfunctional zone (Jews, Italians, Greeks, Chinese and – of
course – blacks) implied that they were in some sense to blame for
that dysfunction and only redeemed themselves (and hence the health
of the city) by moving on into the more disciplined and apparently
normative zones of industrial workers and commuters. In fact, in his
later writings on race and ethnicity (mostly the papers dating from
1917 to 1944 collected together as *Race and culture* [1950], the
majority of which postdate *The city*), Park tended to espouse a less
deterministic view. In particular, in what Banton deems his most
mature statement on race relations (Banton 1987: 90), he stated:
'Race relations . . . are not so much the relations that exist between
individuals of different races as between individuals conscious of
these differences' (Park 1950: 81). That is, although he is not saying
that race is all in the mind, he is saying that the importance given to
race is. It is the consciousness of race, not race itself, that matters.
There is obviously much more that can be said about Park and the
Chicago School in general. Space does not permit it here, but I would
refer the reader to Lal's book (1990), to the relevant discussions in
Banton (1987) and Cashmore and Troyna (1983), and of course to
Park's own essays (1950).

Park, himself influenced by the humanistic and ethnographic
approach of Thomas and Znaniecki in their work on Polish migrants
to North America (1984 [1918–1922], discussed below), was also a
great influence on others, most notably on the authors of a study of

the black community of Chicago published in 1945. St Clair Drake and Horace Cayton dedicated their book, *Black Metropolis* (1945), to Park, describing him as a 'friend of the Negro people'. Park's was not the only influence, however, and I wish to introduce another American anthropologist before turning to Drake and Cayton's book.

In 1929 the American social anthropologist W. Lloyd Warner returned to the United States after conducting fieldwork in northern Australia with the Murngin (later known as the Yolgnu), partly at the instigation of the British anthropologist Radcliffe-Brown (Winters 1991: 739). He decided to begin a series of studies of local communities in the United States, the best known of which are probably the 'Yankee City' studies conducted by him and his team in New England, the results of which were published through the early years of the 1940s. Although one volume of the Yankee City studies had specifically addressed the issue of what we would now call ethnicity (Warner and Srole 1945, discussed in more detail below), a later project that he directed on the 'Deep South' focused far more sharply on issues of race (see Davis *et al.* 1941; see also Powdermaker 1993). Part of this research developed Warner's influential (and controversial) early statement on 'caste' and class in American race relations (see Warner 1936).

Warner proposed that there was an unbridgeable 'caste' barrier between white and black Americans such that no matter how wealthy or 'assimilated' to white society individual blacks became their status would never be comparable to whites. Each 'caste' contained within it a class system of ranking (that is, Weberian status groups rather than Marxist classes), which permitted mobility. John Rex provides a neat diagrammatic representation of Warner's position, showing how a rich, well-educated, 'upper class' black could be seen in one sense to be superior to many middle and lower 'class' whites, but was still debarred from their society by virtue of the 'caste' barrier (Rex 1986: 30, Figure 6). There have, of course, been numerous challenges to this view, not least from South Asian scholars who argue that, whatever the reality of the American situation, the term caste is not appropriate (Dumont 1980: Appendix A). More particularly, the idea (as well as those of Park) was challenged from a Marxist perspective at the time by Oliver Cromwell Cox (Cox 1948).

The caste/class issue also cast a shadow over Warner's work on 'Yankee City' (actually Newburyport, Massachusetts). In the volume he jointly authored with Leo Srole, *The social systems of American ethnic groups* (1945), he touched on the issue, but bearing in mind my comments above about the tendency in American scholarship at this period (and later) to focus on *either* ethnicity *or* race, but rarely both together, the very title of Warner and Srole's book indicates that black Americans were not going to be considered in the substantive discussions of the book. As with Park, the influence of an early model (in Park's case, the ecological model of the city, in this case, caste and class) prevented the kind of integrated analysis that now, after the event, one feels would have benefited the Yankee City work. As it is, Warner and Srole's work is discussed below, when I come to consider theories of the 'melting pot'. Of interest to note, however, is that Warner was already modifying his caste–class hypothesis. In the notorious tables at the end of the work (discussed below in some detail) he and Srole admit mixed and blurred analytical categories, such as 'ethno-racial to class or color caste' as the 'American rank' assigned to or held by '[s]mall groups of Spanish Americans in the Southwest' (Warner and Srole 1945: 291, Table 7). They are clearly experiencing difficulty in trying to square their simplistic and positivist classificatory schemas with the complex reality of the North American population, although the American 'Negroes' are still firmly 'racial to color caste' in rank. They allow their classificatory schemas to drive their analysis of the data.

Let us now return to Drake and Cayton's *Black Metropolis* (1945). Although Park's influence is strong, so is Warner's. Indeed, Warner contributes a 'Methodological note' at the end of the book, outlining the relationship between his Yankee City project, his Deep South project, and Drake and Cayton's work. Drake and Cayton were both black academics (as was Cox, mentioned above): Drake, an anthropologist who had worked with Allison Davis (the chief investigator on Warner's Deep South project) and who would later go on to write about race relations in Britain (for example, Drake 1956); and Cayton, a sociologist and student of Park.

That both were black is not perhaps as significant for my perspective as it must have been at the time, though Drake was from the South originally and to some extent represented the 'Negro problem' that they document (Drake and Cayton 1945: 61, 69, for example). Rather, they present a contrast with the much later phenomenon of the emergence of the non-white anthropologist in British sociology and social anthropology. They followed Warner in quite explicitly doing 'anthropology at home' (cf. A. Jackson 1986), though despite Warner's claim for the value of this over the sociologist's approach lying in the anthropologist's ability to transcend preconceptions by drawing on comparative evidence (Drake and Cayton 1945: 771), there is very little in the way of non-American comparative material to be found in *Black Metropolis* (see, for example, a footnote on pp. 171–2 which discusses cross-cultural standards of physical beauty). The value of the anthropological approach adopted lies rather in the rich ethnography, and the sensitivity Drake and Cayton show towards qualitative data, particularly rhetoric and styles of speech. There are a number of tables and figures displaying quantitative data, but the overwhelming thrust of the book is to document lived experience through authentic voices.

Black Metropolis is not a theoretical work and the theory that informs it is largely implicit. Early on in the book, Drake and Cayton pose a series of research questions that informed the project: how Black Metropolis came to be, why it persists, how its people live, what the rest of the city thinks of it, what its inhabitants think of it and the rest of the city, and whether it will eventually disappear. They seek to answer these questions by looking at a variety of data gathered on employment, housing, class, and so forth. However, I wish to consider only two issues here: skin colour and 'assimilation'. Drake and Cayton realize that skin colour is what seems to set the inhabitants of Black Metropolis apart from other 'groups' in Chicago which is thus the axiomatic variable in American race relations, and for the most part they utilize a (sociologically) unproblematic category of 'Negro' to refer to the people with whom they are dealing. That is, the social problematic of the 'Negro' – as in 'the Negro problem' – is treated by the authors largely as a given sociological category. In this, they follow Warner's 'caste–class' hypothesis. However, at times they indicate that the issue may be more complex and subtle than this, and their most revealing remarks come when they discuss intermarriage, folk notions of biology, black perceptions of skin colour, and 'passing' (light-skinned blacks assuming a 'white' identity – and vice versa).

A popular idea concerning race, heredity and blood at the time held that a single drop of 'black blood' made one black. Although this is still, as far as I know, a popular belief in North America, it is important to realize that this is not by any means a universally held belief. White British belief, in particular, finds this a difficult concept, largely because 'black' as an homogenizing political identity is far less well established in the UK than it is in the US. The situation is even more complex in countries such as Colombia and Brazil where, although the range of skin tones is probably no greater than in the US, the associated cultural or political categories are more fluid and less binary (Degler 1986; Sanjek 1971; Wade 1993).

Drake and Cayton refer to the 'one drop' belief on a couple of occasions. At one point they refer to it as 'a fact' that 'one known drop of "colored" blood is sufficient to make an otherwise completely white person a Negro' (1945: 159), and earlier, discussing 'interracial' (that is, 'Negro' and 'white') marriages, they state: 'Most of the interracial couples studied in Black Metropolis have children. They are, of course, *Negro* children' (1945: 154; emphasis in original).

But it later becomes obvious that these, and other similar remarks, are meant ironically. Referring again to the 'one drop' belief, they show how blacks may claim the belief to their own advantage: 'As Negroes sometimes jocularly phrase it: "Negro blood is powerful. One drop will make you whole"' (Drake and Cayton 1945: 268). In the context of a discussion on 'passing' they make their position clear: 'Americans, white and black, see with their emotions as well as their eyes, and actualities are colored by stereotyped expectations' (1945: 164).

It is this 'seeing with the emotions' that allows many of the cases of 'passing' that they discuss, and they adopt a stance close to that of interactionalist sociology in order to explain how, for example, Robert Park himself (who appears unproblematically white from his frontispiece portrait in *Race and culture* [1950]) could 'pass' as black to gain admittance to a 'Negro' hotel (Drake and Cayton 1945: 164). It is also 'seeing with the emotions' as well as with the eyes that underlies blacks' own views on skin colour. Those blacks who idealize pale or fair skin colour in blacks are said by others to be 'color-struck' and 'partial to color' (1945: 496–7), although Drake and Cayton point out that the preferred skin tone for most is a mid-brown (or 'bronze') – neither 'too' dark, nor 'too' light (1945: 503). But they also make the point that the various colour terms employed – black, bronze, yellow, and so forth – do not refer unambiguously and exclusively to skin colour: '"blackness" ... [is] a whole complex: dark-skin [*sic*] color, pronounced Negroid features, and kinky hair. Sometimes they do not mean color at all!' (1945: 503, footnote).

Of course, even for white racists, stereotypes and derogatory speech concerning blacks call upon other physical and, for that matter, behavioural characteristics. But the point is that Drake and Cayton, like many authors after them, struggled to distinguish between two levels of analysis: between a popular understanding of race as a 'natural' category which required only documentation and not explanation, and a sociological understanding of race that rested upon discourse, perception, behaviour and – crucially in the North American context of slavery – history.

On Drake and Cayton's understanding of 'assimilation' I want to say little, as this is the subject of the next section. Here it is necessary to point out that, although Warner's 'caste–class' hypothesis prevented them from considering the issue with any seriousness, they did veer towards a class-based explanation, as noted. In general, they discuss ideas of 'assimilation' and the 'melting pot' with reference to other groups in Chicago, where they constantly make a distinction between 'native Americans' (by which they mean early white, Anglo-Saxon Protestant settlers) and the 'foreign born' migrants of more recent years (for example, 1945: 17). They also make the point, when discussing 'interracial' marriages, that these are more likely to take place between blacks and recent 'foreign born' migrants who are 'not completely assimilated into American culture' (1945: 139). Again, although they do not pursue the point, they are apparently working their way towards an understanding of a cultural construction of race *and* ethnicity where the two could be considered within the same theoretical paradigm.

Drake and Cayton's book, along with others of the period such as Powdermaker's study of Indianola, Mississippi (1939, recently reissued, with a new introduction by Brackette Williams and Drexel Woodson [1993]), opened up a rich seam of involved local ethnographies of race and race processes in the United States written and researched by members of the groups documented and other Americans, by academics and non-academics (see, for example, Hannerz 1969; Lewis 1964; Liebow 1967; Whyte 1981). In order to maintain some focus in the present work, however, I have chosen not to discuss these works, but to return instead to my central concern with works that seek to document and analyse ethnicity. I shall do this by looking in particular at the 'melting pot' issue.

SHADES OF WHITE IN AMERICA

If, following Warner, black Americans were felt to be for ever excluded (or excluded for the foreseeable future at any rate) from competing equally with white Americans by the 'caste' barrier of race, the same was not thought to be true of other, more recent, migrant groups to the US. In the latter half of the nineteenth century and the first half of the twentieth, ethnicity's equivalent buzz-word to race's 'Negro problem' was 'assimilation'.

To trace the roots of this literature would require us to go back to the European colonization of North America and to analyse the patterns of interaction between the early settler colonies. Such an exercise would allow us to see the structural patterns established by the earliest white Americans to which later, nineteenth- and early twentieth-century, European migrants were expected to conform. Space does not permit such an exercise and instead I start my investigation with one of the pioneering works of this century, William Thomas and Florian Znaniecki's massive five-volume work, *The Polish peasant in Europe and America* (1918–1922; republished in an abridged edition in 1984). This was conceived as a work designed to influence policy (Zaretsky 1984: 2). Yet the data they draw upon include letters and autobiographies written by the subjects, as well as the more conventional quantitative data.

Although Thomas and Znaniecki have little to say about ethnicity as such, they took the unusual methodological step of conducting research in Poland in an attempt to understand the background of the Polish immigrants to America. These immigrants did not simply seek to recreate their old culture (which would have been impossible anyway), but rather sought to make sense of their experience of migration by recreating their group identity: 'the striking phenomenon, the central object of our investigation, is the formation of [a] coherent group out of originally incoherent elements, the creation of a society which in structure and prevalent attitudes is neither Polish nor American but constitutes a specific new product whose raw materials have been partly drawn from Polish traditions, partly from the new conditions in which these immigrants live, and partly from American social values as the immigrant sees and interprets them' (Thomas and Znaniecki 1984: 240; drawn from the introduction to volume 5 of the original).

Earlier in this passage Thomas and Znaniecki note that, as time passes, the immigrants none the less acquire more and more American attitudes, a feature found particularly among the second generation (1984: 240). This acquisition of attitudes and behaviour of the so-called 'host culture' is the process commonly known as assimilation (a term that Thomas and Znaniecki also use) and it became one of the key areas of study for sociologists and anthropologists of minority migrant groups over the next seventy years.

I have already discussed Warner and Srole's *The social systems of American ethnic groups* (1945) above in the context of US race relations, but it is really as a contribution to an understanding of US ethnicity that the work was intended. As noted above, American blacks are largely conspicuous by their absence from the study. Undertaken as part of the Harvard University 'Yankee City' studies, Warner and Srole's study was intended to document 'part of the magnificent history of the adjustment of the ethnic groups [of Yankee City] to American life' (1945: 2).

While this in part is true, Michael Banton has claimed that the study, undertaken in the 1930s, was motivated by a concern among the American public that certain of the European immigrants to the United States in the latter half of the nineteenth century and the early part of the twentieth had still not become, as he puts it, 'Americanized' (Banton 1983: 146). Not that this concern is entirely concealed in the work, for as Warner and Srole quite clearly state: 'The underlying assumption of this study is an examination of the validity of America's conception of itself as the "great melting pot"' (1945: 32). Their conclusion is at once reassuring (for some of their contemporary readers) and revealing; they argue that the 'melting pot' metaphor, with its implications of a new identity being forged out of the elements of all the parts, is inappropriate. What is actually happening is that the minority parts are coming to conform to the greater whole: the 'American system' (1945: 155).

The major part of Warner and Srole's work was to examine the communal life and activities of eight groups of migrants to Yankee City (Newburyport, Massachusetts): Irish, French-Canadians, Jews, Italians, Armenians, Greeks, Poles and Russians, the Irish being the first to arrive (in the 1840s) and the Russians the last (between 1910 and 1920) (Warner and Srole 1945: 28). The reasons for the migrations are touched on only very briefly in Warner and Srole's account and for the most part they subscribe to a standard 'push-pull' model of migration (for example, 1945: 105), where a favourable economic climate in the United States and/or an unfavourable economic or political climate in the sending country provides the motivation. Much of the book is then spent examining, chapter by chapter, a number of key social institutions such as church membership or 'the family', as these are manifested among the eight groups.

For the modern student of ethnicity one of the more interesting features of Warner and Srole's study is the groups they chose to include. Of the eight groups, six are defined by the nation state from which they came, one is defined by religion (the Jews), and one has been pre-defined elsewhere by nationality (the French-Canadians). More interestingly, two groups resident in Yankee City are almost entirely excluded from the discussion: the 'Yankees' who give the city its pseudonym, and the blacks. Blacks appear to be excluded from the main part of the discussion following the logic outlined at the beginning of this chapter – that 'race' and 'ethnicity' are separable categories in much earlier American sociological literature. For Warner and Srole, the stigma and exclusion caused by phenotypical difference is a near-absolute barrier to assimilation; theirs is an investigation of 'ethnic groups' and not a study of race. The exclusion of the white 'Yankees' is perhaps more interesting. Banton's view on their exclusion is that Warner and Srole unconsciously adopted a folk model of ethnicity, one which held that white, northern European Protestants have no ethnicity (Banton 1983: 146). By virtue, in their own eyes, of having arrived 'first' in Yankee City, and in North America, the 'Yankees' felt they had acquired the right to define identity – both their own, and that of those who followed them.

The corollary of two of Warner and Srole's basic themes – that white, northern European Protestants have no ethnicity, and that the minority migrant groups are changing to be like this American majority – is found in the final chapter of the book where they present their by now notorious 'timetable' which predicts the relative rates at which groups will be absorbed into the body of 'American' society (Warner and Srole 1945: 288–92). In this 'conceptual scheme' as they call it, the closer a group is to the culture and phenotype of the 'host' group (that is, English-speaking, white and Protestant), the shorter the period of assimilation. Perhaps wisely, Warner and Srole specified the predicted rates in relative terms only, avoiding any absolute quantification in terms of years. (Robert Park, also a believer in the inevitability of assimilation, also carefully avoided discussing this within any absolute time frame [Park 1950: 353]).

The tangential interest of Warner and Srole in America's black population, and their almost complete avoidance of the white 'Yankee' population is, as I have said, a direct result of their assumptions about the a priori existence of discrete groups and their division of these groups into two types – the 'ethnic' and the 'racial'. This was (and continues to be) a common view, and while Warner and Srole concentrated their efforts on the 'ethnic' side of this divide, the bulk of the literature – then as now – was more concerned with the 'racial' side.

Although some specifically 'ethnic' literature was produced in the two decades following Warner and Srole's book, the next really significant date of publication is 1963. This was the year of the first edition of Nathan Glazer and Patrick Moynihan's influential (and controversial) study of ethnicity in New York: *Beyond the melting pot* (1970 [1963]). Before we go any further, it is worth briefly examining the history and implications of the key term.

The idea of the 'melting pot' was first popularized, if not first used, in the United States in a 1908 Broadway play by one Israel Zangwill, although Glazer and Moynihan find a reference to the idea – 'all nations are melted into a new race of men' – as far back as 1782 (1970: 288). Zangwill's play, *The melting pot*, tells the story of a Russian Jewish immigrant in New York who succeeds, both in money and love and, perhaps more importantly, in becoming an 'American' (1970: 289–90). Over the decades that followed, the term became one of contempt as much as an ideal to be admired or aspired to. Indeed, it is crucially important for the reader to realize that, from Warner and Srole onwards, the academic study of ethnicity and ethnic relations in America is not a neutral process. While Banton needs to look outside Warner and Srole's text, to the historical and political particularities of the US immigration process, to provide a metatextual comment (Banton 1983: 146), this becomes increasingly unnecessary in the later literature. The authors themselves engage in quite explicit polemic, which is enlightening and tiresome by turn.

Warner and Srole's text was quite explicitly a 'melting pot' text. The notorious 'timetable' of assimilation is predicated on the assumption that assimilation to the 'American' way of life is inevitable. In reality, of course, and as noted above, it is not so much a question of all ethnicities becoming blended in the melting pot to form something new, as a question of all 'others' conforming to a relatively changeless core of 'old stock' or 'WASP' identity. Park, too, has been characterized as a melting pot theorist, although his comments on the matter are scattered and less dogmatic than those of Warner and Srole (see, for example, Chapter 16 of Park [1950] – 'Racial assimilation in secondary groups').

Challenges to the very idea of the melting pot had come early on, even from Zangwill himself who became a fervent Zionist after writing the play and advocated a strongly primordialist position of irredeemable differences (Glazer and Moynihan 1970: 290). But the major challenge for most scholars came with the publication of Glazer and Moynihan's *Beyond the melting pot*. The first (1963) edition of this book consisted of a short introduction, extended case studies of five of New York's largest 'ethnic groups', and a conclusion. In the second (1970) edition they added a 95-page introduction, ostensibly to update the original text, but also as a vehicle to defend and restate their ideas. The first point to note is that 'Negroes' are considered as an 'ethnic group' alongside the Irish and Italians, as are Puerto Ricans. Glazer and Moynihan are not blind to race, but they do try to subordinate it to ethnicity (not always successfully, as the introduction to the second edition admits).

Glazer and Moynihan are anxious to establish that ethnicity is a new phenomenon, and that when manifested among minority migrant groups and their descendants ethnic identities are not specifically or solely derived from the 'national' or 'original' culture that the migrants left behind (1970: 16, 313). Early on in the introduction to the first edition they state: '*[t]he ethnic group in American society became not a survival from the age of mass immigration but a new social form*' (1970: 16; emphasis in original). In terms of the positions outlined in the previous chapter, they are explicitly rejecting a 'primordialist' position on ethnicity; they also explicitly endorse an 'instrumentalist' position: '[a] man is connected to his [ethnic] group by ties of family and friendship. But he is also connected by ties of *interest*. The ethnic groups in New York are also *interest groups*. This is perhaps the single most important fact about ethnic groups in New York City' (1970: 17; emphasis in original). However, unlike Abner Cohen who was perhaps the most explicitly instrumentalist of the theorists discussed in the previous chapter, the specific situation that Glazer and Moynihan encounter in New York forces them to consider local patterns and perceptions of race relations. In the book's conclusion, for example, they state: '*except where color is involved*' [my emphasis] the 'specifically *national* [their emphasis] aspect of most ethnic groups rarely survives the first generation' (1970: 313). As we saw with the Hausa in Nigeria, Glazer and Moynihan describe a situation where a number of ethnic identities – Irish, Italian, 'Negro' etc. – are created and recreated as groups jockey for political and economic advantage in the city. A 'national' label is used to describe most of these groups, and 'Negroes' are seen as being equivalent.

In a sense, of course, melting pot theorists, such as Warner and

Srole, also saw blacks as being analytically equivalent to other 'ethnic groups' but for their phenotype (so they could be included in the assimilation timetable along with the others, even if the prognosis for assimilation was extremely pessimistic). Writers such as Drake and Cayton, and later William Wilson (1978), who were more concerned with race than ethnicity, implicitly or explicitly rejected this and proposed instead a class-based analysis that rested on the particular historical experience of slavery and exploitation. Although Glazer and Moynihan explicitly reject the melting pot hypothesis (Glazer and Moynihan 1970: 13), they take its assumption of analytical equivalence between 'ethnic' and 'racial' groups, even if this causes them some problems.

They begin their introduction to the first edition by claiming that it is 'a beginning book . . . an effort to trace the role of ethnicity in the tumultuous, varied, endlessly complex life of New York City' (1970: 1). The resounding turn of phrase is remarkably similar to Warner and Srole's justification of their study (Warner and Srole 1945: 2), but Glazer and Moynihan very quickly go on to describe the main theoretical point: '[t]he point about the melting pot, as we say later, is that it did not happen' (1970: 1). Although they begin the book with the very term that is central to this study – ethnicity – they actually employ it infrequently after that, relying instead on 'ethnic' as an adjective with an appropriate noun. Even in the 1970 introduction to the second edition, the term is used sparingly, and the main adjectival use of 'ethnic' is in the phrase 'ethnic identity'.

Although it would be wrong to make too much of their use of language, it seems clear that 'ethnicity' for Glazer and Moynihan is a relatively unproblematic term, for which the equally unproblematic 'ethnic identity' seems a straightforward equivalent. Their concern in *Beyond the melting pot* is to document the extent to which groups such as the Irish or Italians in New York have continuously manifested an 'ethnic' identity, long after they have ceased to manifest an identity that would be recognizably 'Irish' or 'Italian' in Ireland or Italy. As Stephen Steinberg points out, however, there is an unspoken slippage at work here (1981). While Park and Warner are the focal points for implicit criticism by Glazer and Moynihan, to be fair, they based their melting pot theories on the observation of largely first-generation immigrants. Glazer and Moynihan, writing some twenty to thirty years later, are dealing with a 'revival' of ethnicity among second- and third-generation descendants of those immigrants (Steinberg 1981: 49). History has changed as much as theory.

However, for Glazer and Moynihan, an interesting case of 'non-ethnicity' is found among a collection of individuals who would otherwise be known as the 'German-Americans' (1970: 311–14). There is, Glazer and Moynihan assert, no evidence of a German-American ethnic identity in the way that there is an Irish-American one, or a 'Negro' identity – at least in New York. Presumably the first German immigrants in North America had the same incipient structural potential for an ethnic identity as other groups of immigrants, but it was never realized (or 'crystallized', following Stephen Morris's use of the term to describe inter-group relations in Uganda in the 1950s [Morris 1968: 34]). This is evidenced, Glazer and Moynihan explain, by the fact that there are no 'German' politicians in New York, for example, in the way that there are 'Irish' politicians or 'Italian' politicians (Glazer and Moynihan 1970: 311); that is, politicians who can appeal to and rely on a bloc vote. Their explanation for this is that German immigrants closely matched the 'old stock' Americans (white, Anglo-Saxon Protestants) in religion, occupation and class, and merged imperceptibly with them. The rise of Nazi Germany in the twentieth century was a further incentive for the 'Germans' to ignore their 'national' heritage (Glazer and Moynihan 1970 312–13).

Glazer and Moynihan are both essentially political scientists (Moynihan had in fact worked in government, in the Nixon administration, as well as in academia), and an anthropologist may well have difficulties with the narrow understanding of culture and identity that informs their instrumentalist vision of ethnicity. In fact, an anthropologist might well endorse their claim that there is or was no 'German' ethnicity in New York, but she or he would require far more in the way of evidence than simply the absence of 'German-Americans' as an economic or political force. I will return to this issue below, when I consider Stephen Steinberg, one of the most vocal dissidents from Glazer and Moynihan's point of view, but their (mis)understanding of 'culture' lies at the root of their problems in equating race with ethnicity.

In the first edition of *Beyond the melting pot*, Glazer (the author of most of the substantive chapters) had written a badly phrased comment on the 'Negro' having 'no values [or] culture' (1970: xix footnote, which cites both the original, 1963, text and its revision). What he had apparently intended to point out was that blacks, having been so entirely dislocated from any 'original' culture by the experience of slavery and by virtue of far greater generational depth in the United States than the other groups dealt with, had little to distinguish them in 'cultural' terms from other 'Americans' (that is, the 'old stock'). They shared the same language, religion, and so forth. For this reason, Glazer argued, blacks had less of a core of identity around which their ethnic identity could crystallize (and he tacitly reverts at this point to a more primordial vision of ethnicity) and the middle class blacks 'must' accept 'a higher degree of responsibility' towards advancing the group's cause (1970: 53). The passage is interesting for a number of reasons, not least because it appears to advocate instrumental ethnicity as a social tool for others to use (rather than as an objective analytical tool used by Glazer), but it seems to have been the greatest area of weakness in the book. In the introduction to the second edition, Glazer admits that his passage could be read as claiming that blacks had *no* culture or values at all. He therefore revises the offending passage to seem a little more upbeat: 'The Negro is so much an American, the distinctive product of America. He bears no foreign values and culture that he feels the need to guard from the surrounding environment' (1970: xix footnote, 53). But he then goes on to point out that even in its revised form the passage, indeed the whole chapter on 'The Negroes', was badly awry.

Glazer and Moynihan wrote *Beyond the melting pot* at just the wrong time. Had they waited a year or so more, they would have witnessed a massive politicization of American blacks, that would reach a dramatic peak with Martin Luther King, Malcolm X and the Black Panthers. The introduction to the second edition of the book charts their failings and offers some explanation. The particularities need not detain us here, though in view of their avowed political science perspective on ethnicity their failings must seem all the more embarrassing. Curiously, however, although they seemed to profess unabashed enthusiasm for the failure of melting pot theories and the creation and recreation of ethnic identities in the first edition of the book, they seemed unnerved by the changes that had occurred in the decade leading up to 1970. They claim to be 'saddened and frightened' by '[t]he political costs of separatist rhetoric' among blacks (1970: xxi) and bemoan the use of 'Black, Brown, Yellow and Red' as the then politically correct terms for other 'racial' groups (1970: xiv). 'Human groups', they assert, 'do not exist in nature, or rather, the part of difference that exists because of nature is unimportant' (1970: xiv).

With the final quotation I have no particular quibble: to most anthropologists it is unexceptional. But the earlier quotations indicate that Glazer and Moynihan are having trouble with race rearing its analytical head in their otherwise tidy world of ethnicity theory. They admit that the first edition of the book had failed to determine 'what *kind* of group Negroes would form. As an ethnic group they would be one of many. As a racial group, as "blacks" as the new nomenclature has it, they would form a unique group in American society' (1970: xiii), but one has a distinct sense that they feel that the problem lies with history and society, rather than with their theoretical perspective.

If the tone of the introduction to the first edition of *Beyond the melting pot* had been modestly confident, and the tone of the introduction to the second edition was somewhat conciliatory (at least as far as the ill-judged remarks on 'Negroes' and their lack of culture went), the tone of their next collaboration, the introduction to *Ethnicity: theory and experience* (1975a), is frankly belligerent. Here they bluntly state that ethnicity is new, it is here to stay and that America had better get used to it. Their embarrassment over their treatment of race in the previous book is brushed aside, as 'ethnicity' is asserted to be an analytical category 'that extends beyond the *more limited categories of race*, nationality, and minority group' (Glazer and Moynihan 1975b: 25–6; emphasis added).

They begin their introduction by noting that '[e]thnicity seems to be a new term' (1975b: 1) and give a number of 'first' dictionary definitions dating from the 1960s and 1970s (see Sollors 1989b: xiii for an earlier 'first' use; and Chapman *et al.* 1989: 11–17 for an alternative approach to use and etymology). They then go on to reassert a number of points made in *Beyond the melting pot*: that 'ethnicity' is a new thing, rather than a new way for analysts to describe something old; that a primordialist view of ethnicity is wrong and an instrumentalist view is right, and so forth. No longer are they merely saddened and frightened by the rise of 'separatist rhetoric', they are belligerently scathing of it. Or rather, they object to the fact that the state (the welfare state in the developed world, the socialist state in the developing world) has appropriated ethnicity as a tool for its own increased power (1975b: 8–11). The state – in this case the American state – systematically invades the lives of its citizens and reifies 'ethnic' categories, in the pursuit of the justice and democracy that civil rights legislation was supposed to bring about. In a sense, Glazer and Moynihan have a point: there is a paradox inherent in the idea that, in order to minimize discrimination on the basis of difference between people, differences must be systematically and authoritatively monitored, recorded and hence re-emphasized. But to a European reader, their rhetoric is as much rooted in specifically North American ideas of individualism and the minimal state, as it is in ideas about ethnicity.

There is a theoretical abstraction present in their introduction that is absent from the earlier work. Where, in *Beyond the melting pot*, the persistence of ethnicity among specific groups in New York was explained by reference to equally specific historical factors (for example, Glazer and Moyniham 1970: 292), in the later work the recent evolution and maintenance of ethnic identities are adduced from numerous examples framed within what amounts to a Socratic dialogue. A series of italicized questions – presumably those of the eager but ignorant reader – is presented, and then answered at length by the authors. It is through this dialogue that we learn, far more sharply than in *Beyond the melting pot*, what is new about ethnicity. The authors acknowledge that divisions between groups of people, the struggle for advantage, the ties of affect as well as expediency, are not, in themselves, necessarily new things. 'Ethnicity' is new because the conjunction of these features is new. 'New' as it is used here is rather vague, but seems contingent with the rise, from the early nineteenth century, of nationalism as a political philosophy; in fact, Glazer and Moynihan have little to say on the subject of nationalism, beyond hinting that notions of ethnic identity challenge nationalist ideologies (Glazer and Moynihan 1975b: 18). I will look at this particular idea in detail in Chapter 5.

However, what makes ethnicity different from earlier forms of identification is that it lacks content. At this level, they claim, the melting pot theorists (whose ideas they refer to as the 'liberal expectancy') are right (1975b: 8). 'Culturally' there is little difference between America's 'ethnic groups'; they differ only in their histories and therefore in their position with respect to the structures of the American political economy (1975b: 8). Of course, there is much in common here with Frederik Barth's position. There are also two crucial differences: first, Barth is careful to distinguish between the obvious, superficial aspects of culture – language, dress, food, and so forth – and the cultural *significance* of such items. It is not so much the objective presence or absence of such items of cultural 'stuff' that matters, but the symbolic weight or presence such items have. Barth is happy to accord that the 'stuff' of culture may mutate wildly, but that the idea and symbolic power of 'culture' remains.

As in their earlier work, Glazer and Moynihan treat culture as a 'thin' or ephemeral issue, and see it as unable to sustain the burden of ethnicity. Secondly, Barth argues that ethnic identities cannot sustain themselves: they are forged at the boundaries where they meet other ethnic identities. As political scientists, Glazer and Moynihan look not to the interaction of ethnic identities, but the relation which all such identities (and thus the groups that hold them) have towards the state.

As I pointed out in the last chapter, Barth's analytical indifference to the state, and to centralized relations of power, produces a liberal model of ethnic pluralism that has difficulty in dealing with inequalities of power and resources. Glazer and Moynihan's approach focuses on this almost to the exclusion of all else. As political scientists, the political and administrative processes of the state are all important, and hence they define ethnicity in these terms. The result is that 'culture' is a bundle of ephemeral or indeed non-existent 'stuff' that has no weight in the analysis, and that relations between groups are analytically subordinate to the relationship between groups and the state.

The overwhelming majority of the contributors to Glazer and Moynihan's book are political scientists or positivist sociologists, and to some extent they share their stance over the perceived 'thinness' of culture. For example, Greeley and McCready, in a chapter on 'the transmission of cultural heritage' among Irish and Italians in America (Greeley and McCready 1975), base their research upon an attitudinal survey conducted by questionnaire. The initial hypothesis – that the 'culture' of Ireland and Italy might be a factor in the ethnicity of these groups in the US – obviously has its roots in the primordialist view of ethnicity that Glazer and Moynihan so emphatically reject, so it is a testimony to the volume's catholicity that they are included. We shall see in the next chapter that it is an idea that has appealed to anthropologists working in or out of Britain as well. However, their picture of Ireland and Italy is drawn entirely from rather elderly secondary literature, and the multiple-choice questionnaires they employed in the United States seem to beg as many questions as they ask. This leads them to make statements that an anthropologist would have difficulty in supporting, such as 'With the exception of "fatalism" the Italians were basically similar to the Anglo-Saxons in personality, but different in the predicted direction from the Irish' (1975: 226; 'fatalism' is determined by asking a series of questions about the extent the respondents feel they are to blame

for their problems, how often they feel bored or guilty, and so on).
Notwithstanding this evidence, Greeley and McCready share Glazer
and Moynihan's bellicosity with regard to the 'facts' of 'ethnic
cultural diversity' in the United States: 'a fact which many social
scientists are not yet prepared to concede' (1975: 210).

Similarly, Martin Kilson, in the only contribution to discuss blacks
in the United States (though significant for its inclusion at all),
makes the rather odd assertion that: 'Negroes themselves share the
belief that in some basic way, they do not possess a full measure of
ethnic attributes' (Kilson 1975: 237). Such a statement, of course,
recalls Glazer's misunderstood comment concerning the New York
'Negroes'' apparent lack of culture in the first edition of *Beyond
the melting pot*. The only evidence Kilson gives in support of this
statement is a reference to a 1955 'classic' study of Negro self-
perception of inferiority, *Prejudice and your child*, by Kenneth
Clark. But Kilson seems to be conflating two things: an ethnicity that
is deemed deficient, and an ethnicity that is complete, but includes
a component that subordinates the holding group's status to that of
another. Kilson claims the black 'neo-ethnicity' movement is a
response to one or the other of these – it is not quite clear which.
He does, however, make an important point concerning the self-
ascriptive label 'Afro-American' which became common currency
in the 1960s. Like Talcott Parsons in the same volume (Parsons 1975:
71–2), he argues that this can be seen as an attempt on the part of
blacks to claim categorical equivalence with America's other 'ethnic
groups' ('Irish-Americans', 'Polish-Americans'). He claims, however, that it was a strategy that failed to work, not least because the
conservative Nixon administration sought to demonize radical black
leaders with un-American (and, anticipating an argument of Chapter
5, anti-nationalistic) traits of laziness, crime, freeloading, and so on
(Kilson 1975: 239–40).

In this, Kilson marks an advance on Glazer and Moynihan's initial
treatment of blacks inasmuch as he sees black identity as forged
through the interaction of black and white (even if white almost
exclusively means 'the state' in his vision), rather than somehow a
more passive product of white supremacy, black passivity and the
burden of history. He follows Glazer, however, in restating the
hypothesis that blacks effectively have no culture, as they borrow
much ('though by no means all') from white society, and therefore
have to fall back on an essentially political identity: 'black ethnicity
becomes curiously wedded to politics' (Kilson 1975: 243).

Although not all the contributors to *Ethnicity: theory and experience* share Glazer and Moynihan's view of the inevitability of the persistence of ethnic identities (which Glazer and Moynihan are themselves anxious to note should be taken neither as an endorsement nor a criticism [1975b: 20; the terms they use are 'celebrate' and 'dismiss']), the majority seem to and it is certainly for this feature that Glazer and Moynihan (and hence those associated with them) have become known.

The 'ethnic revival' or 'resurgence' that occurred during the 1960s in the United States clearly caused many academics to reassess positions they might previously have held. It prompted Glazer and Moynihan to write a new introduction to *Beyond the melting pot*, and then to collaborate on *Ethnicity: theory and experience*. One of the latter book's contributors, Milton Gordon, takes the opportunity to revise a highly qualified theory of assimilation he had developed in the 1960s (Gordon 1964, 1975), and so forth. It also prompted what we might call a backlash. In *The ethnic myth* (1981) Stephen Steinberg mounts a sustained attack on what he sees as 'the triumph of ethnicity over the forces of assimilation' and more particularly on those authors who 'celebrate' this apparent fact (1981: 49). Like many if not all the authors I have considered in this chapter (and many more besides) Steinberg combines – and perhaps confuses – the descriptive with the prescriptive. He describes what he sees (analytically) this 'new' ethnicity to be: it is not, as he maintains Glazer and Moynihan and others would have it, a resurgence of ethnic identities that will become more and more entrenched with time, but a last fling, a 'dying gasp' (1981: 51). But he also prescribes: resurgent ethnicity is bad and should be discouraged on the grounds that it is profoundly undemocratic (1981: 260).

He begins the book by making the intelligent remark that, while there is no doubt that ethnicity informs other things (such as consciousness and behaviour) as others have shown, not enough attention has been given to the factors that inform ethnicity itself: 'The tendency in modern social thought has been to treat ethnicity as a given and to explore its consequences' (Steinberg 1981: ix–x). In some senses his goal is therefore similar to my own, to examine the underpinnings of the theoretical status of 'ethnicity' and the historical conditions that give rise to its perception, as well as to its existence. We part company, however, a page or so later when he makes his own position on the matter clear, employing an extended epidemiological metaphor to frame the issue: '[Neo-]Ethnic fever had its origins in the black community. . . . The contagion rapidly spread to other racial minorities. . . . Eventually ethnic fever reached the "white ethnics"' (1981: 3). Thus, although the academic construction of (neo-)ethnicity comes in for attack in the book, it is clear that he as much wishes to attack the thing itself, which in some sense he too therefore treats as 'a given'. Interestingly, Steinberg's epidemiological metaphor was taken up some years later (though without reference to Steinberg) by Ishmael Reed, an American essayist, poet and novelist: 'Ethnicity is treated like a kind of disease [by white Americans]' (Reed *et al.* 1989: 228). The differences between them lie in the fact that Reed is claiming that *blacks* are the only 'ethnic group' in the United States (for reasons I will discuss below), which is quite contrary to Steinberg, and that he employs the metaphor with heavy irony, which is completely absent from Steinberg's prose.

Although Glazer and Moynihan (along with others such as Schrag and Novak, authors of *The decline of the WASP* and *The rise of the unmeltable ethnics* respectively [cited in Steinberg 1981: 49, footnote 9]) are the demons of Steinberg's account, he actually shares much in common with them. He agrees with them that there has been a resurgence of ethnicity in the United States, though as we have seen he disagrees as to its permanence. He also agrees with their later (1975b) comments on the increasing entrenchment of 'ethnic awareness' in the structures of the American state, and the potentially harmful effects of this (Steinberg 1981: 'Epilogue'). Perhaps most significantly, he sets up a straw man of 'primordial' ethnicity to knock down and replace with his own, historically specific and historically limited, theory of instrumental ethnicity. 'Did the ethnic past establish an adequate basis for ethnic preservation?', he asks, 'Or is the melting pot . . . an impending reality?' (1981: 4). Although Steinberg poses these questions as an either/or alternative, the work of several of the writers I have looked at so far shows that this is simply not sufficient. Anthropologists such as Barth or Abner Cohen see ethnicity manifested in a *perception* of common origins, as well as in group interaction; political scientists and sociologists such as Glazer and Moynihan see ethnicity as a product of modernity and manifested in group action. Karen Blu, who supports a modification of the primordialist view, places her conception of it far more in indigenous perception than observation. Only the Soviet ethnos theorists would claim that there has to be an observable core of stable cultural 'stuff' that persists over generations, and even they seem to be less dogmatic on this issue than Steinberg's caricature of primordialism would suggest.

Steinberg thus agrees with Glazer and Moynihan that the facts of migration (involuntarily for America's blacks, somewhat more voluntarily for America's nineteenth- and twentieth-century migrants) effected a cultural rupture – indeed, he speaks of the migrants as being 'ripped from their cultural moorings' (1981: 43). But he agrees with Park and Warner that assimilation is inevitable, because of this rupture. The 'ethnic pluralists', as he dubs those who 'celebrate' ethnic diversity, misread Park and Warner as saying that assimilation would be immediate and thus, when it had failed to happen by the 1960s, assumed that they were wrong (1981: 48–9). As we have already seen, this is quite true: Park and Warner wisely declined to set any absolute time scale on the process and, as Park and other assimilationists (or melting pot theorists) also distinguished between assimilation (moving towards normative conformity with the 'host' majority) and amalgamation ('interbreeding and intermarriage' with the 'host' majority), the argument then becomes one of interpretation rather than fact.

While one can apparently observe and even quantify 'interbreeding and intermarriage' and thus plot the rate of 'amalgamation', argument can rage incessantly over the degree to which a minority group is moving towards a majority group's norms, even assuming one can agree on what those norms are in the first place. Of course, even the observations of amalgamation are only clear-cut if one has a clear-cut notion of what constitutes an 'ethnic group' in the first place. Richard Alba has coined the phrase 'twilight of ethnicity' to cover this interstitial period (Alba 1985b), while another contributor to Alba's edited volume (1985a) argues that the melting pot, even if successful, may give rise to still further types of identity (Lieberson 1985b: 179).

Unlike Glazer and Moynihan, Steinberg is careful to distinguish race from ethnicity. The so-called 'ethnic revival' of the 1960s was really the culmination of historical processes of race relations (that is, relations between blacks and whites) in America. Although the 'white ethnics' appeared to be caught up in this, 'in important respects [the ethnic revival] was the outgrowth of long-range historical trends unrelated to the racial issue' (Steinberg 1981: 51). For Steinberg, the overwhelming pressure on the European migrants to adapt or survive when they first arrived is the issue that will bring about their complete assimilation and perhaps ultimately their amalgamation. The polarization of race issues in the 1960s briefly fanned the embers of their remembered ethnic affiliation, but it was a borrowed impetus and should die away again just as quickly. Indeed, the only block to the final decline of ethnicity in the US is that the state, having been woken up to a conflated vision of 'race-and-ethnicity', is now acting to entrench ethnicity through quotas and pluralist action. As with several of the other authors considered in this chapter, Steinberg's view of ethnicity is moulded by his less well-articulated approach to race. He considers 'ethnicity' a suitable term to describe black identity, but at the same time debars blacks from one of his most important discussions: '[g]iven the different economic and political dimensions of ethnicity in the two instances, it would not be correct to treat the ethnicity of racial minorities and immigrant white minorities as variants of the same phenomenon; the analysis that follows [on the circumstances of migrant arrival and adaptation] deals exclusively with the ethnicity of white immigrant minorities' (1981: 50–1).

The other problematic area with Steinberg's thesis lies with his understanding of 'culture'; like many other sociologists and political scientists he persists in seeing it as a thin, uninteresting thing. The European immigrants, being 'ripped' from their cultural roots, presumably therefore have no culture and are near *tabula rasa*, ready to be inscribed with cultural identities by America. The facets of 'culture' Steinberg examines are the externally observable ones – ethnic food (1981: 63–5), and the 'objects culture' of pictures, books and tablecloths (1981: 61). The former he argues has ceased to be a distinctive marker of particular ethnicities and has adapted itself to non-ethnic tastes, the latter he views as culture in atrophy, as superficial and as a collection of essentially empty symbols. Like most non-anthropologists of the time, he persists in seeing 'culture' as some kind of child's construction kit. 'Objects' and 'attitudes' (cf. Greeley and McCready 1975) are discrete items in the kit, the building blocks, that can be added or subtracted with ease. He seems to have no sense of cultural flow, of interconnectedness, of under-standing the force of culture lying as much in the distinction between things as in the things themselves (Bourdieu 1984). Cultural value imbues things, it is not the things themselves (Leach 1976). It is conveyed through language (as Drake and Cayton richly showed for black culture) and discourse as much as through objects.

There is most certainly a connection between 'culture' and ethnicity and indeed it is often the case that minority migrant groups understand 'culture' in the way that Steinberg and others do. Recent migrants especially tend to reify and objectify their cultural experience and to look to the 'preservation' of cultural artefacts such as specific items of food or clothing. But the reified artefacts are not 'culture' for the anthropologist, rather the process of concretization is a cultural process. I present a specific example of this in Chapter 6 when I look at a particular dispute between white and Asian Britons.

Despite Steinberg's mixture of description and prescription that the US 'ethnic revival' of the 1960s and afterwards will or should peter out, the reification of 'ethnic groups' and academic commentary on this process in the United States continue apace. Two recent edited collections make this point well. First, a collection of essays by folklorists shows that the process of documentation of ethnic difference is undiminished (Stern and Cicala 1991a). In their preface Stern and Cicala claim that '[t]he idea for this book was generated by our dissatisfaction with prevailing academic models of ethnicity, both those which characterize ethnicity as abstract group processes and those which view ethnicity as emerging in small networks of interaction'. They claim these approaches have 'restricted folklorists to thinking about ethnicity in terms of specific stereotypes, identity complexes, values and bodies of tradition' (Stern and Cicala 1991b: ix). It is difficult to see what is wrong with this really, as most analysts of ethnicity and ethnic processes would want to look at stereotypes as well as the 'real' facts of ethnic identity, but Stern and Cicala claim that the contributors develop a 'model of ethnic folklore' that sees ethnicity as dynamic and personal (1991b: ix).

In fact, most of the contributions are descriptive and historical, and make very little reference to any theoretical literature on ethnicity. The 'ethnic' status of most of the groups discussed is taken as given and largely unproblematic, though it is an issue in some, such as Leary and Marsh's investigation into 'Dutchman' musical bands (1991). However, by documenting specific cultural traditions of food, music, rituals and festivals, and more importantly by documenting changes in and revivals of such traditions, the contributors demonstrate the richness of cultural experience that is dismissed by Steinberg and others, even if the congruence with 'ethnicity' is not perhaps so convincing.

By contrast, the contributors to another recent collection go out of their way to problematize 'ethnicity' (Sollors 1989a). Sollors and his contributors come from English and literary studies, or are professional novelists and poets; if nothing else, the Sollors collection and the Stern and Cicala collection demonstrate how 'ethnicity' has taken up a happy residence in ever more disparate fields of study (an idea I return to in Chapter 6). Sollors' introduction to the volume provides a useful account of the increasing relevance of a term such as 'ethnicity' in the humanities, but more importantly he follows authors such as Glazer and Moynihan as seeing ethnicity as a product of modernity (Sollors 1989b: xiii). Ethnicity is 'invented', not in the sense of being inauthentic or contrived or disembedded from social processes, but in the sense that it has been marked as a problematic (1989b: x). In this Sollors is close to my own project and that initially claimed by Steinberg: setting aside for the moment the 'real' existence or otherwise of ethnicity and 'ethnic groups' out there in the world, what is it that has led academics and others to devote so much attention to this term?

Sollors sees it as a project of post-modernity: a whole variety of essentialist understandings of human existence have been challenged in the last decade or so ('childhood', 'romantic love', 'gender', and so forth) and now it is the turn of the complex of ideas and attitudes that surround ethnicity (1989b: x). He therefore – rather late in the day, some might argue – uses the tools of deconstructionism to challenge primordialist notions of ethnicity: '[e]thnic groups are typically imagined as if natural, real, eternal, stable, and static units' (1989b: xiii–xiv). The passive voice used here allows some ambiguity about just *who* is doing the imagining, and it is difficult not to read passages such as this without a sense of *déjà vu*, for the assimilationists and melting pot theorists alike, from Thomas and Znaniecki onwards at least, have challenged such essentialisms. But the literary criticism background of Sollors and his contributors prevents their falling into the easy alternative of instrumentalist theories. Rather than dismissing primordialism as simply false, they seek instead to examine its contours.

For example, Ishmael Reed, who I mentioned briefly above, claims that when he asks his white students in California to write about their own ethnic background they tend to write (presumably fictional) accounts about a 'black' person (Reed *et al.* 1989: 226). This anecdote could, of course, be taken as justification of Steinberg's claim and desire – that there is 'nothing' to be said about being a 'white ethnic' and so instead they turn to the category of 'race' that Steinberg and others usually set aside from the debate on ethnicity. But Reed goes beyond this, to show that of all 'ethnic' categories

'black' is perhaps the least rooted in biology and the most invented
(Reed *et al*. 1989: 227). Following a line of analysis not dissimilar
from Karen Blu's (1980), he argues that regardless of name ('race',
'ethnic') or content (descent from a founding group or ancestor)
categories such as 'black' fulfil a structural need in American society
– in this case an oppositional category outside of which white
America can place itself. This category is – at least in some contexts
– a 'diseased' category (Reed *et al*. 1989: 228), an isolation ward
which reminds the rest that they are healthy. Reed's white students
become 'black', at least temporarily, to articulate difference, not
tradition or history, just as blacks in Robeson County became (by
circumstance as much as by choice) 'Indians' (Blu 1980).

While the classic American works on ethnicity, such as Warner
and Srole's study, ignored the white and black populations of the
country, and the classic American works on race relations considered
the white population only as an unproblematic and 'natural' category
against which the black population could be measured, it is only in
relatively recent times that any investigation into the construction of
a 'white' ethnicity – as opposed to the unproblematic categories of
European national origin – has taken place (for example, Lieberson
1985b; Waters 1990). I shall return briefly to this idea at the end of
the next chapter, but I now wish to sum up what we have learned so
far before going on to look at race and ethnicity in Britain (acknowledging that far more could be said about race and ethnicity in the
United States).

Banton notes that Robert Park's major contribution to the study
of race was to refute the then-prevailing views of race as biology
(that is, some kind of presumed biological determinism) and to
substitute instead a cultural and ecological understanding (Banton
1987: 91). In this, we might include Lloyd Warner too; less
ecologically deterministic than Park and as a mentor if not an author
more inclined to promote a class-based analysis, one that accepted
the historical conditions of slave segregation and saw these as
transformed after the American Civil War into economic inequality.
Later works, such as Drake and Cayton's *Black Metropolis*, provided
the ethnographic and other data to support such a view (see in
particular the introduction to the volume by the black novelist and
documentarist Richard Wilson [1945] which forcefully presents this
class-based reading of Drake and Cayton's data). Over the next half
century Warner's 'caste–class' hypothesis is replaced by a 'race as

class' hypothesis where the conditions of black disadvantage are more and more seen as a result of economic disenfranchisement.

This is succinctly documented by a Chicago successor to Park, the sociologist William Wilson (1978). Wilson advances the thesis one stage further by arguing that economic conditions – class – are no longer sufficient to account for disadvantage. Class differentiations have sharpened among blacks, with the successful middle- and upper-class blacks breaching Warner's 'caste' barrier in recent decades, yet still leaving a majority residue of poor blacks. His explanation is that race has ceased (or is ceasing) to be an issue in the economic sector – that is, there is no longer significant 'racial' competition in the labour market – and the arena of struggle has shifted to what he terms 'the socio-political order' (Wilson 1978: 152). Even this he sees as a false struggle (or better, perhaps, a false understanding) for the real issue he maintains is a structural inequality in the American economic system of industrial capitalism, which disadvantages poor blacks, poor whites, Hispanics and Native Americans equally (1978: 153–4).

As we will see in the next chapter, a similar if more overtly Marxist argument was advanced at much the same time by two authors with respect to the British and western European complex of race, class and economy. At the same time, race was and largely continues to be conceptualized as a 'problem', and as such was never very far away from discussions of ethnicity and 'ethnic groups' in the United States, even those which sought to set it firmly on one side as demanding a different set of analytical tools. With the rise of black radicalism in the 1960s and 1970s ethnicity became a polarizing issue in American public life, to the obvious distress of authors such as Steinberg, and Glazer and Moynihan. While much of the journal literature and many of the essays in edited collections that provide ethnographic and other accounts of particular American 'ethnic groups' are quite happy to ignore broader issues of race and the relationship between race and ethnicity, it is clear from the more wide-ranging and theoretical literature I have looked at that the relationship remains problematic.

Much of what I have written above is an account of the more or less standard works in the North American literature and echoes the relevant parts of other recent surveys (for example, Banton 1977, 1987). There are, however, two important points to be made. First, much of the literature discussed above was produced by sociologists, social geographers or political scientists, not social anthropologists.

Second, much of this literature almost entirely ignores the country's original inhabitants – the Native Americans. The two points are related. The Native American population of the USA had been eliminated or subdued and confined to marginal areas of the country long before disciplines such as sociology and anthropology came on the scene. By the time these and related disciplines came into being the Native Americans had ceased to be considered a significant 'problem' (that is to say, their existence had ceased to be a problem for white America – clearly, white America continued to be a problem for Native Americans). Sociology, in its constant elision of social problems with sociological problems, therefore paid them scant regard.

The position with anthropology was the exact opposite. Long before empirical sociology developed as a tradition in the USA, American anthropologists such as Lewis Henry Morgan were studying Native American populations with a relative degree of disinterest. Morgan, a lawyer, pursued essentially intellectual problems in his study of the Iroquois (Morgan 1851). His aim, typical of the time, was to pose grand questions about remote human antiquity through a study of contemporary 'primitives'. Later American anthropologists such as Boas continued this tradition, though they also concerned themselves with the social welfare of the groups they studied, and their place in American and Canadian society. It was not until much later, however, that studies began to appear of the changing identities of Native Americans and their relations with other sections of American society. Karen Blu's work on the Lumbee, discussed above, must therefore be seen as one of a number of pioneering works that attempted to bridge the large gap that had grown up between American sociological and anthropological empirical traditions in this area.

As we will see in the next chapter, British sociology and anthropology could not remain quite so distinct from one another in their understandings. None the less, the North American cleavage between the sociological study of migrant populations and the anthropological study of indigenous populations was essentially repeated in Britain, though with respect to the same migrant groups under study. Of course, in more recent years the agendas of American sociology, anthropology and a whole host of other disciplines such as social psychology and nursing studies have overlapped in the study of ethnicity. Numerous small studies have been conducted of minority 'ethnic' groups in North America's cities and towns, most of which adopt a fairly specific focus (such as racial segregation in major-league baseball, or intermarriage among mid-west Jews, or ethnic minority access to public libraries, or the role of ethnic sub-cultures in the navy) and many of which refer to Barth's *Ethnic groups and boundaries*, at least in passing. Similarly, numerous journals have sprung up to accommodate the published results of these studies. The growth of this literature and its ethnographic diversity mean that an adequate survey of it would require another book.

Chapter 4

Ethnicity and race in Britain

To the British student of ethnicity, who has neither spent a prolonged period of time in the United States, nor read extensively in the North American literature, the tone of the preceding chapter, and the focus of attention of some North American academics, may have seemed odd (doubtless the same is true for North Americans living for a period in Britain, or on first encountering British anthropological writing on 'ethnic minorities' in Britain). For example, when I was a teenager I encountered a book on my parents' shelves called, dramatically, *I passed for white* (Lee 1956). I had no idea of what might be meant by 'passing' before I read the book and – although I understood the concept in the abstract after finishing it – I had no real understanding of the significance or importance until many years later.

Britain did not have either a 'Negro problem' or a 'melting pot problem'. That is, these terms have never been used (to my knowledge) in British public or academic discourse with any frequency, if at all. Of course, Britain has had social problems (or, more accurately, politicians and others have perceived social problems) to do, loosely, with both 'race' and 'ethnicity', but the historical and political differences between Britain and America are fairly marked in these matters. Most British slaves were overseas, in the colonies not in Britain, and the black British are thus mainly 'twice migrants' or descendants of 'twice migrants'. And the British nation never perceived itself as being built up of migrants and settlers in the way the United States did. There are, nevertheless, roughly analogous perceived 'problems' and certainly an analogous public and political discourse (consisting in terms such as 'swamping [by immigrants]', and predictions of 'rivers of blood' that will flow in 'race riots'). Two issues provide a mooring for the discussions in the section that follows: first, the perception of blacks – and particularly black male youth – as deviant (where it is behaviour rather than mere presence that is at issue and which distinguishes it from the North American 'Negro problem'); and second, the role of migrants in the British economy, especially migrants from South Asia.

Although the British Isles have been subject to waves of immigration and conquest since before the Christian era, most sociologists and anthropologists writing about processes of race and ethnicity in the country confine their historical contextualizing to the period immediately following the Second World War. The obvious reason for doing this (apart, presumably, from laziness) is that it was only in this period that Britain saw large numbers of non-white migrants. In fact, Britain had been the home of a small and diverse non-white population long before this – Chinese seamen, Panjabi travelling salesmen, and black slaves and freemen.

The numbers were not insignificant: Benson cites estimates of up to 30,000 blacks in Britain in the latter part of the eighteenth century (Benson 1981: 3). But the end of the Second World War also effectively marked the end of the British Empire and hence a new set of relations between Britain and the rest of the world. Most of the migrants who arrived during this period were therefore perceived as somehow different from all earlier migrants. Not all migrants, however: one of the effects of the popular and hence academic focus on race was to mask the presence of groups that in the American context were central to discussions of ethnicity. While large numbers of Poles and other east-central Europeans settled in Britain during and after the Second World War, joining the longer-established Irish and Italian populations, they have been the subject of less academic attention (the same being true of other European-origin groups – from Cyprus, Malta, Greece, and so forth; but see Dench 1975, and articles in Watson 1977a; Westwood and Bhachu 1988a).

The major part of British writing on minority groups in Britain has focused overwhelmingly on blacks and 'Asians'. 'Black' in this context generally refers to those who trace their ancestry to the Caribbean former colonies and more recently to 'direct migrants' from Africa, mostly Nigeria, though I shall comment on the term a little more below. 'Asian' is one of the more neutral popular (white) terms to describe people of South Asian descent, mostly from India, Pakistan and Bangladesh, but does not include those of Chinese or more rarely Japanese or Korean descent as it does in the United States (the term 'East Indian' is also largely unknown in Britain).

As in the United States there exists a flotilla of terms ranging from the deeply offensive and abusive through the euphemistic to the self-affirmatory, and they constantly shift in meaning and use. For both countries these would require book length studies in themselves to examine in any depth (see, for example, Reeves 1983) and I shall confine myself to a brief discussion of only one: 'black'. For the remainder of this section I shall employ 'black' and 'Asian' as generic terms. I am fully aware of the problematic status of both terms, and ask the reader's indulgence to suspend judgement on my use.

BLACK BRITONS

The earliest post-war work on Britain's black population is probably Kenneth Little's 1947 study of some 7,000 'African, West Indian, and Arab seamen' in Cardiff (Little 1947). It was undertaken as an anthropological 'community study' equivalent to those conducted at around the same time in the United States, and indeed the first chapter surveys some of this literature, particularly that of the Chicago School and the well-known 'Middletown' studies (Hoover 1990; Lynd and Lynd 1929). What is particularly noticeable is that Little seems to have found few if any models within the contemporary British anthropological or sociological tradition to help him; in fact, most of the book's references are to source material rather than secondary academic material.

Little's stimulus in conducting the study is two-fold. First, he states that he was 'prompted by personal experience, in company with West African friends, of the working of the Colour Bar [in Britain]' (1947: xi). The 'colour bar' or 'colour line' was a phrase current at the time that would perhaps be equivalent to 'segregation' in the United States and in both cases would mark the boundary between the black and white 'castes' of Warner's 'caste'–'class' hypothesis. Little does not elaborate on what his 'personal experience' of the colour bar was: he is not black and so could only have viewed it from the 'white' side. Secondly, he notes a tie with colonialism, pointing out that many of the 'future leaders' of then British colonies were being trained in Britain 'at a most impressionable period of their lives', and might be expected to import British attitudes towards race into their own countries (Little 1947: xi). If these attitudes are allowed to go unresearched and uncorrected, the prognosis is gloomy. For our purposes, the idea that there is some kind of connection between the anthropological study of migrant communities in Britain and the anthropological study of more 'traditional' communities in the developing world is one that will recur throughout this chapter. It is also an issue that marks the British approach to race and ethnicity off from its American counterpart.

Although, as mentioned in the previous chapter, Warner advocated utilizing the comparative approach of anthropology, this was (and continues to be) rarely evident in the United States literature I have considered. American academics tended to look back to the period of slavery within their own country to provide models for contemporary race relations, although interestingly St Clair Drake went on to write his doctoral thesis on race relations in Britain (see Drake 1956). Even within studies overtly concerned with the ethnicity of European migrants these models were not entirely absent, as we have seen above (Thomas and Znaniecki [1984] providing a major exception to this rule). By contrast, British studies of race and ethnicity, particularly anthropological studies, looked sideways to comparative evidence elsewhere, particularly Africa. In part this was because of the British anthropological establishment's rejection of historical approaches under Malinowski's and Radcliffe-Brown's functionalism at this time, but in part it was also because of the fact that the British experience of slavery was intimately bound up with and essentially subsumed by the British experience and understanding of colonialism. Little himself had lived in British West Africa prior to the study (Little 1947: 30) and was conducting fieldwork there by the mid-1940s (1974: 3).

In fact, Little's book is remarkable for 'recovering' the history of race relations in Britain prior to the Second World War, drawing on a large number of primary and secondary sources such as Samuel Pepys's diary and the few existing scholarly studies of slavery and the slave trade. He even devotes a section to 'The Negro in 19th-century fiction', a study taken up some decades later by the anthropologist Brian Street (Street 1975). Although Little makes no explicit reference to work conducted by members of the Manchester School discussed in Chapter 2 (and indeed, he predates their major works on ethnicity by a decade or so) he later went on to specialize in the study of West African urbanization (for example, Little 1965, 1973, 1974) and cited them often, saying in 1974 that their work 'pointed the way ahead' (1974: 3–4). (Little himself went on to become Professor in African Urban Studies at the University of Edinburgh, after a spell as Professor of Social Anthropology there.)

The first, ethnographic, half of *Negroes in Britain*, like *Black Metropolis*, adopts a vaguely ecological approach, particularly in its insistence that the 'community' of blacks studied has sociological validity as a result of its urban geography (Little 1947: 25; see also 53–5). In the second, more general half of the book, however, Little seeks an understanding of British race relations less in terms of cultural ecology and more in terms of the history of British colonialism. Likewise, early on in the book, he considers the issue of whether race or class (in a loose Weberian sense) is the more important variable in defining the life of his chosen 'community' but settles on race on the grounds that 'colour prejudice . . . played so large a part in shaping the general sociological situation' (1947: 26). In fact, the particularities of the Cardiff black 'community' make it rather difficult to follow Little on this. Certainly, prejudice was an important factor and Little gives many examples. But the occupational specificities of merchant seamanship also play a part, and Little makes it clear that such employment amounted to a 'system of slavery' (1947: 37) regardless of colour. In the second half of the book he briefly raises an idea that I will return to shortly: that racism and the 'colour bar' exist as an ideological device by which the white British middle and working classes reassert their position in the class structure: 'The "black man" . . . fitted in, therefore, only on the bottom rung of the social ladder to elevate those hardly less lowly placed than himself' (1947: 218).

As one would expect from a work of the period, Little's attitude towards 'racial' categories is largely uncritical and he tends to accept them as sociological givens. His anthropological training, and perhaps his previous experiences in West Africa, make him more sensitive to internal cleavages and differentiations within his 'community' and he does briefly discuss some 'African [religious] customs' in Cardiff (1947: 148), though without claiming that these are in any way determinative of behaviour. He displays a healthy scepticism of information elicited by way of questionnaires and brief surveys – particularly those which pose hypothetical questions – in his introductory methodological chapter and again in an appendix, (1947: 11, footnote 1; Appendix I), but he does not seem to let this cloud his apparently clear understanding of what constitutes 'race' and 'race relations'.

The 1950s and the early 1960s saw a number of descriptive works on race in Britain, some of them ethnographic studies like Little's, some of them general surveys based on questionnaires, newspaper accounts and secondary material. The titles convey a general feel of the contents: *Colour prejudice in Britain* (Richmond 1954), *Coloured minorities in Britain* (Collins 1957), *Dark strangers* (Patterson 1963). There were also more analytical accounts, though these were rare until the 1970s. One of the earliest was Michael Banton's *White and coloured* (1959). Like Little, Banton is an anthropologist with interests in both race and West African urbanization, but where Little devoted his later career to the study of African urbanization, Banton remained with British race relations and has published prolifically on the topic up to the present day. His first book was an ethnographic study of the 'coloured quarter' of London's East End (Banton 1955) and he also conducted fieldwork in West Africa under Little's guidance (Banton 1957). *White and coloured* (1959) was also undertaken at Little's instigation, and the second part of the book examines a number of race relations situations empirically. But these are presented not so much as data confirming the existence of the 'colour bar', or to galvanize the middle class white liberals. Instead, they are test data to back up a psychological and sociological hypothesis that Banton develops in the first part of the book.

In his later work, Banton has become known for two related theoretical stances (quite apart from the renown he has won for his meticulous and thoughtful scholarship): the idea of 'racial competition' and his use of 'rational choice theory' (see, for example, Banton 1983) which is discussed in more detail below. We can see the seeds of these ideas in his 1959 book. Anticipating the work of John Rex (1970) Banton attempted to provide a sociological understanding of human action that would encompass the specific aspects of 'race relations', but which would be of more general sociological utility: '[b]ehaviour towards coloured people [by white Britons] is not radically different from all other sorts of behaviour but accentuates features discernible in relations between Britons of different class or regional background, or between Britons and white foreigners' (1959: 179; see also 1959: 10).

Banton arrives at this conclusion by a number of routes. First, although he follows Little in seeing the specific pattern of British race relations as located within the broader context of colonialism, he rejects what we might term 'narrow historicism'. He follows Popper and, for that matter, Radcliffe-Brown (1959: 183 footnote, 22) in arguing that sociological analysis is highly specific to certain kinds of human relations. Where the conjunction of relations holds, the successful analysis will remain valid, and is not invalidated by its absence in other times or in other places (1959: 183). Put another way, British race relations in the 1950s were patterned or coloured by a complex of features that included the legacy of colonialism but for which colonialism was not uniquely responsible. Secondly, Banton argues for the supremacy of sociological explanation over psychological explanation or economic causality (1959: 15–22). He does not dismiss other explanatory systems out of hand, but argues that a good sociological explanation is most likely to be aware of its own specificity and construction, what today we might term reflexivity. Psychology – focusing solely on the individual – and economics – focusing solely on the system – fail to see the interconnections between the two; '[w]hen sociologists single out the structure of a situation as a factor exerting causal influence upon behaviour, they see it as defined by people's expectations of particular modes of conduct and the sanctions that can be directed against actors who fail to behave in the prescribed manner' (1959: 20; when Banton speaks here of 'sociology' he includes the analytical framework of much British anthropology of the day).

Today, of course, such extreme positivism seems brashly over-confident in the face of the 'crisis' in anthropology identified by – and, some would say, caused by – post-modernist anthropologists. But Banton's approach contains within it aspects such as reflexivity or critical distance that anticipate post-modernism. In particular, by refusing to take 'race relations' as qualitatively different from other forms of human relations, Banton realizes that race and racial categories are constructs, not givens: '"[t]he coloured man" is a creation of Europeans' (1959: 182).

Banton's book is important in a number of ways not mentioned here, and I have in fact not discussed his main hypothesis: that racial discrimination arises as a result of an increased uncertainty among white Britons about normative values, the 'failure' of migrants to abide by such norms, and the easy but false correlation of skin colour with normative non-conformity ('the coloured man is considered the most distant of all strangers' [1959: 178]). The student of anthropology will spot a Durkheimian background to this and, for that matter, a presaging of Mary Douglas's investigation into category creation and opposition (for example, Douglas 1966, 1970). For my purposes, however, the book is of value in giving an early and clear analysis of race relations in Britain, and for distinguishing sharply between a social problematic and a sociological problematic (see also Banton 1979).

The somewhat clinical approach taken by Banton to matters of race has been criticized on occasion (for example, Miles 1982, cited in Cashmore and Troyna 1983: 11), but he has undoubtedly been influential, not least for his careful exposition of eighteenth- and nineteenth-century theories of 'scientific racism' and the ways in which he considers these to have influenced contemporary academic and popular thought (for example, Banton 1987). However, early British work, such as that of Little and Banton, is largely concerned with mapping contemporary British race relations and with addressing issues of prejudice and discrimination. Little (1947) and Banton (1959) both consider popular white perceptions of blacks, but for the most part they concern themselves with issues surrounding skin colour: that is, the way blacks look. They do touch briefly, however, on sexuality and intermarriage, issues that had been far more to the fore in the work of Park, Drake and Cayton, and other earlier American authors. Aspects of black behaviour (or sometimes, perceived behaviour) – that is, what blacks do – come increasingly to dominate the British literature, as they come to dominate white popular perceptions. No longer are blacks simply 'here', they are 'here' and doing things 'we' do not like. Three issues come to dominate: jobs, sexuality and crime.

I don't want to discuss any of these issues in particular detail, and they are explored fully elsewhere (see, for example, Benson 1981; Hall *et al.* 1978; Miles 1982), but it is worth spending a moment to consider the social construction of these categories in relation to blacks. Despite the fact that mass immigration from the New Commonwealth and Pakistan after the Second World War was triggered partly by a labour shortage in Britain, the perceived problem of 'them' coming over 'here' and taking 'our' jobs has retained currency to this day, particularly in times of economic recession. A related white grudge, particularly with regard to Asian migrants, especially from Bangladesh, has focused on the payment of state benefits to recently arrived migrants.

Similarly, the sexuality issue is stated as 'them' coming over 'here' and taking 'our' women. The gender differentiation here is explained partly by demographic factors – the earliest migrants tended to be men and so unions of black men and white women were more common than the converse – but partly by cultural processes of gender relations already existing in Britain. British women's increased economic and productive activity and autonomy during the war had unsettled men's perceptions of gender and gender relations.

In some senses, white men's fears that they were losing control over women's productive and reproductive services were vested in the image of the predatory black male.

Finally, blacks served as a visible symbol of post-war change, and their arrival coincided with perceptions of rising crime rates and increased social fragmentation. As I say, these issues are explored more thoroughly in other works, and the only point I wish to make is that black identity (and to a lesser extent, the identity of British Asians) became associated with threat and deviancy. This is not to advocate simplistic psychological 'scapegoating' theories, but rather to make the point that the academic literature on race tended to mirror the predominant social perceptions.

The 'demonization' of blacks in the UK began early on in public discourse, with articles and letters appearing in the popular press noting their tendency to 'drift into bad ways' (from a *Picture post* article of 1949 cited in Alexander 1992). Sue Benson cites a number of publications from the 1950s and 1960s, ranging from the *English churchman* to *Honey* (a women's magazine), that discuss – and largely disapprove of – unions and marriages between black and white (Benson 1981: 10–13). Academic mirroring of this 'demonization' takes a while to catch up, but it repeats themes that we have already encountered in the literature on blacks in the US. Sheila Patterson, for example, in her 1963 study of blacks in Brixton, repeats the assertion that blacks in Britain 'lack any distinct and separate culture of their own' (1963: 200, cited in Alexander 1992: 9). As Claire Alexander notes, in one of the most recent and thorough explorations of the literature on race in Britain, 'The black community is thus pathologised socially and culturally [by academics]: British society, by contrast, is presented as "naturally" and understandably concerned with the "alien" presence' (Alexander 1992: 10).

This social pathology is seen particularly in the area of supposedly unstable family patterns in the Caribbean which are imported into Britain (see R. Smith 1963 for a survey of literature on the Caribbean), and in the related issue of black youth as 'natural' criminals. Alexander cites academic studies from as recently as 1979 that accept unproblematically a difficult and rebellious youth culture that problematizes itself, as it were, while a stable, homogenous white society looks on in disgust or pity. Alexander's own study, of black male youth in London, rejects the idea of black identity as a given and sees it instead as a process. The youth she studied are constantly in the process of creating or inventing their blackness, a process which is as much an art form as a tool for survival (the essays by folklorists in Stern and Cicala [1991a] also give some sense of this, though with far less theoretical sophistication).

Alexander herself is insistent that 'blackness' is created, negotiated and challenged, not merely given, and she considers it an issue of ethnicity, not race (Alexander 1992: 60, 63). Otherwise, although a vast literature on race has been produced in Britain during the 1970s and 1980s, much of it is concerned with a range of obvious and pressing social problems and adds little directly to our understanding of race as a theoretical construct and its place within anthropological understandings of ethnicity. This perhaps is as it should be, for issues of discrimination, false arrest, violent attack and murder are of more immediate concern than narrow academic worries over definitions. What is of interest, however, is that much of this literature has been produced by sociologists, not anthropologists. Although the 'community' studies by Little, Banton and Patterson cited above stem directly from an anthropological tradition, ethnographies of blacks in Britain remain at a low level throughout this period (but see Benson 1981; Cashmore 1979; Foner 1979). That is not to say that anthropologists based in Britain have ignored the study of British society; indeed, there has been a steady stream of publications on white, rural communities (discussed in Chapter 5) and on 'ethnic' urban communities.

RACE OR ETHNICITY?

Some works by anthropologists, or popular among an anthropological readership, have acquired an almost talismanic status by virtue, it seems, of their titles alone. I have already discussed one in Chapter 2, Barth's *Ethnic groups and boundaries* (1969a), and will discuss another in the next chapter, Benedict Anderson's *Imagined communities* (1983). A third, often cited in recent writings on ethnicity (for example, Sollors 1989b; Alexander 1992), is Hobsbawm and Ranger's collection *The invention of tradition* (1983). In some cases it seems that mere mention of the title alone is enough to convey a whole set of associations, or theoretical positioning.

Sue Benson has recently coined a similarly apt title for a paper on the anthropological study of minority groups in Britain: 'Asians have culture, West Indians have problems' (Benson in press). In the paper,

Benson comments critically on the way in which anthropologists have tended to view Britain's black population as being uninteresting and have focused instead on the Asian population. Following Patterson and others, blacks in Britain are perceived to have no 'culture', being English-speaking and Christian. Asians quite decidedly do have 'culture': non-indigenous languages, religions, clothing and food patterns. A minor publishing industry (to which, indeed, I have contributed) has grown up documenting the 'culture' of these exotic groups. A further point is that for not entirely clear reasons relatively few British anthropologists have conducted fieldwork in the Caribbean compared to the large numbers who have conducted fieldwork in South Asia. Thus, one of the factors which leads many anthropologists to the study of minority migrant groups – experience of or actual fieldwork in the 'sending' country – tends to prejudice them towards Asian minority groups and away from Caribbean groups (see, for example, Little 1947: 30; also Watson 1977b). By contrast, British sociologists have focused almost exclusively on Britain's black population and, because empirical sociology elides social problems and sociological problems more readily than anthropology, they have focused on 'problems' rather than 'culture'. A division of labour has thus grown up, more sharply than in the United States, and it is this, as much as any abstract theoretical divisions, that characterizes the British writing on ethnicity at home.

This is not to say that British anthropologists writing about ethnicity in Britain have entirely ignored race. But apart from those such as Alexander, mentioned above, who confronts the issue head on (1992: 45–64), the few anthropologists writing on ethnicity who discuss race do so briefly and somewhat cautiously. For example, Chapman et al., in the introduction to a recent volume of anthropological essays on ethnicity, state that 'the discourse of race is an essential background to any concern with ethnicity today' (1989: 14), but within two paragraphs – one of them devoted to summarizing another contributor's views on the matter – they return to defining 'ethnicity' and make only a brief further reference to race.

The contributor in question, Roger Just, refers to 'race' as the 'Joker in the pack' (Just 1989: 76). From the context it is not quite clear in whose deck of cards this Joker is hiding, just as it was not always clear whose the 'Negro problem' was in the United States. Chapman et al. and Just are all anxious to dissociate themselves from the 'scientific' racism of the nineteenth century (which, of course, was inextricably linked to the emergence of anthropology as a discipline); but one senses that in these and a number of other discussions the metaphor of skeletons in the closet is more appropriate than that of Jokers in packs with respect to the contemporary anthropological position on race. While Just sees race as 'a biological substitute for the notion of ethnicity' (1989: 76), Chapman *et al.* interpret him as saying that 'race' is like 'ethnic group' plus biology (Chapman *et al.* 1989: 14). We see at once therefore that there is some confusion between race as an idea, as a notion that has some descriptive or explanatory power, and race as a concrete thing – a group of biologically related people. It is in this second sense that the term was employed in nineteenth-century anthropological writing, in phrases such as 'the races of mankind', and it acquired an abstract quality through meditation on the differences between these 'races', leading to phrases in twentieth-century sociology such as 'the race problem', where race is a quality of and expressed between 'races', just as ethnicity is a quality of and expressed between 'ethnic groups'. The problem is essentially linguistic as much as conceptual: 'ethnicity' is the abstract noun derived from the (supposedly) concrete noun-phrase 'ethnic group', but for 'race' abstract and concrete nouns are the same. (An equivalent problem exists for anthropologists with the term 'culture'.)

Setting aside these terminological quibbles, Just advances an interesting hypothesis. He claims that, in folk conceptions of ethnic identity, issues of biology – that is, folk conceptions of race – are likely to be advanced where the other components of identity (such as common language, history, territory, and so forth) are problematic for one reason or another. But folk conceptions of race do not merely add to the rest of the shopping list as yet another 'proof' supporting assertions of ethnic distinctiveness; they underpin it as an unshakeable truth, from which the other components can be argued (Just 1989: 77). Just goes on to provide an elegant and convincing account of the assertion of Greek ethnic identity in contemporary Greece, where claims to an unbroken history, common language and agreed territory can and have all been challenged; in the end 'the Greeks of Greece and the *ethnos* ['people'] as a whole . . . are Greek because they have "Greek blood"' (1989: 85).

Earlier work on ethnicity by anthropologists shows even less concern with issues of race. James Watson, in the introduction to an influential collection of essays considered below, having noted that definitions of race can vary widely, states that '"ethnicity" is not, as some critics have suggested, simply a euphemism for "race"' (Watson 1977b: 8). He makes the entirely valid anthropological point that '[p]hysical appearance is only one of many possible criteria that can serve as the basis for ethnic divisions' (1977b: 8), and then through the rest of his introduction discusses literature on black and white minority migrant groups without much distinguishing between them. Towards the end of his introduction he returns to the issue of 'physical appearance' and the subjective evaluation of this by members of some of the minority groups under consideration (1977b: 15). But he fails to make the obvious point, and one that was no less pressing in the 1970s than it is today, which is that perceptions of the importance of skin colour play a vital part in the relations of power and domination that exist between minority groups and the white 'host' population (as well as between minority groups). This point is so fundamental to much of the writing on race that I considered in the previous chapter that it is hardly ever stated in this bald form. Works such as Drake and Cayton's *Black Metropolis* (1945) or even popular accounts of 'passing' such as Lee's *I passed for white* (1956) take this understanding as axiomatic and attempt to define its contours and trajectories. Of course, one of the issues touched on in the US literature – is such inequality best analysed as one of race or one of class? – continues to run through the British literature.

In many ways, of course, my own position (for what it is worth) is in accord with Watson, and for that matter Benson, Alexander and a number of other writers: any theory of ethnicity that accepts popular understandings of race as somehow fundamental, inviolate, primordial and ultimately unanalysable cannot be a very useful theory. On the other hand, race is an important issue to consider, both in the cases where it appears to be an issue as well as in the cases where it doesn't. Watson ultimately does himself no favours by dismissing the critics who would hold that 'ethnicity' is an anthropological euphemism for 'race' so lightly, for as Benson has pointed out (in press) they have a point: anthropological accounts of ethnicity have consistently ignored imbalances in power in which perceptions of race are frequently an issue.

'ETHNIC GROUPS' IN BRITAIN

I wish to turn now to consider the British literature on non-black minority migrant groups in Britain, with a particular emphasis on literature about Asian groups. Watson, discussed above, asserts that 'American visitors find it strange that the English categorise South Asians as "coloured peoples"; in the United States, the same individuals would be classed as "caucasians"' (Watson 1977b: 8), and elsewhere he notes that the Chinese in Britain are seen (by the white British) as neither 'coloured' nor 'Asian' (1977c: 206). In fact, the language of popular British race discourse (there being only a rudimentary popular 'ethnicity discourse' – see Chapter 6) is so fluid, so context- and time-dependent, that I would be wary of making any such assertions. What one can more safely assert is that, despite attempts to get them to do so, most South Asians in Britain would reject the label 'black'.

This is a point noted by Westwood and Bhachu in their introduction to a collection of essays on minority women and the economy: '[i]n raising issues we have struggled with a language which consistently reinforces stereotypes by creating sections of the population, both men and women as "others"' (Westwood and Bhachu 1988b: 1). Although they acknowledge that 'black' is a term that has been 'appropriated by black people and made powerful through its politicization', they accept that Cypriots, Chinese and South Asians in Britain do not designate themselves in this way (1988b: 1). None the less, they go on to say: '[t]his book is about British society and British women, but many are BLACK BRITISH women of Afro-Caribbean, Asian, and Chinese descent, who struggle on a daily basis with the racism of British society. This does not mean that Jewish, Irish, or Cypriot people have not been racialized and that they do not also suffer racism – it is quite clear that they do' (1988b: 1–2; capitals in the original). Thus not only 'black' but also 'race' are terms that, as we have already seen in the more recent American literature, have been refocused away from their apparently neutral, primary meanings: 'black' no more refers to colour than 'race' does to genetics. Quite who is doing the refocusing is an issue that would need to be explored in detail in specific contexts; here, Westwood and Bhachu are quite explicitly and deliberately involving themselves in the phenomenon they are writing about (cf. Steinberg 1981: 49). But more significantly, they too are eliding that which the earlier literature tended to keep distinct: race and ethnicity.

As with the early British literature on blacks in Britain, the earliest writings on other minority migrant groups tended towards the broad-brush survey approach. Desai's *Indian immigrants in Britain* (1963), for example, was written at a time when relatively few South Asians were permanently settled in the country and it documents the coping strategies of individuals, as much as saying anything about group identity (see also Aurora 1967). Desai does, however, provide interesting British examples of 'passing': in this case, single South Asian men passing as southern Europeans (Desai 1963: 133–4, 136). He also makes the point that it was only after the initial single male 'target' migrants were joined by their wives and children that a community or ethnic identity could really be built (1963: 7–8, 31, 63). Many later authors have noted this gender dimension in the development of ethnic identities in Britain, especially where South Asian migrants are concerned. It is the presence and cultural activities of women, especially in (re)constituting households and providing a locus for cultural as well as biological reproduction, that provide much of the 'cultural stuff' for ethnicity (see, for example, Shaw 1988: 49). Unfortunately, the role of gender in constructing and transforming ethnic identities is still an ill-researched topic, and much of the earlier literature on ethnicity is effectively gender blind, a blindness that is therefore reflected in this book.

Through the 1970s, however, a number of ethnographic studies of Asian and other groups in Britain begin to appear, many of them derived from doctoral theses and some of them by members of the groups studied (see, for example, Anwar 1976; Barot 1973; Bhachu 1985). The journal *New community*, the official journal of the Commission for Racial Equality, published the preliminary results of many of these studies and tended especially to attract the 'softer' research results of anthropologists, while the journals of the Institute of Race Relations, *Race today* and especially *Race and class*, became the focus for more sociological and more politicized writing. Of the many valuable ethnographies from this time, that of a Gujarati 'community' in London by a Norwegian anthropologist is of especial interest (Tambs-Lyche 1980). Tambs-Lyche conducted his fieldwork in the very early 1970s, and acknowledges a debt to several anthropologists and sociologists we have come across above and in the previous chapter, particularly Frederik Barth and Abner Cohen.

The book explores the life and actions of a group of Gujarati Patidars, members of a land-owning and agricultural caste in India who migrated to Britain (either directly or via East Africa) during the 1960s; Tambs-Lyche completed his fieldwork before the mass exodus of Ugandan Asians in 1972. The Patidars are known colloquially in Britain as the 'Patels', the surname of many of them, and Tambs-Lyche provides an analysis of their mercantile ideology which, he claims, is the significant factor that sets them apart from the white British population and constitutes the major element in the construction of an ethnic boundary (1980: 125).

In his use of the notion of ethnic boundaries, Tambs-Lyche follows Barth (1969b) closely, but he also draws on other elements of Barth's work – particularly the idea of 'choice' and of seeing the 'rules' of society as generative, rather than as static and fixed (Tambs-Lyche 1980: 13–27). I noted in Chapter 2 that Barth's edited collection is possibly one of the most frequently cited anthropological texts of the last thirty years or so, yet Tambs-Lyche, together with the British anthropologist Sandra Wallman (see Wallman 1978, 1986), is one of the few to treat Barth's ideas in detail. Tambs-Lyche acknowledges, however, that there are special difficulties in doing this in his own field situation (Tambs-Lyche 1980: 19–20, 25). In particular, the Patidars are a minority group and there are inequalities in power and control between them and the white British society that encompasses them.

Tambs-Lyche thus deals with the idea of constraint far more than Barth and claims that ultimately the Patidars deal with two kinds of constraint. 'Interactional' constraints on an individual's behaviour are provided by the behaviour of others with whom the Patidars know how to deal – that is, other Patidars. By contrast, 'environmental' constraints are those over which the Patidars have little influence, and are provided by the 'environmental' context of life in Britain, where the important aspects of the political system and economy lie outside Patidar control (1980: Chapter 1 *passim*). Although Tambs-Lyche strongly endorses Barth's point that ethnic groups are not givens, but are the outcome of 'social organization' (1980: 18), one can't avoid the feeling that the argument has a circular aspect to it: the Patidars are different because they are different.

This is particularly evident in his discussion of the economic and occupational 'niche' that the Patidars fill in British society (Tambs-Lyche 1980: 25–6). As shopkeepers catering both to other South Asians (by selling distinctively 'internal' goods such as certain foodstuffs and clothing items) and to the wider British society (selling many of the same goods but packaged and presented in a way that is appealingly exotic yet safe), the Patidars make a living doing things that other British do (selling things) but with a distinctively cultural slant (1980: 63). The Patidars must enter into British relations of production in order to survive; if they also accepted British patterns of consumption (by selling and buying in the way the wider society does – assuming, as Tambs-Lyche seems to, that this is homogenous), their 'ethnic separateness would cease to manifest itself in this respect' and the assumption is either that Patidar ethnicity would disappear, or that it would have to manifest itself in some other way. But the Patidars do not accept British consumption patterns and so remain distinctive (1980: 26). So, they are different because they are different and the ethnic boundary 'has an economic significance' (1980: 26).

In some ways Tambs-Lyche marks an advance on Barth by being forced to confront a minority–majority situation where the expression of ethnicity cannot be assumed to be a matter of neutral 'choice' and where the assertion of ethnic identities is conducted within the wider context of the state. But in other respects he reflects Barth's primordialism, assuming that the question is not so much 'why ethnicity' as 'how ethnicity'.

This is the very issue that is taken up and then dismissed by two authors who reject both 'cultural' factors and ethnicity itself. Although Tambs-Lyche does not refer to Stephen Castles and Godula Kosack's *Immigrant workers and class structure in western Europe* (1973), it advanced a thesis that struck at the heart of anthropological work on minority migrant communities in the 1970s and many later studies found it necessary to deal with it before their authors could move on (see, for example, Bhachu 1985: 7; Boissevain 1984: 34; Watson 1977b: 12–14).

Castles and Kosack are essentially advancing an ethnicity and immigration version of the 'class not race' thesis that some of the US authors discussed above advanced (see, for example, R. Wilson 1945; W. Wilson 1978). They also deny the importance of pre-migration cultural patterns – a position that they share with authors such as Glazer and Moynihan, who argue for the ethnicity of migrant groups as a post-migration phenomenon (see also Abner Cohen 1974b: xi). But where Glazer and Moynihan and others effectively celebrate this newly minted ethnicity as the assertion of proud difference, Castles and Kosack see more sinister forces at work. Indeed, as Marxist sociologists with a predominant interest in labour, they do not refer to either culture or ethnicity. In an often repeated passage from the introduction to the book, they make their position clear: '[i]mmigrants should be looked at not in the light of their specific group characteristics – ethnic, social, and cultural – but in terms of their actual social position. Immigrant workers have come to form part of the class structure of the immigration countries. This in turn has effects on the economic, social, and political situations of all other classes' (Castles and Kosack 1973: 5). That is to say, it doesn't matter where the migrants come from, or who they consider themselves to be; all that matters is that they are necessary to the economies of the western European countries (or were, at least, in the period leading up to 1973), and that they are assigned to the lowest stratum of these countries' class systems (class here being understood in a Marxist, not a Weberian sense).

Castles and Kosack note that the term 'immigrant' in Britain is synonymous with 'black man' in popular discourse and that the two thus become conflated in academic studies, despite the fact that – at the time – around two-thirds of immigrants in Britain were white (1973: 1). As a result, what they identify as being at root a class and economic issue, is mistaken by liberal sociologists and others as a race issue (1973: 1–2). Twenty years later one can still hear white British people, especially of the older generation, talking disparagingly about 'immigrants', even when it is clear from the context that they mean blacks or Asians who may well have been born in the UK, and not, say, first generation white South African migrants. But it is by no means the case that later studies conducted by sociologists and anthropologists 'mistook' race for class in quite the simplistic way that Castles and Kosack imply; rather it is a case of different academic agendas.

Be that as it may, Castles and Kosack, while giving no credence to the idea that immigrants are where they are in economic terms because of some predisposing cultural factor (that is, stemming from a primordial ethnic identity), do not deny the existence of race as an ideology or its outcomes in terms of discrimination in housing, employment, labour union representation, and so forth. On the contrary, they put forward a straightforwardly Marxist explanation: racism exists, and particularly among the indigenous white working class, as a false consciousness designed to prevent class solidarity (1973: *passim*, but see particularly 450–60 and Chapter XI). The ruling class encourages the white working class to fear the immigrant as an employment threat, and simultaneously exploits the immigrant worker by underpaying him for the most unpleasant jobs that no one else wishes to do, while bribing the white workers with minimal privileges. The white workers are distracted by these privileges and by the temptation of advancing themselves through occupational mobility on the back of immigrant workers' labour and fail to notice the essential class solidarity they share with the immigrant workers.

Castles and Kosack's thesis is argued in detail and is in many ways very convincing. For my purposes, however, it adds little to our understanding of ethnicity. That is not to say that other writers have felt the same. Bhachu and Boissevain, for example, both feel the need to point out that the minority groups they are concerned with have more in common with the bourgeoisie or 'ruling class' than Castles and Kosack's 'immigrants' and therefore their analysis is not relevant (Bhachu 1985: 7; Boissevain 1984: 34). The greatest exception to their thesis in the context of ethnicity studies is taken by James Watson (1977b) but, before going on to discuss that, I wish first to make a brief comment about primordial ethnicity and anthropological studies of minority migrant groups.

As we saw above, there was a tendency on the part of authors as far apart as Glazer and Moynihan and Stephen Steinberg to dismiss the relevance of a prior cultural heritage: ethnicity is something that happens when members of the migrant group arrive in the US (or the UK) and, while it is predicated upon the fact of having been born somewhere else (or being descended from those so born), the cultural components drawn from 'home' are trivial and inessential. In the introduction to a volume on urban ethnicity, Abner Cohen appears to be making the same point: 'The differences between the Chinese and the Indians, considered within their own respective countries, are national not ethnic differences. But when groups of Chinese and Indian immigrants interact as Chinese and Indians they can then be referred to as ethnic groups. Ethnicity is essentially a form of interaction between culture groups operating within common social contexts' (Abner Cohen 1974b: xi).

Cohen, an exponent of instrumental ethnicity as we saw in Chapter 2, is not, however, saying that the cultural heritage that 'the Chinese and the Indians' bring with them as immigrants is unimportant. Ethnicity is something that you have, as well as something that you do; although Cohen rejects the primordialism of Barth as being essentially descriptive, not analytical (1974b: xii–xiii), he agrees strongly that ethnicity resides in the recognition, use and manipulation of symbols (1974b: xiv). The symbols may be 'old' ones brought from the home country which are given new meanings and values in a new setting, or they may be new ones. I will examine the power of symbols in constructing and maintaining identities in the next chapter when I discuss the work of Anthony Cohen, but for the moment it is enough to state that many of the political scientists and empirical sociologists I have considered above have only a poor understanding of culture and cultural processes. This leads them to be wary or dismissive of primordialism as an explanation of ethnicity, but to endorse a rather thin and deterministic instrumentality. In fact, as we have seen, primordialism is something of a straw man in these refutations, as few authors I have considered – with the exception of the Soviets – would endorse it in the terms that Steinberg and others reject. It is, however, worth noting that groups such as British Asians are very likely to describe their identity in terms of fixed and ancient (even quasi-biological) attributes, involving distinctive food items, dress and values. As a somewhat banal truism it might be worth stating that subjective understandings of what an analyst would identify as 'ethnicity' tend to the primordial.

Anthropologists therefore have two reasons for considering pre-migration cultural practices and systems very strongly in their understanding of migrant ethnicity. First, 'culture' is what anthropologists study; secondly, from the days of Malinowski anthropologists have been concerned to see the world as the people they study see it. Thus, if the members of a minority migrant group insist upon the importance of certain cultural elements in maintaining their sense of a distinctive identity, and insist that these elements are timeless, distinctive and inherent to their sense of being, an anthropologist must consider them as being so (just as an anthropologist must consider the real presence of witchcraft if people insist it to be so). The question of *why* people hold such beliefs or attach such importance to them is no less important, of course, and it is an analytical rather than a methodological issue. But without a proper understanding of how such beliefs and understandings work, consideration of why they are held at all will be fatally compromised.

With this said, let me return to Watson and his contributors (Watson 1977a). All the authors are anthropologists and all have conducted anthropological fieldwork in both the 'home' country and with the relevant minority migrant group in Britain. Half the contributors had begun research in Britain before they realized 'that they would have to visit the migrants' home society before their studies could really be considered complete', while the other half came 'back' to Britain in search of migrants from the societies they had been studying (Watson 1977b: 2). The essays, together with book-length studies by some of the authors (for example, Foner 1979; Watson 1975), represent the first serious attempt to conduct such a split-location study since Thomas and Znaniecki's work, although none of Watson's contributors appears to acknowledge this.

In some ways the book can be considered analogous to Warner and Srole's *The social systems of American ethnic groups* (1945) and also to Glazer and Moynihan's *Beyond the melting pot* (1970). It is analogous to Warner and Srole's work by virtue of having been triggered by popular British concerns over immigration (Watson 1977a: vii); it is analogous to Glazer and Moynihan's work by virtue of its arbitrary selection of 'groups' for consideration (Watson 1977b: 1) and by the fact that the groups include both 'black' and 'white'. It sits somewhat uneasily between the two over the issue of 'assimilation'. In his introduction Watson is critical of earlier work on race and ethnicity in Britain for assuming, as did earlier American work such as Warner and Srole's, that assimilation was an implicit or explicit goal to which such groups should be directed (1977b: 11).

On the other hand, the very title of the volume implies that the minority groups considered are existing in some kind of limbo-land, having neither one 'culture' nor the other. Of course, Glazer and Moynihan are not very interested in culture at all (to the extent of denying a distinctive culture to American blacks), but they do acknowledge that new ethnic identities are forged by such groups (Glazer and Moynihan 1970: 13, 16). In fact, the tone of some of the contributions belies the somewhat 'neither one thing nor another' implication of the title. Ballard and Ballard, for example, assert that a new pan-South Asian identity is in the process of forming, to which young British-born Sikhs are subscribing (Ballard and Ballard 1977: 54). Similarly, Watson claims that although he can find no evidence of a 'new' identity appearing among young Chinese in Britain, he does not doubt that it will happen eventually. Like many of the contributors, Watson forms his opinion not simply in the light of factors internal to the minority group under study but by considering factors external to them, and emanating from wider British society (Watson 1977c: 206). In the particular case of the Chinese, they remained essentially invisible to British society and were themselves largely indifferent to it until a spate of newspaper stories in the early 1970s which associated them with drug smuggling and extortion rackets. Combined with other factors (such as the handing back of Hong Kong to the Chinese in 1997 and increasingly stringent immigration requirements) the implication seems to be that British Chinese identity will be forced to transform as a result.

But the major thrust of all the contributions is that the ethnicity of minority migrant groups cannot be understood without reference back to the 'sending' country. This is particularly so in the case of groups such as the Chinese, where individuals move frequently between Hong Kong and Britain and where a proportion of British earnings is invested in property in Hong Kong (Watson 1977c). By contrast, political migrants such as the Poles initially mobilized and forged an identity partially on the basis of opposition to the then prevailing regime in Poland (Patterson 1977: 233–6). Most of the contributors none the less are careful to include a discussion of 'external' factors as well as 'internal' factors.

In his introduction Watson stresses the two-sided nature of ethnicity, and tries to balance the element of 'choice' on the part of minority migrant groups in asserting, transforming or even denying their ethnicity, with the element of compulsion or ascription that comes from outside (Watson 1977b). He emphatically rejects, however, at least part of Castles and Kosack's thesis (1977b: 12–13). Although he accepts their comments relating to the essential economic ineffectiveness of remittances sent back to kin in transforming the economies of the sending countries, and agrees that there may be instances in which class takes precedence over ethnicity, he criticizes them for implicitly assuming that migrants 'have only one goal – to join the British working class'. In fact, the large-scale and statistically oriented nature of Castles and Kosack's work means that they have very little to say about what migrants might or might not want. There is little in the way of subject testimony in the book and much of the qualitative description is drawn from secondary sources.

Watson castigates them most for their anti-humanism, for treating migrants 'as if they were a uniform, faceless mass of proletarians' and for treating their 'cultural predispositions' and ethnicity as 'excess baggage that will somehow disappear on the road to a "rational" or classless society' (1977b: 12–13). While I, and perhaps many anthropologists, would have sympathy with Watson's position, it must be admitted that he advances a rather weak argument. He offers no particular refutation, beyond an appeal to liberal humanism, to treat these migrants as people, not labour pawns. The real problem lies in the fact that like is not being compared with like. Castles and Kosack, in their often quoted passage, '[i]mmigrants should be looked at not in the light of their specific group characteristics . . .' (1973: 5), are saying that ethnicity has no salience for their particular style of analysis: Marxist, class-based, macro-sociological. As Marxists, Castles and Kosack are convinced of the 'scientific' objectivity of their analysis, and are concerned to reveal the structural position of immigrant workers within the western European political economy of the late 1960s (the period from which most of their data derive). For Watson – or any other anthropologist – to argue that the members of the minority groups they studied and interviewed do not consider themselves to be members of the British working class is entirely beside the point. A Pakistani factory worker who would like to be an entrepreneurial small businessman is still a factory worker, and as such stands in a particular relationship to the means of production (in Marxist terms).

An anthropological analysis, based on intense ethnographic observation of a small group of people and concerned to understand things as members of that group see them, can only counter Castles and Kosack's position if it meets them on their own ground. Clearly, the anthropologist cannot supply data in sufficient quantity to make the statistical arguments needed to counter their position, and even if they could it might be ineffective: it is entirely possible that the vast majority of European 'immigrants' do occupy the structural position that Castles and Kosack say they do.

Instead, although Watson and his contributors do not perhaps make the point as clearly as they could, the anthropological response to Castles and Kosack lies in challenging their basic frame of reference. If one is concerned to analyse 'immigrants' in terms of their class position, it is obvious that many of those considered by Watson's contributors have an enduring place within the class and other social structures of Italy, Pakistan, the Caribbean, and so forth. Setting class aside, there are a variety of structural features of 'immigrant sending societies' identified by anthropologists which continue to play a part in the behaviour and understandings of minority groups in Britain (and, of course, elsewhere): structural features such as kinship networks, religious affiliations, hierarchies of power and status. That minority groups in Britain can be identified as having a certain class position within British society may be as sociologically significant as the fact that a certain percentage of those migrants will be over one metre fifty in height (which is, presumably, a significant issue for demographers or nutritionists). That is, Castles and Kosack and Watson and his contributors have different research agendas, are interested in different issues and collect differing kinds of data. A far higher, more abstract and more philosophical form of analysis would be needed to weigh the merits of one approach over the other.

Although the 1960s and 1970s saw mostly single-authored ethnographies of particular 'ethnic groups', following Watson's volume the trend moved more towards collections of essays linked by a particular theme. In *Ethnic communities in business* (Ward and Jenkins 1984) the contributors turned their attention to those Castles and Kosack had ignored or whose existence they wished to deny: the migrants who, despite possibly starting out as workers in white British enterprises, aspired to entrepreneurship.

By 1988, Westwood and Bhachu had assembled a group of mostly female academics to explore the gender dimension of this entrepreneurial activity (Westwood and Bhachu 1988a). By focusing the papers specifically on the economy, rather than entrepreneurship, the conclusion that many of the contributors come to is that gender may be a more important variable than ethnicity on occasion (which, of course, is a parallel argument to the class-not-race-or-ethnicity argument we have encountered above). For example, Phizacklea concludes that family structure is a key variable in determining the success of under-capitalized enterprises (1988). While there may be variation, the men of minority migrant groups from as far apart as South Asia and Cyprus can call upon the unpaid or underpaid labour of wives, daughters and other female relatives, following highly authoritarian and patriarchal family structures, in a way that Afro-Caribbean men cannot (Phizacklea 1988: 31).

In a different, but related vein, Westwood notes instances in which women workers in a textile factory can be understood to share a common 'culture' or at least to employ and agree upon common cultural symbols within the factory context, regardless of ethnicity (Westwood 1988). She demonstrates this within contexts as diverse as labour union representation, and wedding preparations, claiming that the 'insertion of reproductive roles and "femininity" into the heart of the production process was both an act of resistance and, simultaneously, one of collusion because the models which inspired this femininity were located in patriarchal definitions of women's roles as wives, mothers, and sex objects' (Westwood 1988: 116).

More particularly, the contributors mount a collective challenge to Watson's notion of an 'economic niche'. In his work on the Chinese in Britain Watson had laid emphasis on the fact that the Chinese occupied a niche in the British economy (for example, 1977c: 193–5). By setting up and running fast-food outlets and restaurants they had found a secure place within the British economy that allowed them to maintain an ethnic identity that was largely immune from influence by wider society (Watson 1977c: 193). This is essentially an ecological model, and while it may go a long way towards explaining the particular case of Chinese ethnicity, it simultaneously serves to homogenize the Chinese and to reify them as a group. More particularly, it obscures the fact that 'the Chinese' can only maintain this safe harbour away from the wider currents of the British economy (though this is also doubtful) because Chinese *men* rely on Chinese *women's* unpaid labour, especially in the fast-food industry as Baxter and Raw (1988) demonstrate. Bhachu (1988), Westwood (1988) and P. Werbner (1988) all make a similar point from the other side of the takeaway counter, as it were: where minority women are involved in the wider labour market, working often in large enterprises such as factories where they may have no kin or even ethnic links with their employers, the entrepreneurial economic niches that their male kin have carved out are frequently dependent upon women's earnings if not their labour.

The 1980s also saw a significant addition to the theoretical literature on race and ethnicity. If Watson's *Between two cultures* was in some ways the British equivalent of *Beyond the melting pot*, Rex and Mason's *Theories of race and ethnic relations* (1986) can be seen as a rough equivalent of *Ethnicity: theory and experience* (though if anything, the contributors to the former are even more gender blind than the contributors to the latter). Among Rex and Mason's contributors there are in fact some North American-based academics, and the majority are sociologists rather than political scientists. The tendency in many of the articles is to the large-scale and the abstract and, as I mentioned at the start of the previous chapter, some of the contributions tend to the elision of 'race-and-ethnicity'; Yinger, for example, in his contribution acknowledges the 'dream of a grand theory' in the social sciences (of everything, not just race-and-ethnicity), but goes on to criticize several attempts that include both race and ethnicity (1986: 20–1). None the less, two articles by anthropologists deserve to be highlighted.

Richard Jenkins looks specifically and critically at anthropological models of ethnicity (Jenkins 1986). He reviews ideas that have been presented in this and the two previous chapters, concerning the troubled relationship between ethnicity and race, boundaries and their maintenance, the shift from (the analytical category of) tribe to ethnic group, and even the Soviet theorists. He also highlights the similarity between Barth's model of 'choice' and Banton's more recent use of rational choice theory (Jenkins 1986: 175; see, for example, Banton 1983), one of the 'grand theories' that Yinger (above) dismisses.

As Hechter points out in the same volume, 'rational choice theory' is in fact nothing new and is to be found under different labels in most, if not all, social science disciplines (Hechter 1986: 264). Predicated on the 'theoretical primacy' of the individual, not the group, rational choice theory holds that individual actors act rationally and in their own best interests, that the results of their actions are cumulative, and that it is the repercussions of maximizing actions which give rise to the structures that facilitate group formation. Its proponents argue that such an approach allows for the observable fact of social change in a way that static, group-based models do not. In anthropology, such an approach therefore runs directly against the grain of Radcliffe-Brownian structural-functionalism. (In sociology it runs against many more such '-isms', as sociological theory seems to breed these more prolifically than anthropological theory.) Probably the major anthropological use of such a perspective in recent years, apart from a model of 'maximizing man' (*sic*) employed in some forms of economic anthropology, is in a loose, Weberian approach to social life known as transactionalism, in which Barth is – unsurprisingly – a key figure (see Kapferer 1976 for collection of essays).

The particular extension(s) of rational choice theory to encompass situations where race and/or ethnicity seem salient are described by Hechter, but for an anthropologist the word 'rational' is enough to sound warning bells. Certainly, the maximizing rationality observable in the maintenance of Gypsy identity that Hechter – citing Banton (1983: 158–64) – describes seems reasonable enough. Gypsies maintain an ethnic identity, and prevent their children from exploring its limits and possibly rejecting it through a combination of ideological and practical means, in order to protect a series of interrelated economic niches (Hechter 1986: 276–7). But we have already seen above how Watson advances a similar argument for the Chinese in Britain, yet does not see the economic niche as constitutive of ethnicity, merely a mould and container for it. For Watson – or rather, for the Chinese – the perceived primordialism of their identity through their enduring links to Hong Kong is the point of departure, their economic niche merely the shaper of that identity in one specific historical context. Furthermore, although rational choice theory is supposed to follow the choices of the actors it is, of necessity, applied retrospectively to the action considered, and hence will always have a tendency to prove itself correct. As a result of this tendency to determinism (which it shares, it must be admitted, with a wide variety of other theoretical positions) rational choice theory runs a very real danger of isolating and objectifying its human subjects in the name of supposedly granting them autonomy.

I admit that my own position on rational choice theory is biased through brief acquaintance and possibly anthropological prejudice, but Jenkins appears to have problems with it as well: 'an emphasis upon the orientations, values and goals of actors – particularly members of ethnic minorities – can appear to be blaming the victims [of racism and ethnic chauvinism] for their own disadvantage' (Jenkins 1986: 177). His solution in this instance is to make a sharper distinction between group identification and the process of categorization (see also Jenkins 1994). From Barth we have already learned that ethnic identity is influenced from both sides of the boundary and that 'ethnic groups' both achieve their identity and have it ascribed to them from outside. Jenkins points out that the two processes are not the same, the latter process of ascription or categorization being particularly dependent upon relative power relations (Jenkins 1986: 177). As for the future of ethnicity theory within anthropology Jenkins proposes a number of possible ways forward, including excursions into social psychology (such as that of Epstein 1978, discussed in Chapter 2), a further look at the Soviet theorists, and a marriage between theories of ethnicity and theories of nationalism (1986: 183–5). Of these, it is the last that has come to dominate in the few years since Jenkins' piece and which forms the subject of the next chapter.

Jenkins spends some time discussing of the work of another British anthropologist, Sandra Wallman, who also has a piece in the Rex and Mason volume. Wallman is one of the few analysts, along with Tambs-Lyche (discussed above), who has made a concerted attempt to work with Barth's ideas of boundary maintenance and construction (Wallman 1986; see also Wallman 1978, 1979). Taking both the notion of boundaries and Barth's notion of generative structures (the cumulative process of actors' choices reconfigures the social system they work within), Wallman attempts to answer a relatively simple question: why does ethnicity appear more salient in some contexts than in others? The question is posed as much for its practical policy relevance as for its theoretical significance, and arises out of her observations and ethnographic investigations in two areas of London: Battersea and Bow. Both have a similarly 'mixed' ethnic population and superficially resemble each other in other ways. Yet Battersea is represented as an area in which 'ethnicity counts for rather little', while Bow (the area that saw the rise and fall of Mosleyite fascism) is represented as an area of continuing race conflicts and polarization (1986: 235, 242).

Wallman is as sceptical of Barth's transactionalist version of rational choice theory as I am, pointing out that the arguments in practice are essentially circular (1986: 232) and cannot explain the Bow/Battersea difference. Her solution is to widen the scope of the context within which ethnic differences are or are not manifest, to the extent that ethnicity becomes almost epiphenomenal, an effect not a cause of a wide variety of other variables. Such variables include housing type and choice, occupational patterns, the strength and density of the subjects' social networks (see also Bott 1971; Mitchell 1969), and a cluster of social, historic and economic factors that make up each area's 'local style'. A slight weighting is given to the local industrial structure in the particular areas under study (Wallman 1986: 245), but she is insistent that all variables are interlinked and none is overly determinate (1986: 236). The actual details of the argument are beyond the scope of my discussion here; the point worth noting, however, is that while relying on Barth for initial stimulus, Wallman does not presuppose the universal significance of ethnicity but seeks to identify the kinds of contexts within which it is likely to be manifest, regardless of whether to the analyst there is any obvious 'rationality' or instrumental gain at work.

Articles such as Jenkins' and Wallman's attempted to demonstrate the state of ethnicity theories within anthropology, but the discipline has always been characterized by an interplay between analysis and ethnography. The last few years have seen a slight resurgence of anthropological monographs on minority migrant populations in Britain after the volumes of collected essays in the 1980s, although edited collections continue to appear, of course; the most recent to contain a high proportion of anthropologists is devoted to a study of political leadership (P. Werbner and Anwar 1991). However, I wish to conclude this section with a brief consideration of two ethnographies that demonstrate very different outcomes of work conducted in the previous forty years or so.

Pnina Werbner and Alison Shaw have both conducted fieldwork with British Pakistani groups, the former in Manchester, the latter in Oxford (P. Werbner 1990; Shaw 1988). Shaw's is the more approachable of the two volumes and, although based on a doctoral thesis, is clearly aimed at a readership beyond anthropology and perhaps beyond the academy as it employs little technical language and few references. There is no explicit discussion of ethnicity in an abstract theoretical sense, but the ethnography is rich and well rounded and the account is informed by a period of fieldwork in Pakistan spent with relatives of those studied in Oxford (Shaw 1988: 1). By contrast, Werbner's book (also based on a doctoral thesis) is highly technical, does include explicit discussions of ethnicity, and is clearly situated in a precise intellectual lineage.

Through detailed ethnographic study, both authors confirm the point made by Westwood *et al.* (Westwood and Bhachu 1988a): an understanding of minority migrant ethnic identity cannot be complete without an understanding of gender relations. Werbner in particular provides detailed information of the way in which women's cycles of gift exchange (the subject in part of her article in Westwood and Bhachu's volume [1988], and also discussed by Shaw [1988: Chapter 6]) are intermeshed with men's trading and business networks (P. Werbner 1990: Part II and *passim*). By introducing anthropological perspectives on gift exchange (dating from Marcel Mauss, but relying particularly on Chris Gregory's work on gifts and commodities [Gregory 1982]), Werbner introduces a cultural dynamic to the rather reductionist account of economic factors in the shaping of instrumental ethnicity seen in some earlier works: '[t]he culturally unique expression of relations through gifting and hosting highlights the ethnic distinctiveness of a group, while at the same time it also allows for transactions to be initiated beyond currently established boundaries' (P. Werbner 1990: 333). Werbner's ties to anthropologists of the Manchester School are obvious and direct, and she makes extensive use of computer-aided network analysis (see, for example, Garbett 1980; Mitchell 1980). Although she talks at times of the Manchester Pakistanis as an 'ethnic group', her analysis of this group is sensitive to the idea of migrant identity (and hence ethnicity) as a process, not a state, and one that is influenced by symbolic as well as material factors.

Shaw too presumes nothing about the existence of a given 'group' or 'community' (despite the book's title), and in a chapter on leadership and politics she makes clear that the political dynamics that shape and define the community need to be understood with reference to the place of patronage in Pakistani society (Shaw 1988: Chapter 7). This is not because patrons who attempt to control affairs in Oxford do so exactly as they would in Pakistan; rather, there is a conflict between such a role and the expectations that (white British) community relations officers, council officials, and so on, have of a 'community representative' (1988: 144–7). As Shaw states: 'Council staff . . . are prepared to accept at face value people who present themselves as representatives working for the benefit of the community . . . [yet] Pakistani perceptions of how the local [government] system operates derive more from Pakistan than from knowledge of British politics and institutions' (1988: 145–6). As with Werbner, Shaw's understanding of an essentially instrumental ethnicity is informed by an analysis of cultural dynamics rather than apparently value-free political or economic factors.

RACE, ETHNICITY AND MIGRATION

An older anthropological approach to minority migrant group ethnicity would argue that it is not so much the cultural symbols themselves that are important, nor how 'traditional' they are, but the way in which – perhaps arbitrarily – such symbols are seized upon as markers of identity and difference. So far, so Barthian. But by itself this does not explain why, on migration, some minority groups appear to invest little in their symbols – such as the 'German Americans' discussed by Glazer and Moynihan (1970: 311–14) or the Maltese in Britain who effectively abandoned their ethnic distinctiveness in the face of hostile press reports that linked 'Maltese' with organized crime (particularly pimping) from the 1930s onwards (Dench 1975). What Barth's approach lacks is a consideration of the relative power balance on either side of the ethnic boundary.

Ethnic identities, according to some authors, are either ascribed or achieved, thrust upon the minority group or claimed by them (for example, Alexander 1992: 58–9; Jenkins 1986: 177; Tambs-Lyche 1980: 24). In a situation of power imbalance and visible differentiation between majority and minority, the ascription of identity by the majority group to the minority group calls not so much on attributes internal or intrinsic to the minority group (such as a propensity for street violence) but on constellations of symbols that are meaningful for the majority group. As Jenkins points out (1986: 177), the majority group does not so much ascribe an identity to the minority group as categorize it, and hence reify its very existence as a group. External ascription can act to bring 'groups' into being. In turn, members of the minority group may attempt to turn stigmatic labels on their heads, to imbue them with new and positive meaning (such as the black appropriation of 'nigger'). This kind of position would be easily endorsed by sociologists, social psychologists and political scientists. More recent anthropological writing on both race and ethnicity recognizes the structural conditions of boundary creation and maintenance, but is sensitive to the cultural power of the symbols that are deployed to that effect.

Such an approach has allowed most British anthropologists of recent years, as well as numerous others in Britain and America (for example, Sollors and his contributors [1989a]), effectively to subsume approaches to race within those taken towards ethnicity. The somewhat idiosyncratic statements of Just and Chapman *et al.* (noted above) on the relationship between race and ethnicity are more the product of working to a slightly different agenda within anthropology than an expression of a radically alternative view. A more typical resolution to the problem is provided by Zenner: '"Ethnicity" and "race" are terms which cover many sins. Both terms suggest biological relationships between those identified with one or another group or classed together in one category; both terms suggest that there are social and sometimes cultural dimensions' (Zenner 1985: 117).

It is none the less the case, however, that few anthropological works on ethnicity or minority migrant communities (especially in Britain) discuss discrimination or ethnic chauvinism at any length. Although structural problems relating to immigration or education may be outlined, the kind of detailed discussion provided by writers who focus on race or who provide ethnographies of black groups is largely absent. While there are certainly practical political consequences of this, there are also theoretical consequences. By seeing ethnicity as a 'social resource' (Jenkins 1986: 176) and by focusing on the study of groups that have 'culture' (Benson in press), anthropologists have enriched and transformed the straw man of ethnic primordialism to a point where instrumental and primordial can be seen as two sides of the same coin. But at the same time they have encouraged a myopia with regard to the minority group's relation to the state, to other minority groups and to actions and interactions in contexts other than those where ethnicity appears to be obviously salient.

As a final point I should return to an issue I raised at the start of Chapter 3: is there some kind of ethnicity that is manifest by minority migrant groups (however analysed and understood) that differs from the kind of ethnicity described in Chapter 2? Or putting it another way, does the fact of migration, and consequent minority status, somehow bring about a new form of identity or merely give a shift in emphasis and content to an existing identity? Political scientists of the ethnic revival 'school' in the United States, such as Glazer and Moynihan, claim that it is obviously a new thing, while anthropologists such as Watson who have a professional invest-ment in the notion of culture would argue for some kind of linkage and continuity. But Glazer and Moynihan also deny that the issue is any longer anything to do with minority status: everyone has ethnicity now, 'even . . . the majority ethnic group within a nation' (1975b: 4).

Thus a synthetic account of the origins of ethnicity would begin in America with the structured inequality of slavery and a polar-ization of the categories of black and white. The white category is then challenged by the first waves of non-'WASP' immigration in the nineteenth century, just as the relationship between black and white categories is realigned in the wake of emancipation. A period of flux follows, during which economic and political inequalities between black and white remain and the new migrants seek to find a categorical space. This persists until economic and ideological shifts following the Second World War lead to the civil rights movement and the crystallization of a new, politicized black identity. The still-in-flux white category follows this lead and fragments into similarly politicized ethnic identities. Finally, the 'old stock' white identity falls into place as an ethnic identity. In Britain, lagging a generation or two behind America and lacking the presence of an obvious black identity until this century, the politicization and reification of identities largely follows the American model and impetus after the Second World War, and an 'old stock' white ethnicity is still to arrive.

This is a just-so story, and is descriptive, not analytical. Indeed, it is not an account of what 'really' happened at all, but an account of the transformation of the concept of ethnicity through the writings of several of the authors considered in this chapter. A different story could be constructed to account not so much for the origin, but the content and maintenance of ethnicity, and this story would involve a description of migration, of class and of gender relations.

There is one problem with the first story, however, which is that of the American 'old stock' ethnicity falling neatly into place. This assumes that the mere existence of ethnicity is a politically neutral issue, even if the uses to which it is put are ideologically motivated and serve to create or reinforce inequality. In the next chapter I examine the relationship between ethnicity and nationalism, and the claim of some authors that the ideology of nationalism precludes ethnic identification.

Chapter 5

Ethnicity and nationalism

If the key term in the previous chapter was 'race' then the key term in this chapter is 'nationalism'. As we saw in the last chapter, the shifting, contested and frankly confusing uses of the term 'race' led to a number of problems in the texts discussed, and possibly also in this one, although I hope the reader placed mental inverted commas around the word while reading the last chapter. 'Nationalism' is perhaps a slightly more neutral term, and although there are many theories of what nationalism is, and how it arose, the term itself seems to be fairly stable. Although the phenomenon to which it refers may be disliked by some, at least in certain manifestations, it is not dismissed as a meaningless or even pernicious term in the way that 'race' has been. That is not to say that it is entirely value-free, however. R. H. Barnes, in a review of a book on nationalism in Australia and Sri Lanka (Kapferer 1988), notes that a Sri Lankan scholar objected to the term being applied to Sri Lanka on the grounds that it has 'pejorative associations'. As Barnes notes, the real objection seems rather to be about observing that a relationship exists between Sinhalese nationalism and inter-ethnic violence in Sri Lanka (Barnes 1991: 93).

I should stress, however, that this chapter is not solely about nationalism, any more than the previous chapter was about race. Implicit or explicit theories of nationalism underlie certain theories of ethnicity and therefore provide me with a hook for the third clustering of ethnicity theories that I wish to discuss. In Chapter 2 I considered theories of ethnicity that derived from observations made by anthropologists working with relatively stable, settled populations. Some of these theories explicitly recognized the existence of the state (usually the colonial state) such as those contained within the work of Max Gluckman and the Manchester School; some of these theories were indifferent to the state – the work of Frederik Barth, for example; and some – those of the Soviet ethnos theorists – were decidedly ambivalent about the state. In Chapters 3 and 4, the ethnographic focus on minority migrant groups brought a consideration of the state back into ethnicity theory. Some authors I looked at in that chapter, such as Glazer and Moynihan, made relations with the state the central focus of their interest, though they tended to treat the state and its ideologies as a given against which minority ethnic identities were formed in a reactive fashion. Other authors, particularly the anthropologists, viewed the state in a rather similar way – detailing its policies on immigration and housing, and so forth – but saw the creation of ethnic identities as far more of a process internal to the minority migrant groups under study.

A consideration of nationalism, however, allows us to examine the role of the state in the construction of ethnicity more closely. By focusing on nationalist ideology employed by the state we can no longer consider the state to be an abstract and neutral force or nexus of interests. It becomes an agent, one which is conscious of the ethnicity of its constituent populations and which itself may be a locus of ethnic identity. This is not quite the same as saying that the dominant white majority of European and North American nations has an ethnicity; rather, the ethnicity of the dominant white population (representatives of which are usually the officers and agents of the state in these countries) exists in some relation to the nationalist sentiments that brought the state into being and which sustain it. Quite what that relation is is the subject of debate among the authors I shall consider below.

The bulk of literature I want to concentrate on in this chapter represents the work of largely European anthropologists working with indigenous minority or majority populations within Europe. In Chapters 3 and 4 a recurring question was: is the ethnicity of minority migrant groups formed primarily by the fact of migration? Although some authors I considered regarded the question as unimportant, uninteresting or missing the point (for example, Castles and Kosack), many would answer yes, even though there was disagreement among them as to the role of culture in this process and the influence (if any) of the migrants' 'home' culture. For the authors considered in this chapter the question cannot be asked. The groups under study have made no significant migration and thus if they are deemed to have ethnicity, it must be caused or influenced by factors other than migration. Minority status within the nation state may also not be a sufficient explanatory factor either, as several studies of ethnicity have applied the concept to the majority population (for example, Just 1989; Forsythe 1989).

Although I referred above to 'indigenous' populations being the focus of the studies considered in this chapter, I do not intend to look at the literature on what are now termed 'indigenous peoples' outside (or, with some exceptions, within) Europe. Although the tribes of India, the Malay Peninsula, Amazonia, and so forth could be considered within an ethnicity paradigm, in my experience they rarely are, although it is quite common to find them referred to as 'ethnic groups' rather than 'tribes' these days. In many such cases there is an apparently sharp and clear dividing line between such peoples and the dominant majority or minority group that defines and gives shape to the modern nation state. Although, of course, there is an empirical blurring between the two – the mestizo populations of central America, be-suited Native American businessmen in North American cities – the prototype identities stand in sharp opposition to one another. Moreover, the dominant population in such cases is frequently non-indigenous.

By contrast, the minority populations that attract the interest of ethnicity theorists are those who are largely incorporated into the state's political and economic structures and who are no more or less indigenous than the dominant population. Within Europe that largely means groups such as the Basques, the Bretons, the Catalans, and so forth. It also means groups, population units and communities (however all these are variously defined) for whom no reifying group name necessarily exists, such as the inhabitants of various Scottish islands or Welsh valleys, yet who, ethnographers claim, express a collective identity that for the moment we can consider as analogous to an ethnic identity. For the former groups, the essays collected together in Sharon Macdonald's *Inside European identities* (1993a) provide a good example of the kind of literature and approaches I wish to consider; the essays collected together in Anthony Cohen's *Belonging* (1982a) and *Symbolising boundaries* (1986a) give a good idea of approaches to the latter 'groups'.

THEORIES OF NATIONALISM

It is necessary at the outset to spend some time considering theories of nationalism in the abstract, before we go on to consider the relevant literature on ethnicity. The reader should be warned, however, that the tie-up between ethnicity and nationalism is less close than the tie-up between ethnicity and race. In fact, with few exceptions (for example, A. D. Smith 1986), very little of the literature mentioned below actually discusses ethnicity at any length. None the less, the issue – that there are perhaps conceptualizations of 'community' beyond ethnicity and that these, by virtue of having political and jural authority, can influence ethnicity – seems to lie behind many of the works discussed below.

So what are these theories of nationalism? Taking a very broad brush approach, earlier theories tended to typologize, tended to be highly Euro-centric, and tended to assume that nationalism is an explicit political ideology, invented at a certain time and for a certain purpose (see, for example, Kedourie 1960; Kohn 1944). Later theories have tended to take a more anthropological approach, to see nationalism more as a process than a conscious ideology, and to be less Euro-centric. It is these later theories I shall discuss, as they are more generally relevant to a study of ethnicity. First, some general outlining is called for.

The chances are extraordinarily high that few if any of the readers of this book have not grown up in a nation state, or unaware of the existence of nation states. Even if you consider yourself Welsh, or Scottish, or Catalan, and feel that your national identity is illegitimately denied political and territorial manifestation (this could also be true if you consider yourself English), you have grown up in a world which from the nineteenth century or so onwards has understood there to be a natural congruence between a country's name (however often changed), a fixed territory (however much disputed), a group of people who are considered citizens (however varied they are), and a political system that administers that country in the name of its people (however much despised). Nationalism is an idea, to quote Ernest Gellner, 'so very simple and easy that anyone can make it up almost at any time, which is partly why nationalism can claim that nationalism is *always* natural' (1983: 126; emphasis in original).

If you are white, if you are European or North American of 'old stock' ancestry, it is quite possible that you may have read the previous two chapters without feeling the issues of race or ethnicity discussed had any personal relevance to you. Only white South Africans and certain others would be conscious of being of 'white race' for most of their lives, only 'ethnic minorities' would be conscious of ethnicity. Of course, if race and ethnicity have any significance at all, they have it on both sides of any boundaries they mark, so the illusion of feeling not touched by them is just that, an illusion. But nationalism is slightly different; there is, apparently, no other side to the boundary in the contemporary world, no obvious condition of non-nationalism. There are few, if any, 'tribes' in the world that are not involved at some level with the states whose borders they now live within, and which claim a seat at the United Nations in their name. And trans-national groupings such as the European Union are rare, fragile and constantly threatened by the interests of their national member states.

I am not claiming that there are *no* contemporary alternatives to nationalism, simply that it is the dominant socio-political condition of our age, and especially for any readers of this book as access to the book itself involves both the printing press and education, which are two key elements in one theory of nationalism's rise (Anderson 1983). As a result, it is very difficult to think around or behind nationalism, to step outside it in any way (in the way that a white reader may feel she or he can step outside the issue of race), and writers on nationalism sometimes use bizarre examples to try to jolt their readers into seeing it for what it is: Anderson, for example, asks you to imagine discovering the name of the Unknown Soldier, or dying for the American Medical Association (1983: 17, 132).

But it was not always so. Before the early nineteenth century, European states consisted of a small band of administrators, aristo-cratic landlords and others such as clerics, and a much larger population of peasants, pastoralists and largely unknown people on the fringes. While these states fought wars with other states, and made deals and treaties with them, there seems to have been no idea that all the people within the state were of a single identity or shared anything in common beyond allegiance to the monarch. They spoke different languages, had different 'cultures', and were often rigidly separated. Some of the groupings recognized kinship or affinity with others in the same grouping in other states, so Catholic priests, or members of royal households, had far more in common with each other than they did with the populations they ministered to or ruled over: as many writers on nationalism are fond of pointing out, there has not been an 'English' monarch in England/Britain since the eleventh century (for example, Anderson 1983: 80).

Most writers on nationalism are therefore agreed that it is a new thing, something that appeared in the eighteenth century and spread around the world. There are many arguments, of course: are there antecedents to nationalism (A. D. Smith 1986)? Is non-European nationalism the same as European (Kedourie 1970)? Is religious nationalism the same or different (van der Veer 1994)?, and so on.

Among anthropologists, three particular works are frequently mentioned and I shall look at them briefly to conclude this section. First, Benedict Anderson and Ernest Gellner both published influential works in 1983, in Gellner's case building on earlier publications (for example, 1964: Chapter 7; 1982). Gellner defines nationalism as being 'about entry to, participation in, identification with, a literate high culture which is co-extensive with an entire political unit and its total population' (1983: 95) and the crucial factors he identifies in the formation of nationalism are power, education and culture (1983: 94). Gellner is an unabashed 'modernist' (A. D. Smith 1986: 7–11). Nationalism marks a sharp disjunction between older agrarian societies and modern industrial societies. It is a modern phenomenon, arising out of a specific set of social conditions that occur only with industrialism. It can only arise when a high culture is established or reified (which none the less may draw upon real or imagined 'folk' elements), a population is relatively culturally homogenous and when there is a sufficiently wide-ranging and stable education system that allows the possibility (if not the actuality) of all members of the nation gaining access to that high culture. The social conditions that differentiate industrial society from agrarian society are characterized by a lessening and blurring of socio-cultural barriers: while these are enforced and celebrated in agrarian society, they are rendered unimportant by cultural homogenization through education in industrial society. Ideologically, a nation differs from a pre-national grouping in that members are part of the nation directly, not by virtue of membership in some lower-level grouping (a class, a kin group, an occupation, etc.).

For Gellner, nationalism does not arise out of the thinking of 'nationalist' thinkers: their thought serves merely to describe and identify the social conditions that give rise to nationalism, but which they falsely assume to be either universal or the product of their own efforts. Finally, nationalism is supremely self-conscious: society does not worship itself through the false mirror of religion (a Durkheimian view), it worships itself directly.

Gellner's overarching emphasis is on the form of nationalism, and though he provides several brief examples, he is relatively uninterested in its content. By contrast, Benedict Anderson's account is more obviously anthropological (though he is not in fact an anthropologist, unlike Gellner) and rests upon the crucial concept of 'imagining'. For Anderson, nations are 'imagined communities' in that 'members of even the smallest nation will never know most of their fellow-members, meet them, or even hear of them, yet in the minds of each lives the image of their communion' (1983: 15). Where Gellner describes how this imagination works (principally through education and a loosening of the bonds that tie individuals to small-scale social units), Anderson describes not only the 'how' of imagination, but what is imagined.

The technology of nationalist sentiment is also slightly different in Anderson's account: he identifies the decline of sacred communities, the consequent decline of sacred texts and languages, and the rise of literacy underpinned by the crucial motor of the printing press. Through printed works in the vernacular individuals gain a sense of being part of the imagined community of their nation, not necessarily by reading about great events of national significance, but rather by reading about the conjunction of the general and the specific. In novels and newspapers, certain events happen on specific days in specific places; while they happen to specific individuals they could happen to anyone – the reader is invited to share the experience of unknown others – and, moreover, a variety of similar (or different) events are happening at the same time.

This sense of simultaneity Anderson identifies as crucial: 'without taking it fully into account, we will find it difficult to probe the obscure genesis of nationalism' (1983: 30). Where pre-nationalist conceptions of time and narrative were founded on notions of cause and effect, of 'pre-figuring and fulfilment', within the nation time is 'empty' and 'homogenous' (1983: 30). 'An American will never meet, or even know the names of more than a handful of his 240,000,000-odd fellow-Americans. He has no idea of what they are up to at any one time. But he has complete confidence in their steady, anonymous, simultaneous activity' (1983: 31). This is where the Unknown Soldier and his tomb are of relevance. We must not know what his name is, or even place some anonymous bones in his tomb; his anonymity means that he can be everyman (or, at least, everyman-within-this-particular-nation). He died, unknown, while you – or your father, or your husband – fought alongside him in the same war.

Anderson's account is richer, in a sense, than Gellner's, and certainly more vivid in evoking the feel of nationalism, as well as its contours. Neither of them, however, has much to say about ethnicity or ethnic identity. Anderson does not appear to use the term or any variation of it at all. He does, however, in an early passage bring up many of the issues that students of ethnicity could be expected to concern themselves with: 'Theorists of nationalism have often been perplexed . . . by these three paradoxes: 1. The objective modernity of nations to the historian's eye vs. their subjective antiquity in the eyes of nationalists. 2. The formal universality of nationality as a socio-cultural concept – in the modern world everyone can, should, will "have" a nationality, as he or she "has" a gender – vs. the irremediable particularity of its concrete manifestations, such that, by definition, "Greek" nationality is *sui generis*. 3. The "political" power of nationalisms vs. their philosophical poverty and even incoherence' (1983: 14).

By substituting the word 'ethnicity' (and cognate terms) for 'nationalism' (and cognate terms) the similarities are obvious: the subjective impression of ethnicity as perduring versus the objective account that it is modern and recent; the widely varying expressions of ethnic identity set against the search for some grand unitary theory; the instrumental uses of ethnicity founded on identities that are shifting, fluid and contestable. If he were writing about ethnicity, Anderson might perhaps be described as a culturally sympathetic instrumentalist, one seeing the force of ethnicity without reducing it to conscious 'rational' trajectories to gain political or economic advantage, one aware of the crystallizing effect of an assertion of ethnicity on neighbouring and distant collectivities that have yet to articulate their own ethnicity.

By contrast, Gellner's broad-brush approach does mention ethnicity and ethnic identity in passing, but treats them casually. He discusses it in two contexts. First, 'ethnic' is treated as a synonym for or as an element within 'culture': 'Nationalism usually conquers in the name of a putative folk culture. . . . At the present time in the Soviet Union the consumers of "ethnic" gramophone records are not the remaining ethnic rural population, but the newly urbanized, apartment-dwelling, educated and multi-lingual population' (Gellner 1983: 57). Thus the 'high' culture which becomes the dominant culture of the nation may well draw upon real or imaginary elements of 'folk' culture in its national construction (other authors too point out the importance of archaeologists, folklorists, philologists, and even anthropologists in constructing a national culture, especially if it has not achieved statehood; see, for example, Chapman 1992; A. D. Smith 1986: 181).

Gellner's second, but related, use of ethnicity is as a differentiating factor. '[E]thnicity enters the political sphere as "nationalism" at times when cultural homogeneity or continuity (not classlessness) is required by the economic base of social life, and when consequently culture-linked class differences become noxious, while ethnically unmarked, gradual class differences remain tolerable' (1983: 94). The implication is that in pre-nationalist situations, ethnicity is singled out as a factor in the building of nationalist sentiment when there is a 'cultural' (ethnic) stratification of class; classes become identified with 'ethnic groups', such as Jewish merchants. In the former use, ethnicity is treated as a rag-bag of cultural elements which are added into the national culture. In the latter use, Gellner is discussing situations where the boundaries or cleavages between particular ethnicities are isomorphic to those between particular classes, so ethnicity is as it were mistakenly identified as the cause of difference. The discussion, to my mind, is not particularly clear, but it is obvious that Gellner, like Anderson, does not see ethnicity as either a necessary or sufficient factor in the rise of nationalism.

In this, they appear in sharp contrast to the claims of Anthony Smith expressed in *The ethnic origins of nations* (1986), one of a number of detailed studies of nationalism he has published. For Smith, the ethnic community is the forerunner of the modern national unit and thus, while he concedes that nationalism as we know it today is indeed a late eighteenth-century phenomenon (A. D. Smith 1986: 11), he disputes both the techno-historical argument advanced by Anderson and the econo-historical argument advanced by Gellner concerning its origins. In fact, Smith is not really so distant from Gellner and Anderson as would at first appear, especially Anderson. Despite lumping both of them together as 'modernists' and distancing himself as an unlabelled '-ist' that lies some way between the modernists and the 'perennialists' (a sort of less extreme primordialist), effectively he is endorsing Gellner's stress on the need for cultural homogeneity, but arguing that the ethnic community or 'ethnie' of the pre-nationalist past can be and has been a site for such homogeneity. Even if these communities cannot be said to express nationalism they express something that one day, with the right conditions, will come to be called nationalism.

His unit of analysis is the 'ethnie', a French term used as a synonym for 'ethnic community', that he feels captures best the range of meanings embodied in the original Greek term *ethnos* and which, he claims, lays a stress on the similarity of cultural attributes in a community rather than biological or kinship-based factors;

ethnie serves to unite cultural uniqueness with historical continuity (Smith 1986: 21–2). The ethnie is defined by a set of features or dimensions that by now should be familiar: a collective name; a common myth of descent; a shared history; a distinctive shared culture; an association with specific territory; and a sense of solidarity (1986: 22–30).

For Smith, cooking lasts and kissing don't: economic and political formations and alliances come and go and, while they may sustain a collectivity in the short term, only a 'myth-symbol' complex is durable enough to sustain an ethnie through millennia until it emerges into the modern world as a nation (1986: 15–16). It is a 'core' of 'myths, memories, values and symbols' (1986: 15–16) that lies at the heart of the ethnie, which is transmitted through and between the members of the collectivity and down through the generations. From the discussion in Chapter 2, it will be remembered that there is a core of ethnos in Soviet ethnos theory that persists through time, while the form of the ethnosocial organism (the political and economic manifestation of the ethnos) mutates. In fact, while Smith makes no reference to Bromley or other Soviet theorists, there is really a remarkable similarity. He is careful, however, to assert that he is not a primordialist (ethnicity as a given aspect of the human condition at all stages of history and in all contexts): 'ethnic and national identities [do not] form some continuum of necessary collective identity, [nor is] the quest for "identity", individual or collective, . . . a cultural universal' but, 'in order to forge a "nation" today, it is vital to create and crystallize ethnic components' (1986: 16, 17).

The major part of his book is devoted to detailing cases of ethnies in the remote and not so remote past, demonstrating that a common culture did indeed permeate a variety of named populations, and that they therefore had a perduring core of ethnic identity that could be transformed into nationalist sentiment when the time came. The cases are too many and too detailed to be examined here and I lack the wide-ranging historical knowledge to engage with them critically. However, I offer a couple of general comments.

First, it strikes me as unlikely that we can ever know what the sentiments of affect were between people long dead, and I don't see how one can prove one way or another that the Elamites (c. 3,500 BC to 500 BC) manifested a sense of solidarity (1986: 70–1), despite Smith's claim that 'it seems incredible to imagine that there was no continuity of ethnic community' given their 'distinctive cultural traits' – though, to be fair, he makes the same point himself (1986: 71). On a related front, I am less confident than Smith that the name by which the 'Elamites' are known from the historical record actually refers to the same population and its descendants at all, a point well made by Chapman with regard to the ancient 'Celts' (Chapman 1992: Chapter 3). Even with populations closer to our own day, we cannot be sure that we have correctly identified all the 'moves' they have made in their game with history (Ardener 1989d).

The second comment takes us back to the previous chapter where I discussed Richard Jenkins' distinction between the categorization of groups by others, which can serve to reify and distil a sense of ethnicity, and the self-willed adoption of a collective ethnic identity by the group itself (Jenkins 1986: 177). Smith's analysis tends either to ignore the distinction or remain focused mostly on self-identification. A brief footnote comment on race makes this point well: '[f]or our purposes, "race" in the *social* sense of an attribution (by self or others) of certain "innate and immutable characteristics", is treated as a sub-type of wider ethnic phenomena' (A. D. Smith 1986: 231, n. 10). The emphasis on 'social' is Smith's and he goes on to make it clear that subjective perceptions of physical or genetic immutability should be discounted. This, however, evades the issue: as we saw in the previous chapter, subjective perceptions of genetic immutability (folk biology) play a very important part in maintaining power differentials between 'ethnic groups'. Both Gellner and Anderson concede this point (Gellner 1983: 64–73, especially the discussion of 'blueness' on pp. 67–9; Anderson 1983: Chapter 8).

If I seem critical of Smith it is only because of the three authors discussed above he devotes so much attention to ethnicity and therefore needs to be taken seriously. On the other side of the coin, there are few authors whose primary interest is in ethnicity who give more than a passing glance to nationalism and its relationship to ethnicity. Two of those who do, Thomas Hylland Eriksen (1993) and Brackette Williams (1989), are discussed in the conclusion to this chapter. For the rest, we must – as I said at the start of this chapter – see the ghost of nationalism hovering over their work and only occasionally inserting itself into the text. My preferred route for tracking this ghost, and the reason for grouping together the literature discussed below, is the stress or emphasis an author or group of authors lays upon the role of the state in forming or maintaining ethnicity, given that the state in all cases discussed is a nation state.

FROM CAMEROON TO SCOTLAND

In 1972 the British anthropologist Edwin Ardener published a short article on population studies which has been highly influential (for example, Chapman 1993b: 2; Eriksen 1993: 89). The purpose of the article was actually to de-objectify the category 'population' which he claimed was seen as 'a reality' and 'infrastructural' in comparison with the more obviously slippery categories of language and ethnicity (Ardener 1989a: 65). As a result, Ardener's understanding of ethnicity must be gleaned from occasional remarks, given that the primary focus is on population studies. Drawing on historical examples from Cameroon, as well as his own fieldwork there with the Bakweri, we learn that a dual scheme of classification was going on between the inhabitants of the area and the German and British administrators, with each influencing the other: '[i]t is by a continuous series of such contrasts and oppositions (to which, I repeat, both foreigners and Africans contributed) that many (and in principle all) populations have defined themselves' (1989a: 68).

He then goes on to give a list, of a kind that we have encountered several times before in the work of Barth, Bromley, Anthony Smith, and so on. However, while their lists are itemized classifications of what an 'ethnic group' is, Ardener's is a list of issues that are important in the classification of such groups. Moreover, it is a five-point expansion of a single one of the items found in most other lists – the item concerning the ethnonym, or name claimed by or ascribed to the 'ethnic group' (1989a: 68). I won't reproduce the list here (it is also to be found in Eriksen 1993: 90), but it makes two important points. First, there is an interplay between self-identification and external classification. Secondly, this process takes place within a 'taxonomic space' which is not neutral. We have seen already how Jenkins (1986) and others working with the concept of race have highlighted the distinction between achievement and ascription, between the claiming of an identity and having one thrust upon one. Ardener adds to this only by highlighting the interaction between the two, although others have come to a similar insight by a different sociological route (for example, Claire Alexander [1992] comes to it via the sociological notion of symbolic interactionalism).

The idea of a 'taxonomic space' links us in more helpfully with ideas about nationalism. It highlights the fact that classifications (by the self or the other) are linked to other classifications and that none of these takes place in a vacuum; an anthropologist will see a

Durkheimian structural influence at work here (certainly in the idea that there are chains or sequences of classificatory action), though Ardener also intends us to see the political and social factors that shape the 'taxonomic space'. This leads Ardener to posit the notion of 'hollow categories' (1989a: 69): 'ethnic groups' that are not biologically distinct populations, that have no necessarily distinctive language, yet which are needed by other 'ethnic groups' for classificatory purposes. The example he gives is of the Kole, a Cameroonian 'group' which appears to have some antiquity, appears to have few members, and which exists in the interstices between a number of larger 'groups' (1989a: 69–70).

In this assessment of 'hollow categories' Ardener is essentially Barthian: an identity exists, but its members and its cultural contents are constantly shifting, to the point where '[w]e can easily hypothesize a situation in which everyone can point to a Kole, but no one calls himself Kole' (1969a: 69). Other, similar 'hollow categories' that Ardener suggests are 'Norman', 'Pict', 'Jew', 'Gypsy' and 'Irishman' (1969a: 70). Though he gives no discussion to how and why these might be 'hollow', we will see below that two of his students go on to explore the category of 'Celt'.

The interest of Ardener's work for studies of nationalism lies in the fact that his uses of the ambiguous tool of ethnicity can undermine both Anthony Smith's certainties in the continuity of ethnic populations through time, and Gellner's vagueness over the narrowing down of a number of 'cultural' or 'ethnic' identities in the pre-nationalistic period, to a single homogenous culture of nationalism. It should not be thought, however, that Ardener's approach to ethnicity is entirely culturist as the earlier similarity to Barth that I highlighted would indicate. In a later paper, also on population studies (Ardener 1989b), he claims that '[e]thnicities demand to be viewed from inside' (1989b: 111), no matter how lacking such claims to identity are in objective terms.

While the quoted part of the statement is somewhat primordialist, the second paraphrased comment is not, and shows Ardener to be adopting an essentially instrumentalist view of ethnicity. It is not there simply as a primeval thing, felt and articulated by all. Even if there are no objective grounds by which an analyst could see a self-proclaimed 'ethnic group' as distinctive, there must be some reason in their claiming such a distinctiveness. The example Ardener gives at this point is of the Ikwerri 'section' of the Ibo 'tribe' suddenly splitting off during the Biafran war in Nigeria and declaring itself to be 'not Ibo'. As he points out, this is rather like 'a stretch of Southern England declaring itself "not English"' (1989b: 111). The point, however, is that the Ikwerri clearly didn't just succumb to some ground swell of internally generated identity crisis and 'realize' that they were not Ibo after all. The Ikwerri section fissioned off in the midst and presumably as a consequence of and reaction to wider nationalist forces in the context of a civil war. A later example that he gives, of the Germanic peoples in Europe between the first and fourth centuries CE, who seemed to shrink in separately named populations over this period, makes a similar point: through a change in self-definition by a process of confederacy their 'effectiveness' was increased (1989b: 113).

In a later paper, however, Ardener effectively abandons the notion of ethnicity as his interests move further away from West Africa and towards groups and populations closer to home, particularly in Scotland. In the two earlier papers 'population' had been the term primarily under consideration and ethnicity had largely been assumed. Although Ardener had pointed out some difficulties with term and ambiguities in its use on the ground, he raised very little doubt concerning its strength as an analytical tool. In 1987, however, he returns briefly to this idea. In the context of a discussion on the definitional problems surrounding terms such as 'minorities', 'embedded groups' and 'plural societies' he states: '[t]he term "ethnicity" was a useful step on the road, which produced its own difficulties' (1989c: 211). He then goes on: '[t]he resort to "identity", as a term, was an attempt to restore the self-definitional element that seemed to be inherent in the idea of "ethnicity", but which was shared by entities other than ethnicities as normally conceived – many kinds of entities have identities. As far as "minorities" are concerned, majorities are just as important for our comprehension of this problem' (1989c: 211–12). The now familiar distinction between self-identification and external classification (familiar from the work of many others besides Ardener) remains although as before there is a bias towards internal labelling, but the utility of 'ethnicity' or 'ethnic identity' to convey this is diminished. At this point Ardener cites Anthony Cohen's edited collection, *Belonging* (1982a), approvingly; the 'fuzziness' of the title concept 'leaves all options open'. We shall see below how it is the openness of 'identity' as a conceptual term that allows Cohen and his contributors to abandon 'ethnicity' almost entirely.

In the course of the previous chapters I have identified a number of schools of thought, some by name (the Manchester School, the Soviet ethnos theorists), and some by inference and influence (the influence of Lloyd Warner and Robert Park on Drake and Cayton, the sociologists and political scientists clustered around Glazer and Moynihan). It would be inappropriate to coin the term 'Ardenerites' in what follows, but the influence of Ardener on a number of his students is palpable and explicitly acknowledged by them.

Under Ardener's guidance, several of his students chose to study what we might call sub-nationalisms or failed nationalisms in Europe. They are sub- or failed because they are nationalist movements that have not (yet) achieved statehood. It is difficult to find a term to describe such movements without seeming to damn them ('failed') and yet keep them distinct from the movements that succeeded (such as Hungarian nationalism creating the Hungarian state out of the fracture of the Austro-Hungarian empire). Gellner pays them little account, uses the term 'nationalism' to cover both those which gain statehood and those which don't, and implies that differences in religion rather than language will lie at the root of success in achieving statehood (for example, in his discussion of the role of Islam in bringing about a 'Bosnian' identity in the then Yugoslav federation, an identity that as I write is being bloodily converted into full statehood [Gellner 1983: 71–2]).

Anthony Smith, on the other hand, recognizes the conjunction of language and nation state in the modern world (so that every nation state has a national language) and argues that this gives greater force to the claims of language-based nationalist movements, such as the French-speaking Québecois in Canada, or the Flemish-speaking Walloons in Belgium (A. D. Smith 1986: 220). He uses a variety of terms to cover such movements, including 'derived or secondary nationalisms' (1986: 223) which indicates a dog-in-the-manger attitude on the part of the older nationalisms: once a nationalist movement has achieved statehood and territorial control, it is highly reluctant to countenance fissiparous tendencies on the part of cultural or ethnic minorities within the state, even if they present claims to distinctive language, culture, territory, and so forth. As Smith points out: '[t]he world of nations is a jealous one' (1986: 223).

Anderson too sees language as a decisive issue; as earlier European nationalisms developed, they marginalized or killed off minority languages within the state, thus reducing the base upon which nationalist distinctiveness could be built (Anderson 1983: 75). Presumably, combining the viewpoints of Smith and Anderson, language-based sub-nationalisms only maintain strength when they are articulated by people who are otherwise relatively wealthy, powerful and closer to the cultural centre, which is why Belgium, Switzerland and Canada have attracted particular attention for appearing – so far – to have contained linguistic diversity within the nation state.

Regardless of terminology and definition, the one thing all these movements share is that they are movements. Although a chicken-and-egg conundrum remains as to which came first, their politicized demands for (usually regional) autonomy or their nationalist character, these are not simply static, or for that matter fluid, identities crystallized around a common sense of being, or history or ancestry. Nor are they 'single issue' instrumentalized ethnicities characterized by their co-ordination in voting, or in demanding indigenous language education, or in monopolizing an economic niche or trade route. They are all these things and more, which means that nationalism encompasses ethnic identity and at the same time contains within it a whole variety of factors that those who have examined ethnicity in other contexts have singled out as being the defining feature. Even race is encompassed as many (but maybe not all) nationalist movements either draw upon folk notions of biology and biological difference or are supported by academic work that identifies such difference (a good example of both is provided by Jeremy MacClancy's discussion of social and biological aspects of Basque-ness [MacClancy 1993]).

In the field of ethnicity studies the most relevant of Ardener's students is probably Malcolm Chapman, whose work has already been cited a number of times. In two book-length studies and a number of articles Chapman takes up the issue of Celtic identity. In *The Gaelic vision in Scottish culture* (1978) Chapman argues that a Gaelic identity is or was essentially a 'hollow category', created and maintained by the larger Scottish and English society and then 'filled in' or given substance by the self-conscious efforts of 'Gaels' themselves. In *The Celts* (1992) the thesis is much the same, but extended to all the constituent Celtic identities: Gaelic, Welsh, Breton, Manx, and so forth. In 1978 he stated: 'Gaelic culture is only present in English literary discourse in a shape that has been imposed upon it from without; Gaelic culture has been subject to what I term "symbolic appropriation" at the hands of the majority and dominant culture' (1978: 27–8), and in 1992 he reaffirms: 'I have argued throughout this work that the Celts, as we know and remember them, have been constructed to serve the interests of a discourse external to them' (1992: 262).

Both books chart the course of these constructed identities; in the case of the Celts Chapman also discusses the ways in which the constructed identity has been re-appropriated by Celts themselves (especially young, middle-class proto-nationalists) and by certain academics who have wittingly or unwittingly colluded in establishing 'the Celts' as an oppressed minority in Europe (Chapman refers to such identities as 'balloons', puffed up with the hot air of academic discourse and given substance in the modern world of nationalisms and anti-nationalisms [1992: 235]). In both books the main effort is devoted to showing that, despite what certain authors say, there are few if any historical or cultural continuities in Gaelic/ Celtic identity of which the Celts themselves have been self-consciously aware.

Chapman also points out, particularly in the Gaelic case, that there has been a relatively recent elision between Gaelic identity deriving primarily from a distinctive language and (lowland) Scottish identity more generally, such that 'a language not understood by 98 per cent of the Scottish people, with a modern literary tradition that only begins to assume importance in the late eighteenth century and is still very small . . . and spoken by a people who have been regarded for centuries by their southern neighbours as barbarians, should now be regarded as the quintessence of Scottish culture' (1978: 12). Similarly, Rosemary McKechnie recounts how Oxford colleagues and Corsican informants alike assumed Gaelic elements to form a part of her own Scottish identity (McKechnie 1993: 123–8). In this way, the oppositional pairing Gaelic (language)/English (language) comes to mean Scottish (national identity)/English (national identity) (see Chapman 1992: 208–17 for an extended discussion of such structuralist pairings). Thus, what we can call an ethnic identity becomes elevated or broadened into a national identity.

The questions then arise of how and why such identities were constructed, and what, if anything, does this have to do with nationalism? For the how and why, Chapman draws on Ardener, structuralism and European nationalist politics. In the eighteenth century, the time at which the Gaelic identity is established, the Gaels and other Celtic but more generally peripheral peoples were identified as an oppositional category to the newly emerging state nationalisms of Britain and France. Their supposed wildness and primitiveness were both celebrated in the work of Romantic writers and used as a measure of all things that the 'civilized' English (and later French) were not. Here we see the influence of Ardener, as Chapman endeavours to demonstrate the interplay of categories and the way in which the national centre – the majority identity – creates an oppositional, minority identity within the 'taxonomic space' of certain classificatory schemes. The primary agent in this process is the discipline of historical linguistics. Along with ethnologists, the precursors of modern anthropologists, historical linguists were endeavouring to map out the 'natural' divisions of humanity. Infected by the growing idea that nations were themselves natural units, it was inevitable that the tree diagrams of language relationships they drew up (for example, the Indo-European language family dividing into Germanic, Hellenic, Slavonic and Celtic branches) should be read as divisions of biological populations. Thus, 'the adjective "Celtic" denoted a language, a society and a race, forging its unique path through time' (1992: 18), which of course is the same logic that Ardener identified in his articles on population with reference to colonial understandings of West African 'tribes' (1989a, 1989b).

Chapman, like Ardener before him, is conscious of the minority–majority relationship in his work. Like Ardener too, he is interested in the study of ethnicity only for the light that it sheds on the processes of human classification more generally (Chapman 1993b: 21–2; see also McDonald 1989: 310). Although he stresses at various points in his work that his primary interest lies with self-identification – ethnicity studied from the inside as it were (for example, 1993b: 2; cf. Ardener 1989b: 111) – and chides other scholars for failing to conduct fieldwork and for relying on accounts written by outsiders or a militant minority (for example, 1992: 234–5), the strength of Chapman's own work lies very much in giving us a clear view of ethnicity from the outside, as a construction of non-Celtic nationalist thinking. As he himself admits, 'It is difficult to look at the ancient [and, we might add, modern] Celts directly, without one's gaze passing through the various distorting lenses that romanticism and Nationalism put in the way' (1992: 209).

This insight into the embedding of (minority) ethnic identities within national(ist) identities, and the reification of those ethnic identities into minority national(ist) identities by dominant national identities is seen in the work of several of Ardener's former students and associates. Maryon McDonald, for example, in a study of the Breton language movement is less concerned than Chapman to flesh out her (acknowledged) debt to Ardener, but reinforces many of their observations and findings regarding the 'invention' of the Celts from outside, the conflation of taxonomies between the classification of languages and the classification of 'races', and the importance of the national centre in defining the identity of the peripheral subjects (McDonald 1989). This last point is perhaps particularly acute in the French context as, by contrast to Britain, the French state is far more preoccupied with its own centre and with maintaining centralist control. As McDonald notes, the irony is that '[t]he French government, in seeking to oppose minorities in the name of national unity, nurtures the very nightmare it wishes to dispel. Movements such as the Breton movement grow and blossom on opposition' (1989: 313). As the French state lays particular stress on the contiguity of language and nation (to the point of periodically purging the language of foreign, usually English or American, loan-words) it is no surprise that the dominant assertion of Breton identity is through a language movement.

Like Chapman, McDonald pays some attention to nationalism (although at the level of 'identity' she is happy to talk of 'what we like to call national or ethnic identities' [1989: 20]), and again reinforces the point that it is not just any old dominant majority that is imposing categories on minorities (which the minorities in time come to reflect back) but the national majority of the nation state that is doing so. In turn, the Bretons and other similar groups forge their identities as much with respect to the state as they do to the dominant classifying group. McDonald relates an anecdote concerning the wedding of a Breton- and Cornish-speaking Cornish boy to a Breton-speaking girl that illustrates this point well (1989: 118–19), as do numerous other passages.

The same theme emerges from a collection of papers edited by Sharon Macdonald, another student of Ardener's, on the subject of European identities (Macdonald 1993a). Macdonald notes in her introduction that '[n]ationalism, ethnonationalism and colonialism – all deeply rooted, one way or another, in Europe – are, then, among the wider movements which shape the Europe within which more localised identities are realised' (1993b: 4), while another contributor, Rosemary McKechnie, makes a similar point: 'the whole of society participates in the creation of peripheral identities . . . [and] images of "otherness" located in the peripheries have played a definitional role for centres of power in Europe down the centuries' (McKechnie 1993: 118, 121).

McKechnie's article concerns the interplay between her own (assumed) Celtic identity as a Scot, and the expression of Corsicanness. Like McDonald and Chapman she found her initial fieldwork investigations on Corsica frustrated by the fact that 'accounts of "real" Corsicanness were already theorised [by Corsicans]' (1993: 120) and so she needed to investigate the processes of construction as much as any supposed content. In doing so, she came to realize that other minority identities could well be implicated. 'It had simply not occurred to me', she writes, 'that immigrant workers [from North Africa] could have very much to do with Corsican identity, and it was some time before I revised this point of view' (1993: 134). Her conclusions on the matter are straightforward enough – that North Africans act as a 'pariah' group at the bottom of the social hierarchy, but also as a point of contrast against which Corsican values can be measured – but her very inclusion of the discussion raises an important matter and provides a link back to material I discussed in the previous two chapters.

Like Maryon McDonald, Sharon Macdonald points out in the introduction to the volume that Europe experienced an ethnic 'revival' in the 1960s in the face of expectations of homogenization (McDonald 1989: 11–12; Macdonald 1993b: 8–9). As we have seen in Chapter 3, a similar 'revival' among minority migrant groups in the United States at the same time brought about a huge sociological interest which, as usual, has taken a little longer to be reflected in British anthropology and sociology (two major 'revivalist' works on European ethnicity are Edwards [1985], especially Chapter 4, and A. D. Smith [1981]). In the context of the United States the literature on ethnic 'revival' was refracted through a paradigm of race but, as noted in the previous chapter, some of those mentioned above have a distinctive understanding of race. I noted there how Chapman *et al.* tie the word almost exclusively to its uses by (European) Victorian anthropologists (Chapman *et al.* 1989: 14), something Chapman repeats and expands in a later article where he again claims that '"ethnicity" is "race" after an attempt to take the biology out' (1993b: 21). The meaning of this is somewhat enhanced by Maryon McDonald's linkage of race and nation in nineteenth-century thought (1989: 10). 'Race' in the nineteenth-century biological or genetic sense indeed gave rise to so-called scientific racism which underpinned the interlinked movements of European colonialism and nationalism, and which has been rightly eschewed by modern anthropologists.

But as we saw in the previous chapter, 'race' also gave rise to an academic and popular discourse about *categories*, especially in the United States. By treating such a classificatory system seriously, rather than just dismissing it, Karen Blu (1980), for example, was able to come to a context-specific understanding of ethnicity and ethnic processes. In this sense, race should have been of more interest to the students and colleagues of Ardener than it appears to have been, although Maryon McDonald's contribution to Sharon Macdonald's volume goes some way towards this (McDonald 1993).

The problem really arises out of a nexus of confusion between disciplinary background and fieldwork experience. The American and British academics discussed in the previous two chapters studied migrants and descendants of migrants who had arrived on their doorstep, as it were. Though they could quite easily have discussed their findings with reference to theories of nationalism, the dominant concerns of the wider society (the national concerns one could say) about such groups were articulated through a discourse of race, and this discourse rightly or wrongly provided the framework within which the analyses were conducted. By contrast, the academics discussed in this chapter are mostly working with minority groups who consider themselves to be as settled and indigenous as their ethnographers, if not more so. For all the reasons that Chapman, McDonald and others outline, nationalism is both the framework within which these kinds of majority–minority relations are understood, and the framework within which the analyses are conducted.

I have not discussed above what in many cases is the main theme of the books or articles I have cited, but instead concentrated on picking out discussions that pertain to ethnicity and trying to link these with what are sometimes implicit references to nationalism. It should by now be clear that many of those above are discussing nationalism (by name or otherwise) at two levels. First, there is the nationalist identity of the minority group under discussion – the Bretons, the Corsicans, the Welsh, and so forth. It is this identity I take Macdonald to mean when she refers to 'ethnonationalism' without any further gloss (Macdonald 1993b: 3, 4) and which, as I mentioned earlier in this section, is perhaps best understood as a movement which has not achieved statehood. While this is predicated on what in other places and by other authors would be termed ethnicity, it should not be confused with Anthony Smith's idea of the ethnic origin of nations (A. D. Smith 1986), although several of the authors above mention his work in passing.

The main reason for this is that, following Ardener, most of the authors above are clear that they are concerned with *categories* of identity, not populations, and that these categories tend to be both defined and filled through the work of external agencies and at a particular time. This is where the second level of discussion comes in. The external agencies that fix and fill peripheral or minority identities are doing so in order to define (by opposition) state-level national identities, and they are doing so from the late eighteenth century onwards – the time of European nationalisms. Paraphrasing Chapman (1992: 209), it is only through the lens of state-level European nationalisms that we can understand the 'ethnicity' of groups such as the Bretons, and for precisely this reason we understand that ethnicity in terms of nationalism.

On a more personal level, it was only by considering it within a paradigm of nationalism and theories of nationalism that I could begin to understand the discourse on ethnicity employed by Ardener and his students and colleagues (which began with the confusion I referred to in Chapter 1 when I attended a conference the latter had organized). It is for this reason that I have presented the material in this fashion. By the same token, it is this perspective that informs my reading below of the 'new British ethnography' and its relevance to an understanding of ethnicity, despite the fact that this body of literature rarely if ever mentions the term.

A CELEBRATION OF IDENTITY

I said at the start of this chapter that the key term was 'nationalism'; while that is true overall, it takes second place in this section to another key term: 'identity'. In the context of this chapter, and in the context of this book generally, the two terms stand somewhat in opposition to one another. Disregarding for a moment the real presence of either nationalism or identity in human affairs, as analytical terms or as analytical tools, they represent two very different offspring from their parent ethnicity. Ethnicity is their parent not in any etymological sense, nor even within the intellectual development of the social and human sciences more generally, but because within the genealogy of literature set out in this book they both claim to spring from and to go beyond the parent concept. Both, in a sense, acknowledge that ethnicity as a term has failed to encompass satisfactorily the variety of inter-group interactions that it has been applied to, but while nationalism has been taken from the political scientists and applied in a new, culturally sensitive way by anthropologists, the exponents of identity in anthropology tend to eschew its psychological origins and to celebrate its very everyday-ness. Sharon Macdonald, for example, takes the term from Edwin Ardener as an expansion on what they saw as the more limited term ethnicity (Macdonald 1993b: 11; Ardener 1989c). Although the term has long been used in a casual sense by social scientists (and a more specific sense by social psychologists) it, like 'ethnicity' before it, is now being raised to the status of an analytically specific term even if its exact meaning rests on its broadness. In the middle of 1994, for example, a new academic journal was announced: *Identities: global studies in culture and power*. The eight-page advertising flyer noted discreetly that the new journal was to replace the journal *Ethnic groups* and claimed, among other things, that the new journal 'transports the field of ethnic studies beyond descriptions of cultural diversity'.

In a rather different way, identity as an analytical tool to unpick cultural diversity is employed by the author to whom I now wish to turn: Anthony Cohen. Cohen has been an influential figure in recent British anthropology and through the 1980s was a veritable one-man publishing industry, producing an ethnography, a short theoretical work, and two edited collections of articles that celebrated the diversity of British cultures (A. P. Cohen 1982a, 1985, 1986a, 1987). Through his work and influence he clustered around himself less a coterie of students and more a loose gathering of academics to contribute to what is now known as 'the new British ethnography' (Bradley and Lowe 1984: 9).

In fact, the term identity is used sparingly, although it forms part of the subtitle to the two edited collections, and Cohen is perhaps better known for rehabilitating the term 'community'. It is not of direct relevance to discuss the term here; briefly, earlier anthropo-logical studies of rural Britain (known as 'community studies') had tended to treat isolated rural communities as closed social units, unresponsive to change and locked in 'traditional' ways. The term 'community' came to assume a specious, almost bogus air – a false quality of togetherness but also backwardness in the face of modern industrial metropolitan society; it was also open to the accusation that it acted as a masking device, concealing the 'real' structuring principle of class (A. P. Cohen 1982b: 3). Cohen and his colleagues change all this by introducing a Barthian notion of boundaries and by focusing on the use and manipulation of symbols in sustaining these boundaries. The rural 'community' reappears, formed not by supposedly objective factors such as its economic isolation and stagnation, or by clinging blindly to past traditions, but by a self-willed process of active identity maintenance. Cohen's communities are self-aware social formations, internally divided and differentiated but subsuming their complexity 'within shared and relatively simple forms for the purposes of . . . interaction with the outside' (A. P. Cohen 1982b: 8).

Cohen is adamant that these local identities are formed primarily from within: the social forms discussed by the contributors 'acquire their significance from the meanings which their *own* members perceive in and attribute to them' (1982b: 9; emphasis in original), although he acknowledges that external political and economic factors can act as constraints to this process (1982b: 12). As he points out, the nearshore fishing industries of Whalsay (a Shetland island), Lewis (a part-island off the western coast of Scotland) and Aberdeen 'are affected by common influences of technology, economics, government policy and declining marine stocks', yet the industries have very pronounced local forms (1982b: 12). A man on Whalsay is never merely a fisherman, he is a *Whalsay* fisherman (1982b: 9).

Cohen's two edited collections (1982a, 1986a) are both devoted to celebrating the diversity of British cultures. For Cohen, there is no single, homogenous British (or national) culture. There are dozens of diverse cultures, founded often on a sense of locality or 'belonging'. Although the inhabitants of these cultural fields may share features in common with the rest of the nation – watching a popular soap opera on television, for example (1986b: 2) – they invest this common property with locally specific meaning. Everyday words, actions, circumstances are similarly invested with local meaning so that the boundary between members of the community and 'outside' may in fact be invisible to the outsider who, of course, is placing her or his own meanings on such words or actions and assuming that they are universally shared meanings.

Cohen's own work is based on extensive field experience on the Shetland island of Whalsay and his ethnographic monograph is a sensitive piece of 'interpretativist' anthropology, owing a heavy debt to Clifford Geertz (1975). More so than many of his contemporaries he rejects the structural-functionalist paradigm of British anthropology in favour of a search for meaning (1987: 17–19, 203–4; see also 1986b: 12–13). However, my own interests are slightly different, and in what follows I shall focus just on Cohen's approach to ethnicity and nationalism, while acknowledging that his ethnographic project and his commitment to creating a new understanding of symbolism are his main contributions to the discipline (see also the recent work of an early Cohen contributor, Simon Charsley [1987, 1992]).

In the previous section I noted a curious paradox. Despite Edwin Ardener's claim that '[e]thnicities demand to be viewed from inside' (1989b: 111), his own work, and more particularly that of his students, tended to emphasize the 'hollow category' nature of the ethnic identities they chose to examine. They devoted far more space to discussing how such identities had been constructed from the outside, even if these had subsequently been appropriated and 'filled' by those so categorized. Although his theoretical underpinnings are very different, Anthony Cohen's work in many ways represents the outcome of Ardener's demand (issued first in 1974). In a more or less phenomenological vein, Cohen and his colleagues take the demand very seriously, resolutely placing themselves 'inside' and seeking an understanding of what it feels like to be 'inside'.

But surely Cohen and his colleagues are not discussing 'ethnic' identities? The identities they consider are enclosed by boundaries that range from those within single households (Bouquet 1986) to those between the Scottish and English (Charsley 1986). Although by the second edited volume the scope of 'British cultures' had been widened to include urban cultures, in both volumes only a couple of articles on Northern Ireland (Larsen 1982a, 1982b; McFarlane 1986) contain subject matter that one would normally expect to find in a collection of essays about ethnicity. Even then, McFarlane, for example, is anxious to challenge the notion that the only salient and meaningful boundary is between 'Catholic' and 'Protestant' (which, although apparently religious, is interpreted by many academics as an ethnic boundary: for example, Glazer and Moynihan 1975b: 7). The sectarian divide is 'only one part of the cultural reality of people in rural Northern Ireland' (McFarlane 1986: 88) and there are many 'folk sociologies' to explain and articulate difference of various kinds.

Cohen's understanding of ethnicity is largely unexplored in his work, although there are more extended discussions in his short theoretical work, *The symbolic construction of community* (1985). Although he mentions it as a kind of identity from time to time (for example, 1985: *passim*, 1986b: 11) it is clear that he sees it as but one kind of identity. Ethnicity is just a 'sectionalism', a way of making and articulating us/them sentiments: '[w]e can make germane contributions to the debate [about definitions of ethnicity] if we slightly alter their focus from the causes of "ethnicity" to the generation of some form of sub-national, sub-state, communal sentiment' (1985: 107).

The 1960s and 1970s saw the 'revival' of ethnicity in the United States, a fact that was noticed and celebrated by authors such as Glazer and Moynihan. The 1970s and 1980s saw the rise or 'revival' of ethnic or sub-national identities in Europe. Anthony Cohen notices this too, but adds a slightly different spin. He points out, first of all, that 'community' as a term and focus of analysis had been replaced by 'class' in the 1960s among sociologists and that in turn 'class' had been displaced by a focus on gender, race and employment status (1985: 76). But, he argues, these shifts seem to depend as much on definition, on academic fashion and – crucially – on externally imposed academic categories as anything actually happening in the 'real' world (1985: 76; 1982b: 10). By contrast, 'it is empirically undeniable that the 1970s and 1980s have seen in the Western world a massive upsurge in sub-national militancies founded on ethnic and local communities' (1985: 76).

Several of the examples (drawn from the work of others) that Cohen gives in *The symbolic construction of community* could well be interpreted from a standard instrumentalist viewpoint on ethnicity: the mobilization of Saami reindeer herders of northern Norway against a planned hydroelectric scheme which would have flooded their pastures, for example (1985: 77–9), though he tends to focus on reactive cases of ethnic assertion, rather than on the more proactive demand for rights through to calls for positive discrimination that we are familiar with from literature on the United States. But his own work, and that of many of the contributors to the two edited volumes as well as several of the other examples in *The symbolic construction of community*, would not be so easily amenable to such an analysis.

The islanders of Whalsay are never discussed as an 'ethnic' group, nor is it very clear what they stand to gain by asserting their identity. Although Cohen provides the example of the Whalsay fishermen joining a blockade of Lerwick harbour (the main port of the Shetland Isles) against a number of recent national and international events and policies, he is clear that this extraordinary event was not the focal point in the creation of a Whalsay identity, or the start of some kind of class or occupational-based identity (1982c; 1987: 163–5). The Whalsay identity had been there all along and the blockade simply provided the community with a chance to 'speak for itself' (1987:

164). More generally, the Whalsay islanders seem to spend much of their time creating and manipulating their identity boundary with no specific external 'threat' in view. Similarly, Simon Charsley's Scottish brides and grooms would appear to have nothing to fear from English marriage practices (Charsley 1986). Yet Cohen is able to discuss or encompass all these expressions of identity within a single analytical framework, even though the examples range in scale from the household to whole villages and islands.

The key to understanding his position is nationalism. Cohen has very little to say about nationalism directly, whether of the state kind or the non-state kind ('sub-nationalism'). But it is clear that he regards national identities as deficient or unfulfilling in some way. Faced by national and transnational units (such as the European Union) people become 'politically introspective and reach back to a more convincing level of society with which to identify' (1985: 106). Which particular level they 'reach back to' would appear to depend on the specificities of local context: it could be an ethnic identity, a sub-national one, or simply the familiarity of a local community. Whatever it is, it is preferable to a national identity. 'The suggestion is, then, that people assert community, whether in the form of ethnicity or of locality, when they recognize in it the most adequate medium for the expression of their whole selves' (1985: 107). This is exemplified by the case of the Norwegian Saami again. 'To be Norwegian is *only* to be different from Swedes or Danes', while to be a Norwegian Saami 'is to have a range of interests which, in discriminating you from "white" Norwegians, paints a much fuller portrait' (1985: 107; my emphasis). While this sounds dangerously close to saying some cultures are better than others or at least more interesting and satisfying, presumably Cohen would claim that no one is 'only' a Norwegian and that even the non-Saami Norwegians will have rich and satisfying local identities that are as good as the Saami one.

In some respects Cohen's view of nationalism, and of the state, is a caricature. The nation state exists as a vague impersonal force that imposes itself upon local people, that demands linguistic and other kinds of homogeneity, but which appears to have no purpose about it, no agency. At times, he seems almost to define it out of existence: local communities are not merely parts of the national whole, they are the vivid and fleshy contents of its otherwise empty categories (1982b: 13). The nation state represents a threat and provides material for symbolic manipulation, but it is often a diffuse ill-articulated threat – looming modernity, if you like – rather than a sharply focused attack as in the case of the Norwegian Saami. This is largely a consequence of Cohen's focus on the touchstone of the authenticity of local experience (in sharp contrast to the scepticism expressed by Malcolm Chapman [1992]).

Although Cohen makes passing reference to Barth in pointing out that boundaries distinguish one thing (an identity, a group) from another, that they do not section off something from nothing (for example, 1985: 12), the ethnographic focus on peripheral minorities tends to mean that the emphasis lies rather more on one side than the other. Indeed, one of the contributors to *Symbolising boundaries* (1986a) complains rather aggrievedly that Barth's model has 'little utility for an analysis of the social boundaries between crofting settlements' on the Isle of Lewis because it doesn't place enough stress on the symbolic manipulation of the 'cultural stuff' that the boundary encloses and cannot explain (symbolic) boundary differences in cases where there is a great deal of apparent cultural homogeneity (Mewett 1986: 73). In fact, as we saw in Chapter 2, a criticism of Barth is that he places rather too much emphasis on 'cultural stuff' and diacritical markers, a point reinforced by Abner Cohen (1974b: xii–xiii).

It should be clear that there seems to be a fundamental gulf between Anthony Cohen's claim that national identities are rejected in favour of local identities and Benedict Anderson's claim that it is the very impersonal-ness and even transcendence of national identities that makes them powerful, so powerful that people will die for them. Can this circle be squared? Cohen thinks it can; in the case of the Lerwick harbour blockade a trans-local event can act as a focus for local boundary definition – the solidarity of community, alongside others and against the rest. More generally, the symbols and institutions of 'the nation' only have power and validity because they can be imbued with *local* significance and meaning: '*[l]ocal experience mediates national identity*, and, therefore, an anthropological understanding of the latter cannot proceed without a knowledge of the former' (1982b: 13; emphasis in original).

Crucial to Cohen's understanding of symbolic meaning is that people can refer to and manipulate the same symbol under the misapprehension that others refer to it in the same way. The symbol is common, so people think they have something in common, even though their interpretations vary (1986b: 2). A common 'British' culture of soap operas, newspapers and politicians' rhetoric, presents symbols that all recognize but which each interprets in her or his own way. And this is a thin, pitiful thing compared to the vibrancy of local culture, which has its own symbols, as well as appropriating those from the common stock.

However, Cohen's ethnography lacks the historical depth that Anderson brings, the historical depth that Chapman and McDonald use to demonstrate that the 'cultural stuff' of Celtic or Breton identity may be local but it is crafted into an identity from the outside. At one level this is unimportant to Cohen's analysis. His focus on symbolic practice means that it doesn't really matter whether supposedly 'traditional' and local touchstones of identity are in fact recent innovations or imported from outside. What matters is that locally specific symbolic meaning is generated by such cultural artefacts. But on another level the absence is problematic. In this world of relativist interpretativism, history becomes a casualty of symbolism; indeed it is the symbolic power of a sense of timelessness that matters and for which history is just a 'masquerade' (1985: 103). Not only are the present and past actions of the nation state rendered vague and impersonal, they are rendered impotent. The very real relations of power and inequality that exist between Britain's centre and its peripheries are diffused and overlain. This makes it difficult to accept the force of Cohen's statement that there is some 'empirical' reality in the 'upsurge of . . . militancies founded on ethnic and local communities' (1985: 76) when his own example of the Lerwick harbour blockade is presumably supposed to demonstrate, in Mc-Farlane's words, that 'it's not as simple as that' (McFarlane 1986).

DO MAJORITIES HAVE ETHNICITY?

Like most authors writing about ethnicity who I have considered in the previous chapters, Edwin Ardener, Anthony Cohen and their various students and colleagues have focused their ethnographic studies overwhelmingly on minority populations. The obvious question is: minorities in relation to what? And the obvious answer is: in relation to some national majority. Of course, around the world there are exceptions to this rule – the dominant, nation-defining white minority of South Africa during the years of apartheid, for example. But, in general, minorities who for political, cultural, economic or geographical reasons are peripheral to the nation-state centre have been the focus of most anthropological and sociological studies of ethnicity and identity. There are a variety of reasons why this might

be so, including some straightforwardly practical ones – it's easier
to get to know everyone on a small Scottish island than everyone in
a European nation state. But there are also some theoretical implications. We saw in the last chapter that Abner Cohen thought that
ethnicity was only salient for Chinese and Indians when both were
together as minority groups in a common context; apart, in China
and India, they were national groups (Abner Cohen 1974b: xi).
Although his point here is really about interaction and a common
context, not about the relative size of the groups ('Indians' are a
numerically dominant migrant group in Fiji, for example), it still
raises the issue of what kind of identity the majority group, the group
that claims to be synonymous with the nation, has.

Several authors writing about ethnicity see no particular reason
why everyone should not be considered to have an ethnic identity,
minority and majority alike. Glazer and Moynihan claim that a
'WASP' or old stock identity is emerging in the United States, in
reaction to ethnic minority assertions of identity (1975b: 4), and
Stanley Lieberson documents this process (1985b). Edwin Ardener
points out, in the context of a discussion of identity, that one must
understand majorities to comprehend minorities (1989c: 212), and
Chapman *et al.* claim that they deliberately invited contributions on
majorities to facilitate this process of comprehension (Chapman *et
al.* 1989: 15). Two of these contributions are of particular interest,
as they inform us about ethnicity and nationalism, and the relationship between them.

In discussing the Greekness of Greece and Germanness of (West)
Germany respectively, Roger Just and Diana Forsythe throw some
doubt on the obviousness and taken-for-grantedness of the nation and
national identity (Just 1989; Forsythe 1989). The picture they present
from within each of these European nation states is of a kind of
jellyfish identity, constantly wobbling and never quite fitting neatly
into any rigid container. Their ethnography challenges some of the
remarks with which I opened this chapter and some theories of
nationalism, particularly Anderson's otherwise rather hypnotic accounts of simultaneity. Both Just and Forsythe take as their starting
point the uneasy classificatory fit between the modern states of
Greece and Germany and the criteria for defining the populations that
are supposed to inhabit, define and be defined by those states.

Forsythe deals with an obvious problem: the fact that, at the time
she was writing, a conceptual 'Germany' was split between the two
nation states of East and West Germany. West German passports

claimed their holders to be merely 'German' (Forsythe 1989: 155, n. 5), and until 1972 an official statistical yearbook contained a map of 'Germany' (Deutschland) – dating from 1937 – that covered East Germany, West Germany and sections of Poland and the Soviet Union (1989: 139–40). Yet her own research revealed that the (West) Germans she interviewed considered Germany and Germanness to be defined in relation to a sliding scale of factors where contemporary state boundaries and political realities played their part, but so too did perceptions of history, language, race and culture. Simple oppositional categories – 'We know we are German, because we know we are not something else' (Austrian, Italian, black, and so forth) – were not sufficient to describe or explain the variety of anomalies and ambiguities that Forsythe encountered; for example, some people she spoke to objected to her referring to herself (a white non-German) as a 'foreigner' (Ausländer) as there were contexts in which the term was restricted to the Turkish minority in Germany (1989: 149).

In the end, Forsythe claims, 'Germanness is ephemeral . . . to be German is to feel vulnerable and at risk' (1989: 152) – a conclusion that many outside Germany (especially in Britain and after German reunification) would find strongly counter-intuitive. Yet Forsythe's data are convincing and her argument is credible. A 'national' identity, drawing upon many factors that have been claimed in the name of ethnic identity definition (common language and culture, folk notions of biology, and so forth), is as fluid and shifting as many ethnic identities when examined up close. Most crucially, it seems to have no centre or core, but to be 'hollow'. Although the majority, supposedly dominant identity within the state, it seems to draw no security or stability from this. It understands itself in part by opposition to other identities, but there are so many anomalies and contradictions in this (Forsythe and other white northern Europeans are 'not really' foreigners, ethnic German minorities in Poland or elsewhere are 'not really' German) that it seems to envelop or encompass other identities as much as marking them off to define its own boundary.

Just also considers the 'hollowness' of the Greek national identity and the attempts that have been made since the existence of a Greek state (around one hundred and fifty years ago, after the Greek War of Independence) to fill that identity with historically rooted components. The problem, as Just identifies it, has been to bring the recent Greek state – the *kratos* – and the supposedly long-standing Greek identity carried by the Greek people – the *ethnos* – into conformity. Just – who considers it a 'retrograde step that ethnicity should ever have entered into the *analytic* vocabulary of the social sciences' (Just 1989: 76; emphasis in original) – is in the unusual and perhaps difficult position of working as an ancient historian and contemporary anthropologist in the society and language that gave rise to much of our analytic discourse. The Greek term *ethnos* (essentially, 'people') and its derivatives, while translating conveniently as 'nation' or 'national' on some occasions (as in National Bank of Greece – Just 1989: 72), have also given rise to the English term 'ethnicity', and in modern Greece it can act as a convenient mask to conceal any suspicion that a complete contiguity of people and state might not exist (Just 1989: 85–6). As in Forsythe's 'Germany', Just notes that there are several instances where the lack of fit between *kratos* and *ethnos* is evident: well over twice the number of those defined as Greek living outside the borders of the Greek state at its founding than those within it; the 'Macedonian question' (all the more burning since the break-up of the Yugoslavian state and the emergence of the independent state of Macedonia); and the presence of minority populations such as the Vlachs within the state borders.

The Greek case could quite easily be understood from Ernest Gellner's position – the smearing over or eroding of weaker, ethnic and regional, cultures by a dominant culture to form the national identity. Indeed, Gellner does discuss the Greek case briefly, referring to it as a case of 'diaspora nationalism' (Gellner 1983: 106), in view of the fact that the impetus for the founding of the Greek state came from an alliance of Greeks outside the territory and romantic philhellenes such as Lord Byron. (Indeed, for non-Greek champions of the Greek cause in the nineteenth century, the actual people living in what became the state of Greece were something of a disappointment, falling far short of the standards of world civilization set by the ancient Greeks.) But Just instead attempts to understand the 'national' identity from inside, taking as his starting point a five-point definition of criteria associated with ethnicity:

1 Political incorporation into a sovereign state
2 Geographical circumscription
3 Historical continuity (some sort of 'origins')
4 Culture

   and

5 Biological self-reproduction

(after Just 1989: 75–6)

In many respects this is similar to the lists we have seen before, enumerating features such as historical continuity, common culture and territorial boundedness. But there are also significant differences. First, the five points are not external analytical ingredients in a recipe for ethnicity; they are criteria invoked from within, four of them being 'evidence', as Just terms it, for something that is already known. Second, the fifth point in the list – biological self-reproduction – is, for Just, the one that really matters. The other four items act as a confirmation of notions of folk biology. The modern Greeks know themselves to be a race, a biologically self-reproducing group, and factors such as their ties to the land of Greece, their ancient history, and so forth should merely be evidence mentioned in support of this.

In fact, as Just details, all the evidence that could be adduced in this way is problematic or unsatisfactory for the Greeks for a variety of reasons. As with Forsythe's Germans, the modern Greeks are profoundly uneasy with their claims to Greekness on cultural, historical and territorial grounds alone (Just's first criterion – political incorporation into a sovereign state – from all the literature I have considered so far would more normally be seen as an aspect of nationalist rather than ethnic ideology and, while relevant to his Greek case, would be aberrant elsewhere). So it is that the Greeks fall back on the idea that one 'is Greek because one has *elleniko ema* – Greek blood' (Just 1989: 77).

Just in some ways combines the best of Gellner and Ardener. He listens to Ardener's call to examine an identity from within and finds there an essential stability, despite much 'manufactured' evidence (as Just notes, the 'problem' of Greek ethnicity is really a problem for the historian and anthropologist, not the Greeks themselves – 1989: 71). But, because many of the historical influences that have shaped the Greek *kratos* and *ethnos* have come from without, he also considers this identity within a broader framework of European nationalism. It must be noted, however (as I did in the previous chapter), that Just's remarks on 'race' are coloured by both the Greek case and his specific anthropological background and he devotes comparatively little attention to quite what constitutes an understanding of 'Greek blood'.

Both Just and Forsythe, but especially Just, seem to see a difference between minority identities and majority identities, but even within the modern world of nation states it would be oversimplistic to say that dominant majorities either have or do not have 'ethnicity'. By the very fact of their peripherality and subordination, minority identities seem sharply focused and sharply defined and 'ethnicity' has been used by vast swathes of earlier literature to convey that sense of definition, even while the groups so defined may feel themselves under continual cultural threat from outside. Yet those who subscribe to the national identity, and appear to reject any idea of a subordinate 'ethnic' identity (as the metropolitan English appear to do in my experience), would appear from Forsythe's and Just's arguments to be engaged in a continual process of boundary negotiation and definition, seeing threats to the integrity of their identities on every side (one such English case is discussed in the next chapter).

Anthony Cohen's argument, of course, is that no one has a national identity – or at least, not one that is unfiltered through some local identity – but I think that rather evades the point of how it is that national identities can be seen quite clearly in formation and promulgation (especially at times of 'national crisis' such as war). The nation state has the power and more particularly the authority to promote nationalism through national channels, such as the media and the education system. It also has its problems, problems which are as much cultural and cognitive as they are political and economic. The identity and the experience of nationalism clearly share much in common with features that authors have identified for ethnicity – a commonality of cultural symbols, an appeal to history and continuity, a constant redrawing and redefining of boundaries in opposition to like others (alike as conceptual entities, crucially unalike in aspirations, power, economic strength, and so forth). The expression of nationalism is, however, unlike that of ethnicity in that it is harnessed to the machinery of modernity and linked to the structures of the state.

The issue of the relationship of ethnicity to nationalism is taken up by two authors I wish to consider finally. In a recent book, *Ethnicity and nationalism* (1993), Thomas Eriksen reviews a number of existing theories of ethnicity, before moving on to a chapter in which he considers nationalism. He performs a valuable task in outlining the previously unacknowledged parallelism between theories (and manifestations) of ethnicity and theories (and manifestations) of nationalism. For example, in their manifestation both employ the idiom of kinship as a central metaphor: 'ethnic groups' invariably stress common ancestry or endogamy, while nationalist ideology invokes the idea of a fatherland or motherland. Eriksen notes that, in the period leading up to the fall of the Shah in Iran,

Islamic revolutionaries represented Iran as a virtuous woman, raped by the US personified as an infidel (1993: 108).

Similarly, at a theoretical level, national identities, like ethnic identities, 'are constituted in relation to *others*; the very idea of the nation presupposes that there are other nations' (Eriksen 1993: 111; emphasis in original). Employing Diana Forsythe's data on Germany, however, Eriksen notes that fundamental 'us/them' distinctions are rarely possible in real life and that, however much nationalist ideologies are built upon such binary oppositions, empirical evidence suggests that people tend to think in terms of graduated scales of more alike and less alike (1993: 113–16). As Eriksen remarks, a similar understanding was reached by members of the Manchester School (particularly in the work of Clyde Mitchell – see Mitchell 1974) and this leads him to conclude that from an analytical perspective ethnicity and nationalism can manifest themselves in what he terms analogic and digital forms (Eriksen 1993: 116, 66–7). That is, either as a series of relations between people that consist in classifying others along either a continuum of 'more like us'/'less like us', or in sharp binary (digital) terms, where outsiders are simply an undifferentiated other.

As students of anthropology will realize, this is akin to the modifications made to 'pure' Lévi-Straussian-style structuralism by Mary Douglas and Edmund Leach. Eriksen's work seems to imply that the distinction is one between 'official' ideology (which would, of course, be more apparent in nationalist ideology which is usually codified in official rhetoric and government publications) and day-to-day cognition. As Forsythe's work shows, and as Eriksen acknowledges (1993: 116), neither the official ideology (manifested in this case in the changing maps in the statistical yearbooks of the West German state) nor day-to-day cognition of otherness can maintain binary or digital distinctions in practice.

As well as demonstrating the parallels between ethnicity and nationalism, Eriksen is careful also to note the differences. The major one concerns the relation to the state: '[a] nationalist holds that political boundaries should be coterminous with cultural boundaries, whereas many ethnic groups do not demand command over a state' (1993: 6). Even in cases, such as the Breton case, where control over the state is not realized, it is none the less a plank in the agenda that turns a possibly ill-defined ethnic identity (as held by many Bretons) into a political, proto-nationalist movement (as advocated by a generally youthful, middle-class Breton minority).

As we saw in the treatment of American ethnic minorities by Glazer and Moynihan and their colleagues, Irish-Americans or Italian-Americans demand a relationship with the state which privileges them or at least which does not foster disadvantage, but they do not seek control over the entire state apparatus, nor do they seek to promulgate Irish-American or Italian-American values as the dominant values of the nation. Returning to the distinction I made earlier in this chapter between achieved nationalisms and proto-nationalisms we can appreciate the force of Eriksen's observation that (proto-) nationalism can act against the state (1993: 109–11; see also Breuilly 1993: Chapter 16). Irish-Americans or Italian-Americans do not seek to cede from the state, and form a new state. Parts of the Breton movement, however, do seek just this, as do many others such as the Quebec separatist movement. An academic discourse of ethnicity has been used to make sense of all these cases, yet it is clear that there are obvious differences. It is only by reference to the state, and more particularly to nationalism, that we can make sense of such differences.

Eriksen's demonstration of parallelisms and divergences between ethnicity and nationalism is undoubtedly helpful. Slightly less helpful is a model he develops in relation to this. He claims that in the writings of others such as Ernest Gellner an equation is made such that nationalism equals ethnicity plus the state (Eriksen 1993: 99). As we have seen from the above, this is a fair enough statement in general, regardless of Gellner's position. But Eriksen advances it as a straw man hypothesis in order to highlight his own counterclaim that it is possible to have a non-ethnically based nationalism, one that transcends or bypasses ethnicity (1993: 116–18).

There are several problems with this position. First, as I said at the start of this chapter, Gellner and Anderson at least devote very little attention to ethnicity. Anderson in fact has no sustained discussion of it at all, and Gellner tends to refer to it only as a principle of cultural distinctiveness which provides a boundary between the culture that will be reified into the national culture and the cultures that will be effaced or emasculated in that process. Nowhere does he indicate that a specifically ethnic identity is the only one capable of such a transformation. Of the authors I have considered, only Anthony Smith (1986) could be said to be explicitly arguing for an all-embracing position that saw nationalism as transformed ethnicity. At this level my objection is no more than a quibble over interpreting what Gellner means when he refers to 'culture' (a word he uses often). But the reading of Gellner's position in this way tends to hide the value of Eriksen's counter-position.

Eriksen advances as an example of non-ethnic nationalism the case of Mauritius where he has conducted extensive fieldwork. The population of Mauritius has a varied ancestry, combining Indian, African, Chinese and European strands, although the Constitution acknowledges four 'communities': Hindus (52 per cent), Muslims (16 per cent), Sino-Mauritians or Chinese (3 per cent), and a residual 'general population' (29 per cent) (Eriksen 1993: 26). But, as Eriksen notes, while these communities are invited to explore and celebrate their heritage (through learning 'ancestral languages' in school, for example [1993: 116]), the 'national' culture carefully avoids specific ethnic reference. English, for example, is the national language, although it is neither an 'ancestral language' nor in fact the language of everyday life, which is a French-based creole. He concludes, therefore, that Mauritius is in the process of inventing a collective history that will be the root of the national culture without appearing to favour any one group over another.

Eriksen's knowledge of Mauritian society is extensive and exemplary (see, for example, Eriksen 1992) and I do not wish to cast doubt on his analysis in this case. I do, however, doubt the extension of this analysis to many other areas of the world. Eriksen claims, for example, that 'in many African countries, as well as in Mauritius . . . no ethnic group openly tries to turn nation-building into an ethnic project on its own behalf' (Eriksen 1993: 118). This could be disputed. At the time of writing, anthropologists have been arguing about the civil war in Rwanda and whether or not there is an ethnic dimension to the conflict (see de Waal 1994a, 1994c; Pottier 1994). Similarly it could be argued that a number of present and past conflicts in post-colonial African states represent the attempt by one 'ethnic group' not only to gain control of the state apparatus but, if successful, to impose its norms and values as 'national' norms and values. This is not to say, of course, that ethnicity *explains* such conflicts, merely that for descriptive purposes it has been used as a framing device.

But I don't mean to suggest that Anthony Smith is right, or that Eriksen's claim about previous theories of nationalism, which see it as the successful control by one 'ethnic group' over the machinery of the state, is correct. In fact, I think Eriksen is right, but doesn't make the point clearly enough. It is not that there are cases such as Mauritius in which a nationalism, unusually, is constructed that bypasses any local ethnicities. Rather, I think it is the case that all nationalisms, once state control is achieved, actively seek both to enhance and reify the specifically ethnic identities of deviant others within the nation state, and at the same time to efface the idea of ethnic particularism within the national identity.

The homogenizing tendencies of the national culture and its institutions appropriate local forms (whether these would be identified by an anthropologist as specifically 'ethnic' or not) which it labels, in English anyway, as 'folk elements'. Thus 'folk' themes are taken up and transformed in the music of composers who are later or at the time celebrated as 'national' composers, as many writers on nationalism, including Eriksen, have frequently pointed out. The point, however, is that such activities and their products communicate a message of continuity, not difference. The nation is a continuous whole, enlivened, as it were, by variations in local colour, but not riven by them. No local difference is valorized or elevated above others in this way. Today the composer uses themes from the music of the mountain peasants in his symphony; for tomorrow's symphony he will turn to the music of the coastal fisherfolk. The aesthetic criteria for preferring one symphony over the other are the criteria assigned by the national high culture and are to do with the skill with which the composer manipulates the encompassing form. One symphony is not preferred over the other because the mountain folk music is in some sense deemed better than the coastal folk music.

In certain cases, however, the differences between those living within the nation state's borders are too great to be encompassed and arranged upon a national continuum in this way. This is particularly true if certain individuals collectively form a minority or are already politically disenfranchised in some way, or speak a different language (one that cannot easily be redefined as a dialect of the national language), or have an essentially non-industrializable mode of production, such as pastoral nomadism, or have taken up residence within the nation state within the last few generations. Attempts are, of course, made to rectify such differences, by forcing the minority to conform to the majority's norms, but such attempts frequently crystallize in the minority a sense of collectiveness. An ethnicity is created by reaction. As McDonald points out for the French-Breton case, the harder the state pushes, the more the newly crystallizing ethnic minority pushes back (McDonald 1989: 313).

Given particular circumstances the emerging ethnic identity may be transformed by militants into a proto-nationalist identity, one that seeks a degree of state control or autonomy. Whatever the case, the national identity is very decidedly not an ethnic identity in its own view of itself, whether it arose from one or not. Tom Nairn claims this to be a hypocrisy: nationalism claims to be for and about all the citizens of the nation, but is really only for and about part of them; it is 'Janus-faced' (Nairn 1977: Chapter 9). Thus 'British' national identity is really only about and for the English. It is their values, their language and institutions that are promulgated. As Chapman shows (1978), the lowland Scots can be accommodated within this framework to some extent, but not the Gaels – the Highlanders and Islanders. They are too irredeemably 'other', and besides, their (constructed) presence does valuable cultural work in sustaining what Britishness/Englishness is by contrast, as do the North Africans in Corsica mentioned by McKechnie (1993).

Eriksen is aware of Nairn's argument (Eriksen 1993: 119) and he is also aware that (ethnic) minority identities can be ascribed, stigmatic and exclusionary (see 1993: 123–4, for example); but he does not make enough of the link between constant and perhaps integral processes of ethnic effacement within mature nationalist ideology, on the one hand, and the reification of otherness through ethnic stigmatization, on the other.

This link is explicitly to the fore in an article by Brackette Williams (1989), which I discussed briefly at the end of Chapter 2. Williams' argument is rich and complex: the title alone indicates the scope of her enterprise: 'A class act: anthropology and the race to nation across ethnic terrain'. In short, she is attempting to outline a synthetic account of the role of ethnicity in nationalism that is cognizant of factors of race (particularly notions of 'blood' and descent) and class. From this, I wish to extract only a few insights on the effacement of ethnicity in nationalist ideology.

Williams cites Stanley Lieberson who asks the reader to consider the following two sentences:

1 Americans are still prejudiced against blacks
2 Americans still earn less money than do whites
        (Lieberson 1985a: 128, cited in B. Williams 1989: 430)

What is it, ask Lieberson and Williams, that makes the second sentence seem odd or confusing? The answer lies in the fact that 'Americans' in both sentences is used synecdochically (the whole is named but a part is understood), but in the first sentence the synecdoche has the 'natural', normative meaning of 'white Americans' engendered by nationalism. As white America sets the nationalist agenda, 'black Americans' cannot be the normative reading of the second sentence.

Williams goes on to discuss the processes of exclusion and effacement which deny to some full membership in the nation, while masking the part-for-whole nature of others' inclusion. There is, she says, 'a magic of forgetfulness and selectivity, both deliberate and inadvertent, [which] allows the once recognizably arbitrary classifications of one generation to become the given inherent properties of reality several generations later' (1989: 431). She argues that a conflation of race, class and nation exists, in which an élite group (class), that claims better or purer blood (race), defines what it is to be a member of the nation. Individuals who cannot match up to the standards or criteria set fall behind or lose out in the 'race' for state control or hegemony (1989: 435–6). The agenda-setting group assigns such individuals to categories, and their 'failures' become categorical failures; named 'ethnic groups' become 'liabilities to the nation-as-state' (1989: 436). They can achieve 'success' only by reducing their ethnicity to external, folkloristic forms (music, dances, costumes) and by sacrificing individual and collective interests to those of the nation.

It is in this way that the music of the mountain peasants becomes part of the national heritage. This sacrifice is rewarded by jam tomorrow, of the assurance that an individual's self-sacrificial achievements (and hence, their collectivity's achievements) will be rewarded by a place in national history. This Williams describes as 'bleeding for the nation' (1989: 436). Those who cannot or will not sacrifice their identity in this way become the nation's 'ethnic groups', its problem groups. The nation's defining group, the one that claims the national label as its own ('Americans' in the above example), is not then simply another 'ethnic group', it is very deliberately and self-consciously everything and nothing; its name is synonymous with the national name, not a hyphened adjunct to it (Lieberson 1985b).

Chapter 6

Ethnicity unbound

So far in this book I have concentrated almost exclusively on the way terms from the ethnicity discourse ('ethnicity', 'ethnic', 'race', 'nationalism', and so on) have been used and understood by academics in writings primarily intended for an academic readership. It must be clear to anyone who has stepped outside the academy, however, that several of these terms are also in use in popular and non-academic official discourse. Prominent among them is probably 'race' and its derivatives. They are officially enshrined in Britain in the title of a statutory body (the Commission for Racial Equality) and a number of Acts of Parliament, and in popular speech the epithet 'racist' is frequently applied to others and denied for oneself (as in 'I'm not a racist, but . . .').

'National', of course, is to be seen in dozens of formulations, ranging from the titles of banks and motor recovery services, to a convenient way of describing countrywide phenomena – the local television news bulletin always follows the national news bulletin, for example. Frequently, in fact, 'national' is an unmarked term, just as national identity is an unmarked identity as noted at the end of the last chapter, so that in Britain we tend to speak of watching 'the news' and only use an adjective to mark the noun if we watched the local news, or the regional news. It is my impression, however, that the term 'ethnic' is not so frequently used in popular speech, and the term 'ethnicity' hardly at all. While I was writing this book I told people who asked that I was writing about ethnicity. With anyone other than academics in social science disciplines this tended to produce a nod and a silence by way of response – a sort of 'I've heard the word but I'm not sure what it means' look. After a while I began to reply that I was writing about 'ethnicity . . . er, ethnic issues – race, nationalism, the way people from different groups get on or don't get on'.

Otherwise, the term 'ethnic' seems to be used on occasion as a euphemism for 'racial groups' ('They're always wanting something, those ethnics') – though this is more common in the United States than in Britain – and as an all-purpose adjective to mean 'exotically different'. In this sense it is used frequently by the fashion industry – ethnic décor, ethnic jewellery, revitalize your wardrobe with the warm rich colours of ethnic fabrics this season.

There are, however, occasional uses that link more directly with academic uses, and it is on these that I wish to focus here. Quite how, when and why these terms entered popular discourse it is hard to say. Almost all of them came from ordinary speech in the first place, of course, but it seems to me that they have re-entered it, or been popularized within it as a result of contact with academic discourse. Thus 'race', which had a pre nineteenth-century meaning in English of 'kind' or 'lineage' was transformed through a discourse of natural history and later sociology into the complex multi-faceted and highly contentious term we know today (Banton 1987: 2 and *passim*). A great deal of detective work would be needed to track down the exact exchanges between academic writing and popular speech usage for even the few terms I have mentioned above.

My suspicion is that the language of multicultural educational theory in the 1970s and 1980s was probably a key cross-over point, and that the workings of the process were probably similar to those which exported psychological and psychoanalytical terms into the variant of speech sometimes known as psychobabble. Today, the public language of ethnicity seems increasingly associated with violence and disorder. A British newspaper recently reported on an electronic database of contemporary English created by Collins, the dictionary publisher, and Birmingham University. With reference to the database and the way language use is changing, John Sinclair, Professor of modern English at Birmingham, was reported as saying 'If you say someone has ethnic tendencies you are taken to mean that he is a murderer' (*Guardian* 14.7.94). The article makes it clear that this linkage has arisen in the context of the Bosnian conflict (discussed below).

With reference to other parts of the world it is also clear that such a linkage is being made. A newspaper article from 1989 that I mentioned in Chapter 2 employs the terms 'ethnic', 'communal', 'ancient communities', 'nationalist' and 'multi-racial' all in the context of unrest and bloodshed in the then Soviet Union (*Observer* 3.9.89). Generally one could say that journalistic accounts such as this understand a curious mix of instrumental and primordialist sentiments to be implicated in ethnicity. The accounts are instrumentalist inasmuch as the expressions of ethnicity appear to have some clear purpose – usually linked to territorial control – and there is no corresponding discussion of neutral, non-directed ethnic sentiment. On the other hand, the tone of the reports tends on the whole to assume that inter-ethnic hostility is somehow only to be expected. Human beings are naturally troublesome and quarrelsome, and the natural (hence primordial) lines of cleavage between human groups will be ethnic.

In general, journalists tend to use the terms 'race' and 'ethnic' fairly interchangeably, certainly when reporting on Britain. An article headed 'Black police officers form ethnic force to fight for equal rights' (*Guardian* 12.8.94), for example, talks consistently of 'ethnic minorities', but makes it clear that both the association within the Metropolitan Police and the journalist are apparently focusing exclusively on black and Asian police officers. Here as elsewhere, the issue is phrased in terms of conflict if not violence, the conflict arising over allegations of racism towards black officers within the police force itself. Quite who is 'ethnic', however, is not a trivial issue or merely an academic question of definition.

In a law report headed 'Rastafarians not ethnic but religious', *The Times* (29.4.91) described the latest round of appeal and counter-appeal in a case involving a Rastafarian who had been turned down for a job when he refused to cut his dreadlocks. The man had taken his case to an industrial tribunal arguing, under the Race Relations Act of 1976, that he had been subject to 'unfair discrimination on the ground of his race'. It is clear from the report that the judges and magistrates in the various hearings had wrestled with the issue of ethnicity and ethnic distinctiveness. On the one hand, it seemed that Rastafarians were not a 'racial group' or an 'ethnic group' (both phrases are used at various points in the article) because there was 'insufficient evidence' that they had either a 'long shared history' or a long shared 'cultural tradition', and because it could be doubted 'whether the majority could claim that they were of group descent'. On the other hand, 'placing them in the context of a formerly enslaved people striving for an identity, there might be a sufficient cultural tradition to satisfy the test' [of ethnic distinctiveness]. One of the most intriguing arguments advanced was that the Rastafarians could not be an 'ethnic group' because they had 'very little structure, no apparent organisation and customs and practices which had

evolved in a rather haphazard way'. While not strictly an instrumentalist point of view, this seems to argue that a group cannot just *be*,
it has to *do*, and that in doing a communal identity is forged and a
boundary wrought. Only subsequently can the issue of whether this
boundary constitutes an ethnic/racial boundary be addressed.

It is perhaps unlikely that an anthropological intervention in this
case would have unambiguously clarified the issue, though the terms
of reference were certainly those that anthropologists deal in ('group
descent', 'cultural tradition', 'striving for an identity'). Social
scientists' interests in ethnicity have, however, been invoked in other
areas of public policy and concern. One sociologist, for example,
refuted the claim of a *Guardian* editorial (28.12.87) that 'social
researchers' were united with the Government, the Commission for
Racial Equality, and the Office of Population Studies and Censuses
in wanting the inclusion of a 'race' question on the 1991 British
census. In a letter, Robert Moore claimed that the 'only scientifically
correct answer' to a question on 'race' would be 'human'. He went
on, '[t]he new line seems to be to ask about ethnicity. Ethnicity is a
very difficult concept . . . [and] the short-answer and box-ticking
methods of the census . . . are not appropriate to questions of
ethnicity' (*Guardian* 30.12.87; see also Ballard and Kalra 1994).

Elsewhere, however, anthropologists have seen it as the profes-
sion's duty to get involved with public issues of ethnicity. In two
articles that appeared in the summer of 1994, the anthropologist Alex
de Waal, co-director of a human rights organization focusing on
Africa, outlined his view of the Rwandan civil war (de Waal 1994a,
1994b). In both pieces he decried the tendency of journalists to
describe 'the current mass killing in Rwanda as the expression of
age-old tribal animosities' (1994a: 1) and blamed the (German and
Belgian) colonial administrations for mistakenly transforming an
occupational stratification between Hutu, Tutsi and Twa 'groups'
into a distinction between separate 'tribes' or 'ethnic groups'. This
reified a notion of 'racial' difference between the groups, that in the
context of the war was inevitably seen by journalists to lead to
conflict, bloodshed and even genocide. De Waal cites the anthropologist David Turton: '[i]f groups such as the Mursi [of Ethiopia] are
treated . . . as "given in nature", then the conflict which is seen to
define their boundaries is also given in nature' (Turton 1994: 20,
cited in de Waal 1994b: 3).

These pieces were interpreted by one anthropologist as 'stabbing
[anthropological] colleagues in the back and implicating them . . . in

this genocide' (Pottier 1994: 28). Although in fact de Waal had clearly stated in one article (admittedly, not cited by Pottier) that '[a]nthropologists and historians unite in deriding the descriptions of the Hutu and Tutsi as "tribes", and even as distinct "ethnic groups"' (1994b: 3), he partially agreed with his critic. Past anthropologists were indeed to blame for giving academic respectability to what is elsewhere known as scientific racism, and their professional descendants must share some of their sins; at the very least, argued de Waal, 'we should popularize our refutations of our ancestors' errors' (de Waal 1994c: 28). Of course, at another time it might well be anthropologically useful to consider relations between the Hutu, Tutsi and Twa 'groups' in Rwanda within a general paradigm of ethnicity – to look at issues of self-perception, boundary creation, maintenance and crossing, notions of descent, and so forth. The point that we can take from de Waal is that 'ethnicity' seems to have become fatally conflated with 'race' in the popular or journalistic mind. And not 'race' as a contemporary sociological category and tool of analysis, but 'race' as a nineteenth-century category of spurious biological worth.

Similarly, a year earlier a group of British anthropologists had organized a working group under the name 'Anthropologists against ethnic violence', prompted in part by the conflict in Bosnia. In their initial statement the group argue that 'it is the responsibility of anthropologists to expose the seductive simplicities which invoke primordial loyalties to ethnic origins' and call for a 'greater public awareness of how dangerous will be the consequences of an illusory concept of ethnic or racial purity'. One member of the group, Pat Caplan, later wrote a review of a booklet on Bosnia, put together by journalists and academics and published to accompany a series of programmes broadcast by Channel Four in 1993 (Caplan 1994). In the review, Caplan repeats again the claim made by many that 'explanations' of the Bosnian conflict in the mass media tend to rest on primordialist understandings of ethnicity (1994: 38).

While there are exceptions (and Caplan notes that they tend to be found in the *Guardian* newspaper) this is probably a fair assessment. In the light of some of the academic work I discussed in earlier chapters, however, it needs to be noted that news reporting, by its very nature, tends to focus on *change* (good or bad, peaceful or violent, actual or anticipated). Away from the features pages and the magazine programmes, a journalist would see little point in describing the 'age-old' tribal or ethnic loyalties of the Pathan and

Baluchi, for example, unless there was some conflict between them. For this reason, there tends also to be an instrumentalist strand to journalistic accounts. The As and the Bs may draw up the battle lines between them along an 'age-old' fault line of ethnic difference, but they are fighting *for* something – for territory, for jobs, even for survival.

Below, I present two examples of a non-academic conflated race-and-ethnicity discourse that reveal this mixture of primordialism and instrumentalism. The first is a brief account of a single, chilling term – 'ethnic cleansing'; the second concerns an educational dispute in which the discourse is more than usually hidden under a layer of self-consciousness and euphemism. My interest in both cases is primarily academic, at least within the context of this book. In examining the journalistic discourse of ethnicity I do not wish to trivialize the pain and suffering involved in these conflicts (particularly the first) or in the Rwandan conflict touched on briefly above. My aim is to highlight some of the ways in which the ethnicity discourse seems to structure public knowledge and understanding, in the hope that clearer understanding may lead to easier solutions in the future.

'ETHNIC CLEANSING'*

We have seen above how the term 'ethnic', and more rarely 'ethnicity', have entered the vocabulary of everyday British English speech. One of the newspaper articles cited above made a specific link between ethnicity and violence, grounding the link to the conflict in Bosnia. The article, which reported on trends in contemporary English usage, claimed that 'the word "ethnic" is being redefined thanks to Bosnia, which means it can no longer be used for groups differentiated by race alone' (*Guardian* 14.7.94). Setting aside the confusion, noted above, between the terms 'race' and 'ethnic' in both popular and official discourse, the article confirms our opinion that in journalistic use at least the term 'ethnic' was used most frequently in British English in the first half of the 1990s with regard to the Bosnian conflict. It tended to appear in phrases such as 'ethnic populations', 'ethnic characteristics', 'ethnic fights', 'ethnic segregation' and 'ethnic hatred'. But the phrase that took greatest hold and was repeated again and again was the phrase 'ethnic cleansing'.

---

* This section was co-authored with Monica Laptoiu.

It is difficult to write about the Bosnian conflict, not least because at the time of writing it is still continuing. Since it started, there have been so many shifts in the fighting, and so many twists and turns in policy (local and international) that the task of deciding which were the focal points, which were the decisive events must be left to future historians. Similarly, the task of outlining the situation as it stands currently would need far more knowledge of the region and its history, of political science and strategic studies than we can provide. None the less, it seems unlikely that any future account of the conflict could avoid reference to the policy and practice of 'ethnic cleansing'. We therefore offer some brief notes and comments on the term as it was used by the British press, in the hope of providing materials and leads for future writers.

Early on in the conflict the phrase 'ethnic cleansing' appeared in the British press. It was used in a variety of contexts but was generally used to describe the actions of the Bosnian Serb forces, backed initially by the Serbian administration in Belgrade, to drive Muslims and Croats out of their homes and villages in areas of Bosnia-Herzegovina that the Serb forces considered 'Serbian'. The actions took place, of course, in the context of the break-up of the state of Yugoslavia into its constituent republics following the death of Tito and the collapse of the Soviet Union.

Although the phrase only seems to have entered the British press vocabulary in mid-1992, it began to lose its quotation marks a year or so later (especially when Bosnian Serb authorities were being quoted), though for the most part they were retained. The phrase was used by the press throughout 1992 and into 1993, but by 1994 was becoming rarer (probably not so much because the actions it described were becoming rarer, but because journalistic attention had shifted to other matters).

Some journalists were opposed to the use of the phrase from the start – 'journalists should take more care before they repeat this Nazi epithet so blithely on radio or television' (*Independent* 15.8.92). The reference to the Nazis made here links to two historical strands from the Second World War: first, the German Nazi policy of rendering parts of the territory of the Third Reich *Judenrein* (clean or pure of Jews); second, the Croatian Ustashe (fascist) policy of expelling Serbs (and others) that was described as 'cleansing' (*čišćenje*) during the brief existence of the independent Croatian state under Nazi tutelage. Some journalists at least explicitly noted these antecedents (*Independent* 27.6.92 and 15.8.92), and parallels were made with the Holocaust: '[a]re the people of Sarajevo, like the Jews of the Warsaw ghetto, to be starved and shelled into submission while armed troops go from house to house in their chilling "ethnic cleansing" operation?' (*Times* 29.6.92). The phrase does not seem to have been used in reporting of the war between Serbia and Croatia (1991–92), but first surfaced in the post-war period in the summer of 1992 in the context of the Bosnian conflict (see, for example, *Guardian* 1.6.92, *Independent* 25.5.92, *Times* 5.6.92).

The phrase was widely used by the press during 1992 and was usually defined as a forcible expulsion of population (for example, *Independent* 22.8.92, 28.8.92, 29.7.92), although some journalists attempted to examine the meaning of the words a little more closely. The 'cleansing' part was relatively easy: 'The reality behind the Serbian government's clinical phrase is that villages, suburbs or streets inhabited by ethnically "unclean" and unwelcome minorities are deliberately targeted for rocket and shellfire' (*Independent* 27.6.92); 'houses are empty, cleansed of their inhabitants' (*Guardian* 21.8.92). In fact, many people were not so much shelled out as simply ordered out, and indeed had to pay towards the cost of their own 'cleansing' by paying compulsory 'evacuation taxes' and bus fares.

Somewhat more troublesome was the 'ethnic' component. Most journalists tended to refer either to 'populations' or to a group name (Serb, Croat, Muslim) without further comment, so that 'ethnic cleansing' was a policy of 'kicking out minority populations' (*Independent* 29.7.92), or the 'mass expulsion of non-Serbs' (*Independent* 12.8.92). But some were a little more reflective: '[t]he callous and cynical gratuitousness of the idea that millions of people should uproot themselves at the behest of politicians and regroup themselves under the meaningless labels of Serbs, Croats and Muslims appalled us all' (*New Statesman and Society* 11.12.92). This idea of the 'meaninglessness' of the labels harks back to the discussion earlier in this chapter of the Rwandan 'ethnic groups'; the *Guardian*, for example, declared that '[d]espite the horrible expression "ethnic cleansing" there are no ethnic divisions among the Slavs of Yugoslavia' (12.8.92) and went on to claim that the inhabitants of the former state were the same people, divided along religious and cultural lines.

The 'religious' issue is a complex one. The presence of an indigenous Islamic minority within Europe had long been of interest to observers, including some early ethnographers (see, for example,

Evans 1877; Lodge 1941: Chapter 7). Although a religious division between the Orthodox Serbs and Catholic Croats had occasionally been noted during the Serbian-Croatian war of the early 1990s, for largely Protestant Britain this was a rather flimsy and minor distinction, despite the parallels with Ireland. By contrast, the otherness of Islam, particularly in the aftermath of the Iranian Revolution, the Gulf War and the *Satanic verses* controversy, created a strange and paradoxical focal point. On the one hand, the Bosnian Muslims were Muslims – if of an apparently rather secular sort – and therefore would normally be placed in a 'feared other' category. On the other hand, they were also clearly the underdogs, the victims of 'ethnic cleansing', not its perpetrators (despite an early claim to the contrary by Franjo Tudjman, the Croatian president – *Independent* 29.7.92).

We have already seen in the previous chapter how several authors, but particularly Ernest Gellner, identified the spread of a common culture or a common religion as integral to the development of nationalism. Gellner (writing, of course, a decade before the Bosnian conflict) describes the 'transition from faith to culture, to its fusion with ethnicity and eventually with a state' for the Bosnian Muslims under Tito: '[they] secured at long last the right to describe themselves as Muslim, when filling in the "nationality" slot on the census. This did not mean that they were still believing and practising Muslims . . . identifying as one nationality with other Muslims. . . . They were Serbo-Croat speakers of Slav ancestry and Muslim cultural background . . . [and] thereby Bosnian, Slav ex-Muslims who feel as one ethnic group' (1983: 71–2). Gellner is clear that their 'Muslim' identity was as much oppositional to that of the Serb and Croat Christians as it was a thing in itself.

For our purposes, however, the claim of the *Guardian* that there are no 'ethnic groups' in former Yugoslavia, merely cultural divisions, seems to indicate the by now familiar conflation of popular understandings of race and ethnicity. The *Guardian* writer seems to feel that religion and 'culture' are both transient ephemeral things, not worthy of being deemed 'ethnic'. Ethnicity then is clearly about rootedness, permanence and clear-cut categories – in short, all the attributes normally brought under the label of primordialism. This perspective is apparent in much of the press reporting of 'ethnic cleansing' in Bosnia. The practice is enforced, for example, 'to create ethnically pure regions' (*Independent* 29.7.92), as though this were a straightforward task, however distasteful. As the normalcy of the idea of unambiguous ethnic difference resulting in unambiguous groups became established, so too the phrase itself became normalized. Journalists ceased to define it and used it as a name, like that of a disease, an item in a catalogue of disaster. The *New Statesman and Society* informed its readers that '[our] commitment must be to the civilian population of Bosnia suffering daily bombardment, ethnic cleansing, starvation, hypothermia and God knows what else' (23.10.92).

Some journalists elevated 'ethnic cleansing' to the top of the list of privations by identifying it as a central goal of the Bosnian Serb war effort – it was the *'subject matter*, not a side-effect of the war' (Vulliamy 1994: 96; emphasis in original). Others disagreed that it was necessarily the original aim, but implied that an inexorable logic made it so as the war progressed. Misha Glenny, for example, a journalist with extensive experience of east-central Europe who produced a book on the war, comments: '[i]nitially, "cleansing" is a military tactic which is mistaken for the central war aim because it is executed in such a horrifying fashion. Of course, as the war continues . . . the idea of including a minority population in the conquered territory becomes less acceptable as the doctrine of "national purity" strengthens' (1992: 187). Glenny's use of the ironic 'of course' and his placing of 'national purity' in inverted commas indicate that he is sceptical of any naturalism implied in this process. His comment also reveals again the mixed strands of primordialism and instrumentalism in journalistic discourse on ethnicity.

Even if the ethnicity of 'Serbs', 'Croats' and 'Muslims' is seen as perduring, obvious and a natural focus for group division, it is thought to be expressed for a purpose, for some reason. The reason given in the accounts is almost always territorial gain, and the logic underlying it is the logic of nationalism. As we saw in the previous chapter, successful nationalisms must always lay claim to territory, and strive for a congruence of the political, the national and the territorial. This assumption is reflected by most journalists writing about the Bosnian conflict, revealed by the fact that the terms 'ethnic cleansing' and 'national[ity]' frequently occur together in their writing (perhaps aided by the terminology of the former Yugoslavian state which, like the Soviet Union, employed the notion of 'national' [*nacija*] populations).

The phrase 'ethnic cleansing' has been employed by all parties in the Bosnian conflict, and reported as such by the media. It has progressed from being a shocking new term requiring a definition, to being an accepted fact. Journalistic explanation of the Bosnian conflict has largely been in terms of shifts and changes of local and international policy, with an occasionally expressed historical 'explanation' that the roots of the conflict lie in the Second World War. The first reports of ethnic cleansing were from the Banja region in north-western Bosnia, the area that had suffered apparently similar atrocities in the Second World War. The aggressors at that time were the Croats, and their victims were Serbs, Jews, Gypsies and Muslims.

On the whole, however, the term has tended to provide its own explanation by resting on largely primordialist understandings of ethnicity. The term has also spread, to be applied to other, apparently similar conflicts: '[t]alk of ethnic cleansing is growing louder as another Balkan feud unfolds [in southern Albania], this time pitting Muslims against Orthodox Christians' (*Guardian* 8.6.94).

We are not in a position to 'explain' the Bosnian conflict, or even to offer any firm clues as to why 'ethnic' became a key term in the reporting of that conflict. We would note, however, that a number of strands came together in the 1990s that made it a handy term, in which description could stand for explanation. Those strands include policy decisions in the former Socialist states of east-central Europe (informed in part by academics) to administer culturally heterogeneous populations, a terminological confusion surrounding the relevant terms in Slavic languages (such as the Russian *natsional'nost'*, or Serbo-Croat *nacionalnost*), a rise in the use of the term 'ethnic' more generally in British and American English, and a general conflation of 'race', 'ethnic' and 'blood' in the popular imagination which can, in part, be traced back to the scientific racism of Victorian anthropology.

THE SCHOOL ABOVE THE PUB

The second case study I want to present brings together many of the themes discussed earlier in this book, particularly ethnicity, race, culture and nationalism. It also provides some support for my earlier suggestion that the academic discourse of ethnicity was introduced to the public realm through the practice of multicultural educational theory, at least in Britain.

The bare facts of the case are straightforward. On a September morning in 1987, twenty-six children aged between seven and eight arrived for their first day at junior school in the Yorkshire town of Dewsbury, accompanied by their parents. They were initially refused entrance but finally came into the school. They were not registered or taught. The next day they came again and were also not taught. By the third day their parents had been sent a letter by the headmaster of the school warning them that their children would not be allowed into the school, but they came anyway and were allowed in for an hour. The children and their parents continued to arrive at the school door for a few more days, but by the end of the second week they were being taught by their parents, friends and a retired headmaster in a large room above a pub. The following year the parents successfully called for a judicial review in the High Court of the local Metropolitan Council's actions, during the course of which the Council suddenly backed down and offered the children places at the school (and another one nearby) (Naylor 1989).

The issue had begun earlier in 1987. Following the reforms of the Education Act 1980 the idea of school catchment areas was effectively abandoned. Children were no longer assigned to a junior school on the basis of where they lived but their parents could choose (within limits) where they would attend. All twenty-six of the children had been attending the same Church of England infant and nursery school; in their final school year their parents were offered a choice of three junior schools by the Education Authority: Headfield (the nearest to their current school), Overthorpe and County (about a mile away). The parents of fifty children selected either Overthorpe or County, while a further thirty-four elected for Headfield. All the applications for Overthorpe and County were refused, though on appeal sixteen children were offered places at the two schools before the new school year started. What with several children moving from the area or eventually enrolling at other schools, that left the rump of twenty-six children who had no school place and whose parents demanded they be admitted to Overthorpe (the majority) or County (Naylor 1989: 13–21). More specifically, the parents were adamant that their children would not attend Headfield.

Even before the 1980 Education Act parents all over Britain had tried to circumvent the strictures of the catchment areas policy, and after the Act disputes were bound to arise as local Education Authorities struggled to balance available school places, the best use of available resources and the wishes of parents. The Dewsbury dispute, however, became a focus of interest for the national press, attracted the attention of right- and left-wing political activists, involved a right-wing educational policy group (PACE – Parental

Alliance for Choice in Education) and became the subject of a book-length study (Naylor 1989), all for one reason: race. In fact, Naylor and the Dewsbury parents constantly denied that race was the issue, but in view of the attention given to it by the media, they were also constantly forced to confront it. For our purposes, the issue is best regarded as a complex nexus of ideas about race, ethnicity, nationalism and 'culture', with two 'sub-plots' concerning religion and multicultural educational policy.

Like many other towns in the north of England, Dewsbury became the home of substantial numbers of South Asian migrants (mostly Pakistani Muslims) from the 1960s onwards. They settled largely in one area of the town and their children attended the two local Church of England infant schools. Under the old catchment area system, these schools fed into Headfield junior school, together with the infant school that the twenty-six children in the dispute had attended. By 1987, 'the percentage of Muslims [had] reached 100%' at the two infant schools in the area settled by the Pakistanis according to Naylor (1989: 11). Naylor, the Secretary of PACE and 'educational adviser' to the parents of the twenty-six, places consistent emphasis on religious affiliation in his account. He does initially, however, write in terms of race and origin and it is interesting to see how he frames his opening discussion. He begins by briefly describing the town and its history, being careful to mention the ruins of a twelfth-century Cistercian convent in the district (1989: 8). He then goes on to describe the South Asian migrants as 'a peaceful close-knit community of some 4,000 souls in Savile Town, a former white working class district' (1989: 9) and stresses that '[t]hey wish to live their own way of life and to preserve as much of their culture as possible' (1989: 10). Similarly, Thornhill Lees, an area about half a mile away and the site of both the infant school attended by the twenty-six and Headfield junior school, is described as a 'white working class area' which is formed into 'a close-knit community' through the presence of the infant school and the pub, which later became the focus of the dispute (1989: 13).

The picture then is very clear. Two 'close-knit communities' of different origin live peacefully side by side, but desire little or no contact with one another. When the children of one 'community' begin to outnumber the children of the other 'community' at the local junior school (Headfield was estimated to have 85 per cent 'Asian' children according to Naylor – 1989: 13), the parents of the children from the first 'community' seek to take advantage of the new policy of educational 'choice' to send their children to other, largely white, junior schools in the area. Quite why the Metropolitan Council refused their applications is a murky and complex issue, though Naylor and the parents seemed convinced that it wished to avoid a *de facto* apartheid developing in the district, with some schools becoming exclusively Asian and others becoming exclusively white. Naylor became involved as PACE's representative very early on, and his account makes fascinating reading. He claims that PACE would not have involved itself if the parents' reasons for preferring one school over the other had been 'too trivial . . . to justify support' and he notes that the 'colour of the skins of the pupils' would have been just such a 'trivial' reason. However, '[a]fter speaking to some of the parents I concluded that they were acting from cultural rather than racial motives' (1989: 33) and that PACE could get involved.

Judging by the press reports, the parents were also anxious that visiting journalists should be clear about this 'cultural' not 'racial' motivation: 'It is not a racist issue. They have got their right to their culture and their choice of school and we have ours' (*Independent* 5.9.87); 'Our objections are cultural, not racial' (*Independent* 7.9.87); 'It is not about race at all. Perhaps cultures, but not race' (*Independent* 9.9.87); and, in the words of a reporter, 'the parents seem genuine in their insistence that race has nothing to do with their preference for Overthorpe which is based on tradition and family loyalty to the school' (*Sunday Times* 13.9.87). A number of press commentators (who had not necessarily visited Dewsbury) clearly agreed with the parents. Barbara Amiel, a *Times* columnist opined, 'Is this racism? It seems to me that it probably isn't – at least not in the sense of the noxious idea that one group of people are inherently inferior or superior to another. For most of us, whatever our race, our cultural self-identity is an important part of our human identity' (*Times* 11.9.87). Amiel receives Naylor's praise for '[d]istinguishing properly between race and culture' (Naylor 1989: 67) as does Robert Kilroy-Silk, a former Labour MP, who proclaimed that 'there is nothing wrong with being British, English even, and proud of it' (*Times* 12.9.87). On the other hand, a number of journalists and columnists were in no doubt that the issue was in fact one of racism: '[t]he real issue of the Dewsbury affair is racial prejudice' (*New Statesman* 11.9.87); 'Dewsbury court appeal smacks of apartheid', and 'race not culture' (both quoted in Naylor 1989: 73–4).

Naylor himself is insistent upon this 'culture not race' interpretation of the affair (for example, 1989: 33, 135–6) and it is worth examining this position more closely. He defines 'culture' as 'the sum total of the material and intellectual equipment whereby a people satisfy their biological and social needs and adapt themselves to their environment' and claims that this is an 'anthropological definition' (1989: 127); the most important elements of this 'culture' are 'language, religion, morals and political and economic organization' (1989: 136). By contrast, '[i]t is physical characteristics such as skin colour, hair texture, shape of face etc. that alone determine a person's race' (1989: 136). The definition of race is both biologically inaccurate (race as biological species) and sociologically ignorant (race as a social category) but Naylor's concern is obviously to minimize and trivialize it (cf. 1989: 33) in order to forestall any criticism of racism. He does not explain how the elements of 'culture' (language and so on) perform their task of satisfying social and biological needs, nor does he explain why different 'cultures' (which he understands as discrete bounded entities) should necessarily be unable to coexist or 'adapt' to one another.

Within the educational world (and apparently, the wider world) Naylor regards the complete assimilation of 'ethnic minority citizens' as unenforceable (1989: 129), but he is also strongly opposed to multiculturalism, a situation in which the constituent elements of all 'cultures' represented are given equal weight. His preferred option supports a situation of diversity in which 'members of the minority and majority cultures alike strive to maintain their separate identities' (1989: 129). This is largely because a Christian could never, for example, 'respect a religion based on the caste system, or the worshipping of idols' (1989: 137); equally, of course, he accepts the claim of Muslims that their religion is more worthy of respect than Christianity (1989: 96 and 113). Indeed, the following year, PACE advised a group of Muslim parents seeking local authority funding for an independent Muslim girls' school in the nearby town of Batley (1989: 193–4).

Readers of several of the newspaper articles cited above noted the weakness in such definitions of 'culture', pointing out among other things that 'British culture is not uniform and static' (letter: *Times* 21.9.87) and that dividing children along cultural or religious lines would only foster intolerance and misunderstanding (letter: *Independent* 11.9.89). Journalists and letter writers picked up on two main inconsistencies. First, one of the parents' major objections to Headfield school lay in the claim that their children's command of the English language would suffer through exposure to 'Asian languages' in the playground and even the classroom (for example, *Independent* 3.9.87). This was constantly refuted by the education authority, educationalists and teachers. Naylor cites this objection in passing (for example, Naylor 1989: 64), but he does not press the point, perhaps realizing it would be difficult to defend. Instead, he vigorously promotes the idea of a Christian 'culture' under threat. This was treated somewhat incredulously by some participants, who noted that very few of the parents of the twenty-six sent their children to church on a regular basis (1989: 17).

Secondly, there was the vexed issue of 'British culture'. Quite what was wrong with 'Asian culture' and why it would be harmful to the twenty-six children in a multicultural educational context seemed to boil down to a (refuted) allegation that chapatis (a flat dry bread) were made in the classroom instead of pancakes on Shrove Tuesday (*Independent* 3.9.87; *Guardian* 4.9.87). Far more space was given over to quite what 'British culture' consisted in and how best to defend it. Somewhat bizarrely the parents claimed that their children would not be able to learn about Roman Britain at Headfield school 'because of the number of Asians' (*Guardian* 7.9.87). Barbara Amiel claimed that 'British traditions are indifferent to the colour of a person's skin' and went on to ask rhetorically: '[w]ould it really matter – culturally speaking – if a few hundred yards down the road, the people calling themselves British were largely of Asian or East Indian stock, so long as they had acquired all the habits of the original people?' giving few clues as to what these 'habits' might be (*Times* 11.9.87).

Robert Kilroy-Silk, however, was the most strident in defending 'British culture' (*Times* 12.9.87). Under the title 'No shame please, we're British', he claimed that 'The British have a fine culture that has contributed a great deal to the benefit of the rest of the world'; he later defines this as 'the language, the values and the rest that go to make up the culture'. Like Amiel, however, he also offers no insight into what these 'values and the rest' consist in, beyond noting that the Dewsbury parents 'quite naturally and properly, wish [their children] to have a Christian education with an emphasis on British cultural values'.

Like Amiel (with her talk of 'stock') and Naylor, Kilroy-Silk seems to have a folk-biological notion of race (he talks of both 'other races' and 'their culture') that is a value free category of purely and insignificant biological relevance, unconnected to 'culture'. This is, of course, a white conceit, as the anthropologist Roger Ballard notes in the different but related context of the notorious 'ethnic' question on the 1991 British Census: '[i]f the white British are . . . deeply imprisoned within the assumption that "'black' and 'white' are fixed, permanent and antagonistic social categories" (Marable 1994), it is hardly surprising that they tend to deny their own role in the creation of racial disjunctions' (Ballard 1994: 14). This conceit is linked to an insecurity, which lies at the heart of much of the pro-parent rhetoric. Naylor briefly refers to this insecurity: 'a weakening of the sense of national identity' (Naylor 1989: 128).

As noted above, English 'ethnic' identity is crucially unmarked because it is the main constituent of 'British' national identity. It is defined oppositionally in terms of what it is not (in this case, pancakes not chapatis, English not 'Asian languages', and so forth), but there seems to be difficulty in defining it in its own terms except in the empty rhetorical flourishes that Kilroy-Silk employs which consistently conflate 'English' and 'British'. As all the Asian children attending Headfield school in the late 1980s were pre-sumably British, there is an innate contradiction in arguing for 'British culture' and against 'Asian culture'; the religious issue is settled on as the best bet, although Christianity could hardly be said to be either indigenous to Britain or exclusive to it. As we saw in the previous chapter, it makes sense for national identities to include tokenistic representation of all cultural traits within the nation state wherever possible for most of the time, while effacing or minimizing the dominance of the majority group's norms and values. Such a policy backfires or causes difficulty when a group such as the Dewsbury parents are able to see through this construction and exploit it for their own ends.

In some senses the Dewsbury parents were correct, the issue was not one of racism, it was an issue of ethnicity and ethnic conflict. From the reports I have looked at the term 'ethnic' and its variants were never employed by the parents (and only very rarely by Naylor), but if they were aware of the term at all they probably avoided it because of the popular conflation with race. That is, any mention of the term would have been seized upon by their opponents as proof of their racism. They probably did believe, along with Amiel, Kilroy-Silk and Naylor, that race is of no consequence and that 'culture' is an independent variable (ignoring, of course, the fact that their own white 'British' culture places crucial and axiomatic importance on race in its account of itself). In a sense they were not employing 'culture' as a euphemism for 'race' but as a euphemism for ethnicity or ethnic chauvinism.

A NOTE ON RACISM

I am not particularly concerned with the rights and wrongs of the Dewsbury case. Naylor's account seems to indicate that the parents' High Court case was won on the basis of inconsistencies in the Metropolitan Council's application of its own stated policies; however, a similar High Court ruling three years later confirmed that parental choice over schooling enshrined in the 1980 Education Act took precedence over the 1976 Race Relations Act (*Guardian* 19.10.91). In the context of this book the Dewbury case, together with the discussions earlier in this chapter, indicate two things.

First, that although ethnicity has become inextricably linked with race in the public mind, underpinned by a strong notion of primordialism, accounts of the Dewsbury case (for pragmatic, context-specific reasons) maintain the linkage but posit 'culture' (ethnicity) as a malleable variable. In these accounts 'culture' is usually insisted upon as unchanging by its holders and transmitters, but it is open to the possibility of complete rewriting (for example, Barbara Amiel's hypothetical people of 'Asian stock' who might 'acquire all the habits of the original people'). Such hypothetical rewriting is, of course, only possible in one direction – towards greater conformity with 'national culture'. But as national culture is almost always the reification of the dominant ethnicity or identity and, in the British case at least, this itself is strongly shot through with understandings of race, complete conformity is always impossible. If to be 'British' is ultimately to be 'white' then those of 'Asian' or any other 'stock' can never become 'British'.

The second point follows on from this. Although some anthropologists tend to see race only as a mistaken scientific prejudice of the nineteenth century and dismiss any discussion of it, they fail to appreciate the significance of it in popular discourse. It is significant by its conspicuous absence, denial or 'sanitised' presence (Reeves 1983) in dominant white discourse (as well, of course, by its unashamed presence in the rhetoric of certain anti-immigration and far-right groups), and it is therefore significant in structuring white or, more generally, dominant perceptions of minority groups. As one of the lessons of Chapters 3 and 4 was that minority group ethnicity or identity is constructed in relation to the dominant group and to the state, there is also a sociologically relevant discourse of race among minority groups. For this reason, the salience of race as a social category is as important in the understanding of ethnicity manifested by apparently 'white' groups (such as Greek and Turkish Cypriots, or Poles and Ukrainians, in Britain) as in the ethnicity of apparently black or brown groups.

Several commentators on the Dewsbury case accused the parents of the twenty-six of 'racism', but it should be clear by now that the term must be as unclear and unambiguous as 'race' itself. Let me give an example. The mother of a friend of mine has a habit of identifying individuals as Jewish on the basis of their physiognomy. For example, while watching television she will turn to her daughter and say, 'He's Jewish, you know', of a news reader or announcer. When challenged as to why she made the remark, she will say, 'But it's a fact! [that is, she has deduced it as a fact to her own satisfaction]. What's wrong with stating it?' (Drake and Cayton, the authors of *Black metropolis* discussed in Chapter 3, note that many people, especially United States white southerners, believed they could always tell a black who was 'passing' for white [1945: 165].) On further questioning, my friend's mother strongly denies any imputation of racism – indeed, she is offended by the suggestion. We can go some way towards understanding her behaviour when we know that she grew up in wartime continental Europe, a period and place when knowing who was and who was not Jewish were of strong significance. This does not, however, help us to explain why she should announce the result of her deductions in the 1990s.

My friend says she remembers her mother making similar remarks – without attaching any value-significance to them – throughout her childhood, and it is possible that the mother is unconsciously still striving to socialize her children with 'skills' that are no longer relevant, in a context where such 'skills' are irrevocably tarnished. One could, of course, say that while the individual is not necessarily racist in this case (or not consciously and intentionally so), she reflects the institutional racism of her culture (white middle class European). Or, one could argue that she is performing the kind of cognitive mapping operation that Clyde Mitchell's Copperbelt workers performed (Mitchell 1974) and that an effectively neutral cognitive action becomes 'racist' by context. That is, certain attitudes and actions are not inherently racist, rather that 'racist' and 'racism' have become a container for a particular culture at a particular time for the pigeonholing of these attitudes and actions.

More generally stated, we have a problem that feminists and others have encountered: are key terms such as 'feminist', 'racist', 'sexist' universally applicable at all times and in all places, or are they ideological constructs of our own time and place, that only have meaning in that context? For example, can one call women writers of earlier periods who seemed to espouse the 'cause' of women in some general or specific sense 'feminists', or is the label applicable only to western women born in this century (and possibly only white women at that)? Similarly, can one label (or, in the jargon, 'claim') figures such as Sappho or Alexander the Great as being 'gay', because they appear to have entertained homosexual preferences, or is being 'gay' only possible today, when the term denotes a taste in music, clothing, and patronizing certain bars and clubs as much as it denotes a form of sexual activity? In these or similar cases anthropologists have generally argued that the labels are not cross-culturally applicable (which would mean cross-temporally, as well).

Throughout this book, but particularly in Chapters 3 and 4, I have been trying to keep the two terms 'ethnicity' and 'race' distinct for analytical purposes. Unfortunately, popular or non-academic English recognizes only one '-ism': 'racism' (as far as I am concerned the term 'racialism' is an outdated equivalent). Even academic English can only come up with a circumlocution to give an '-ism' to ethnicity: 'ethnic chauvinism'. This is unfortunate only insofar as I am unable to construct neatly analogous parallel discussions on racism and 'ethnicity-ism'. The inability to do so lies not with language, but with the concepts themselves. Popular British and American English usage holds that 'race' has some kind of real existence and the concept is understood through folk notions of biology. If 'ethnicity' (as opposed to the adjectival use of 'ethnic') has any popular currency at all, it is understood either as an epiphenomenal characteristic of persons roughly equivalent to popular uses of the word 'culture', or – more commonly I think – as a euphemism for 'race' or 'racial characteristic'. It is in this sense that we tend to hear 'ethnic' being used as a noun rather than an adjective, usually disparagingly ('Those ethnics, coming over here and . . . '). 'Racism' thus is used to describe perceived prejudice by whites of one ethnicity against whites of another ethnicity (so that the telling of 'Irish' jokes in England, or 'Polack' jokes in the US, can be deemed 'racist' and the term carries far more force than the awkward 'ethnic chauvinist' would).

These comments most certainly do not satisfactorily cover what racism actually is, how it is perceived and manifested, but there are plenty of works that cover these issues thoughtfully and in great detail (see, for example, Braham *et al.* [1992], Miles [1989, 1993], Wetherell and Potter [1992]). Instead, taken together with the two main cases described above, they should go some way towards mapping out the new life that 'ethnicity' and its derivatives are living beyond the confines of the academy.

Chapter 7

Conclusions

So, what conclusions can possibly be drawn from all this? The overly trusting reader may be hoping that I am going to perform some conjuring trick, to pull out some hypertextual highlighter pen and go back through the previous chapters drawing together points before declaring, 'Hey presto! look, that's what ethnicity is!'. The next sentence should therefore be some kind of definition – 'In conclusion, we can say that ethnicity is . . .' – that can be cited in undergraduate essays and other texts.

It should be apparent to the more observant reader that I am unlikely to do anything of the sort. The very diversity of texts I have discussed should have demonstrated the point that, regardless of whether ethnicity 'really' exists out there in the world or not, it has had a rather insubstantial and chimerical life within academic discourse in its own right. From the heyday of the 1960s and 1970s it has looked increasingly tired and threadbare, despite Ronald Cohen's confident assertion with which I opened the book (R. Cohen 1978: 379). 'Ethnicity' has only really flourished when allied to some stronger (though not necessarily any more 'real') partner, such as 'race' or 'nationalism' (or, more rarely, rather obscure and unlikely partners such as Wittgensteinian 'language games'). Indeed, in many cases, it seems to have been something of an absent partner, contributing little or nothing to the alliance. Whether 'race' (for example) is an analytically useful tool or not, it seems to have managed quite well without ethnicity in many cases, as Chapters 3 and 4 demonstrated. And Daniel Bell warns, after discussing the resurgence and salience of ethnicity in the US in the 1960s and 1970s, that ethnicity is not necessarily 'the central concept to analyse social change in the world today. The forces of nation and class are latent and other circumstances could readily bring them to the fore' (1975: 172–3).

But while ethnicity has an ever more insubstantial place within the narrow world of academia I hope the previous chapter showed that it appears to be increasingly important in the wider world. Since the end of the Second World War, and especially since the end of the so-called Cold War, small-scale conflict within once apparently stable nation states (or confederations such as the former Soviet Union) seems to be on the increase. In some cases the conflict has been expressed through language and the courts alone, in others it has been marked by bloodshed and the deaths of tens of thousands of people. In most cases it seems that ethnicity is somehow to blame. As the discussions of Chapter 6 showed, however, the 'ethnicity' that lives in public (or at least journalistic) discourse is no less chimerical than its academic sibling.

So, if I have no 'hey presto!' revelations up my sleeve, no advice on what ethnicity 'really' is, or on which is 'the best' theory of ethnicity, what can I offer? Perhaps in keeping with what I have said above I first of all offer a number of thoughts, not so much on ethnicity itself, but on reading, writing and thinking about it. I finally conclude with a brief and cautious statement about future research directions.

WAYS OF THINKING

I said in the introduction to this book that there were a number of possible ways in which the material I have been considering could have been presented. I outlined two possible approaches that I could have used: I could have divided the material up by ethnographic area or by topic, or I could have divided the material along already existing theoretical lines. I chose instead to organize it by grouping together clusters or 'schools' of authors. As I pointed out, this approach to some extent subsumes the other two, as groups of authors tend to work in similar ethnographic regions and to exchange ideas among themselves. All these approaches have something to recommend them and at the same time involve classificatory draw-backs. The approach I chose, however, served to insert two related sub-texts or sub-themes into my discussion and I should make these a little more explicit.

The first is relatively obvious and straightforward. In Chapter 2 several of the authors I was concerned with had conducted fieldwork abroad with groups of people who considered themselves to be 'at home'. The anthropologists of the Manchester School were a slight exception to this pattern as they concerned themselves (at least in the works I discussed) with rural to urban migrants. But the anthropologists were still working in what were for them, and for the majority of their readers, exotic and distant locations. In Chapters 3 and 4 the direction of travel was reversed. Here I discussed the work of sociologists and anthropologists who had stayed 'at home' and studied the migrant populations who had come to Britain and the United States. A dominant theme of this literature was how well, if at all, the migrants were fitting in with the normative values of the 'host' society. This apparently trivial difference – who had travelled to whose country – gave rise to a really rather sharp cleavage in the literature. A further cleavage became apparent in Chapter 5 when both the academics and the people they studied could be considered to be 'at home'.

It was not, of course, always possible to keep to a neat 'at home'/ 'abroad' dichotomy in these four chapters, but I think the distinction is none the less an important one. The ethnicity of minority migrant communities, for example, has been treated very differently in the literature from the ethnicity of groups which in the earlier anthropological literature would have been described as 'tribes'. The distinction also highlights differences in disciplinary perspective. Sociologists and political scientists have in the past tended to stay at home and study social phenomena on their own doorsteps, anthropologists by contrast have tended to study ways of life that are radically different from their own. Today the boundaries are more blurred in terms of fieldwork but by and large disciplinary assumptions still persist.

One problem with my use of the terms 'at home' and 'abroad' is that they could be taken to endorse certain nationalistic sentiments, embodied in Norman Tebbitt's infamous 'cricket test' remarks. (Norman Tebbitt was a Conservative MP who viewed the support of British Asians for visiting cricket teams from India and Pakistan as an expression of disloyalty to the British state – see P. Werbner [forthcoming] for further details.) In the context of this book the issue was summed up by a colleague, who is familiar with much of this literature, who told me that the difference between North American writing on minority groups in the US and British writing on similar groups in Britain lies in the fact that the North American writers consider those they are writing about to be American, while the British writers persist in seeing their subjects as foreign or alien.

I can see some truth in this opinion, though there are many

exceptions and the different historical processes need to be taken into account. But while it is true that many American 'ethnic groups' that have been written about extensively (basically, white groups of European origin and black groups of African origin) are technically groups of migrant origin, many of these groups have an historical depth of residence in the United States stretching back centuries, and to say that the US was not 'home' would no doubt be deeply offensive to many. The labels 'home' and 'abroad' are in no way meant to legitimate or deny the permanence or right of any group to reside within the boundaries of any nation state. Rather, they reflect the approach that earlier ethnographers took (and that some today still take) towards their objects of study. With regard to the United States, the earliest debates on ethnicity took place within the context of debates on assimilation and against a background of continued in-migration. Later work on ethnicity in the US rests on this foundation (of necessity, to some degree) and to discuss US approaches to ethnicity demanded that the literature be treated as a single corpus.

The second sub-text or sub-theme is more abstract and concerns the location of ethnicity. The primordialist approach to ethnicity tends, as I noted on several occasions, to see it as a permanant and fundamental aspect of human identity, expressed either alone and for its own sake, or in relations with differently ethnic others. By contrast, the instrumentalist approach tends to regard it either as a position or outlook that is adopted to achieve some specific end or to see it as the outcome of a set of particular historical and socioeconomic circumstances. That is, ethnicity is adopted by 'choice' by those such as the Hausa traders discussed in Chapter 2, or is thrust upon people, such as the migrants discussed in Chapters 3 and 4, by circumstance. In both cases, the location of ethnicity resides with the ethnographic subject, the person or persons studied by the anthropologist or sociologist. Primordial ethnicity could therefore be considered to be of or in their hearts, while instrumental ethnicity could be considered to be in their heads.

The first, primordialist, approach is relatively uncommon. It is usually a view of ethnicity that authors cite only in order to distance themselves from it. When it is claimed by an author it is often with the understanding that because the people studied assume their ethnicity (or what the author terms their ethnicity) to be a fundamental and permanent part of their identity, she or he has chosen to follow them in this (just as most anthropologists accept the belief of people in witchcraft). The only authors who consistently seem to think that ethnicity really does exist and really is a fundamental aspect of the human condition are the Soviet ethnos theorists who I discussed in Chapter 2. The second, instrumentalist, approach is by far the more common. As with the supposedly outdated anthropological theory of structural-functionalism, it is difficult not to see *some* kind of gain or advantage that is linked to the expression of ethnicity.

But there is a third perspective on the location of ethnicity, one which in some ways subsumes the other two. This locates ethnicity in the observer's head; it is an analytical tool devised and utilized by academics to make sense of or explain the actions and feelings of the people studied. There are a number of advantages to this perspective. First, it shifts the 'responsibility' for ethnicity from the ethnographic subjects on to the analyst. This is not to say that the ethnographic subjects are not responsible for their 'ethnic' actions: they are fully responsible for their actions but it is for the analyst to decide whether – if at all – ethnicity is a useful tool to make sense of those actions. I hope that one of the lessons of Chapter 6 was that to project one's own understandings of race, ethnicity and nationalism on to others under the impression that one is deriving those understandings from them is to make a profound mistake that leads to confusion at best, and to violence and bloodshed at worst.

Another advantage of this perspective is that I believe it to be the most intellectually honest and accurate. In recent decades anthropologists have become accustomed to the idea that key concepts such as 'kinship' may not be out there in the world of social relations at all, but are an invention of the academy (Needham 1971). To view them in this way need not invalidate the concepts, or reduce their utility, but it does necessitate a repositioning of the analyst with regard to her or his subjects. Finally, while viewing ethnicity in this way is not especially novel (Eriksen, for example, briefly flirts with the idea [1993: 16], though he does not go on to develop it), it does help us in reading much if not all of the older literature. Ethnicity was very much located in Warner and Srole's heads when they wrote *The social systems of American ethnic groups* (1945), for example, and not in the heads or hearts of the citizens of Newburyport.

Figure 1 gives a diagrammatic overview of these three locations of ethnicity. The reader will perhaps see that there is a rough analogy between these three locations and the three possible ways of organizing this book's structure that I discussed at the start of this section. Organizing the literature on ethnicity by ethnographic theme

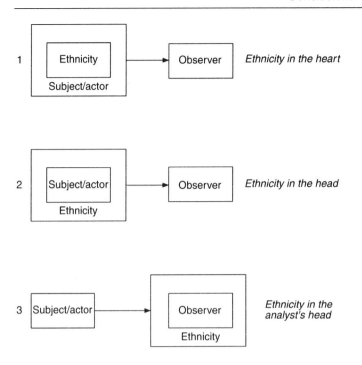

Figure 1 Locations of ethnicity

or region ties in well with the assumptions of primordialist ethnicity, which often include a component of territorial rootedness. Organizing the literature by clusters of theory or ideas similarly ties in with bringing together all the situations in which 'different' kinds of ethnicity are expressed for different kinds of reason. But organizing the literature by related groups of authors (who often, of course, work in the same kinds of ethnographic area and often subscribe to common or related theoretical positions) locates ethnicity very firmly in the heads of the analysts.

WRAPPING IT UP

Writing this book has been a largely descriptive exercise, but it has also been deconstructive, inasmuch as I have tried to break down a number of writings on ethnicity to see if the idea itself can stand up to intellectual scrutiny. To that extent I am aware that the argument has been somewhat circular at times as on occasion I have used one author's approach to highlight weaknesses in another's approach, and then later undermined the first author's approach. To that extent also it has been a project influenced by the deconstructionist or post-modernist turn in the social sciences and humanities over the past decade or so. Although writing the book took a fair amount of effort, it is an easy enough trick to pull off. The difficult part is to try to put it all together again.

It is not so much a question of whether this is possible, but whether it is worth it. If one were to reconstruct – or rethink or reconstitute – a theory of ethnicity, would it serve any uniquely useful purpose? Or is the work that a shiny new theory of ethnicity could accomplish already adequately managed by other areas of theory in the social sciences? Malcolm Chapman and Maryon McDonald both argue (following Edwin Ardener) that, in Chapman's words, '"ethnicity" should be subsumed under the general study of the classification of people (by themselves and others), and that this "classification of people" should be subsumed under the study of classification in general – an area which is the characteristic speciality of modern social anthropology' (Chapman 1993b: 21–2; see also Chapman *et al.* 1989: 17, and McDonald 1989: 310).

It's a fair enough demand, but a trifle abstract. Human beings classify everything, all the time. It leaves unanswered why and how we should mark some kinds of classification off (itself a classificatory process) as processes of ethnicity. The contributors to Chapman *et al.* (1989) invoke history and, to a lesser extent, nationalism as the relevant variables. Others, such as Blu (1980), Keyes (1976) and B. Williams (1989) invoke notions of 'blood' and race. Still others, such as Rex (1970) and Banton (1983), invoke political considerations of power and inequality. The list is potentially as long as the number of authors who have written about ethnicity, all of whom could be said to be dealing with 'classification' implicitly or explicitly.

As a result, a number of authors have either called for or predicted the demise of ethnicity as an analytical term. Roger Just regrets that it ever entered the analytical vocabulary at all (1989: 76), Edwin Ardener indicated that it had had its day (1989c: 211), and Thomas Eriksen provocatively entitles two subsections of the concluding chapter of his theoretical work, 'Beyond ethnicity?' and 'The end of ethnicity?' (Eriksen 1993: 156–60). Citing Ulf Hannertz and John and Jean Comaroff he points out that there are other axes along which people differentiate themselves, axes which may be missed if one focuses single-mindedly on ethnicity (Eriksen 1993: 157). I would most certainly concur with this. As a small experiment I would ask the reader to look at random passages from this book, or any other theoretical work on ethnicity, and mentally substitute the names of other, non-ethnically defined, minority or subordinate groups every time (ethnic) 'group' is mentioned. Try 'children' or 'women' or 'gays and lesbians' or 'the elderly'. While some passages will appear to make sociological sense, others will not, and there will be lacunae – places where a discussion relevant to the particular group in mind is apparently not relevant to 'ethnic groups' and the issue is not raised.

Unfortunately, as I hope I demonstrated in Chapter 6, it is too late to kill it off or pronounce ethnicity dead; the discourse on ethnicity has escaped from the academy and into the field. Tracing the contours of this new life will be necessary for understanding the biography of this idea for as long as anthropologists and other academics continue to use it. Whether or not there was, in some innocent past age, a real social phenomenon fluttering around that could have been trapped in the butterfly net of fieldwork methodology, brought back to the academy and pinned on to cork boards by words like 'ethnicity', there is certainly a designer organism out there now, bred in the laboratory and released into the world to be fed by politicians, journalists and ordinary citizens through their words and actions. As Edward Said said of the academic construct of Orientalism, 'there is some reason for alarm in the fact that [Orientalism's] influence has spread to "the Orient" itself: the pages of books and journals in Arabic (and doubtless in Japanese, various Indian dialects, and other Oriental languages) are filled with second-order analyses by Arabs of "the Arab mind", "Islam", and other myths' (Said 1985: 322).

For what it's worth, my opinion is that the continued study of ethnicity is probably worth it, but only if the approach taken recognizes that to study it is to bring it continually into being. Like the natives in the old anthropological coffee-room story who, when asked about their customs and traditions by the newly disembarked anthropologist, say 'Hang on, we'll just go check what the previous anthropologist wrote about us', the manifestations of ethnicity we study today contain within them the ghosts of previous academic formulations. In the modern world ethnicity is indissolubly linked to nationalism and race, to ideas about normative political systems and relations, and to ideas about descent and blood.

The fragmentation and reformulation of macro political structures since the end of the Cold War, and the rise of the 'new genetics' (which will alter ideas about human reproduction if not everyone's practices), mean that new folk systems of knowledge are being thrown up every day. These systems, while local in colour and character, are neither particularistic nor bounded. They are linked in nested hierarchies, feed off each other, and make competing claims to authoritativeness and universalism. Ethnicity lives self-consciously within these systems. Because of a constant conflation between description and explanation in folk theory, a conflation analogous to and perhaps derived from mumbo-jumbo academic jargon, ethnicity is constantly produced as explanation: the reason why the As are slaughtering the Bs, the reason why the Cs are 'clannish', or 'dirty', or 'unreliable'.

There is a constantly changing terrain of human relations to be mapped out by anthropologists and others. Recognized for what it is – a collection of rather simplistic and obvious statements about boundaries, otherness, goals and achievements, being and identity, descent and classification, that has been constructed as much by the anthropologist as by the subject – there is no particular reason why ethnicity should not be the name given to at least part of this mapping enterprise.

Bibliography

Akiner, Shirin (1983) *Islamic peoples of the Soviet Union*, London: Kegan Paul International.

Alba, Richard D. (ed.) (1985a) *Ethnicity and race in the U.S.A.: toward the twenty-first century*, London: Routledge and Kegan Paul.

Alba, Richard D. (1985b) 'The twilight of ethnicity among Americans of European ancestry: the case of Italians', in Richard D. Alba (ed.) *Ethnicity and race in the U.S.A.: toward the twenty-first century*, London: Routledge and Kegan Paul.

Alexander, Claire (1992) *The art of 'being black': the creation of black British youth identities*, Unpublished doctoral thesis, Oxford University.

Anderson, Benedict (1983) *Imagined communities: reflections on the origins and spread of nationalism*, London: Verso.

Anwar, Muhammad (1976) *Between two cultures: a study of relationships between generations in the Asian community in Britain*, London: Community Relations Council.

Ardener, Edwin (1989a [1972]) 'Language, ethnicity and population', in Edwin Ardener (ed.) *The voice of prophecy and other essays*, Oxford: Basil Blackwell.

Ardener, Edwin (1989b [1974]) 'Social anthropology and population', in Edwin Ardener (ed.) *The voice of prophecy and other essays*, Oxford: Basil Blackwell.

Ardener, Edwin (1989c [1987]) '"Remote areas" – some theoretical considerations', in Edwin Ardener (ed.) *The voice of prophecy and other essays*, Oxford: Basil Blackwell.

Ardener, Edwin (1989d) 'The construction of history: "vestiges of creation"', in Elizabeth Tonkin, Maryon McDonald and Malcolm Chapman (eds) *History and ethnicity*, London: Routledge.

Arutjunjan, Yulian (1974) 'Experience of a socio-ethnic survey (relating to Tatar ASSR)', in Yulian Bromley (ed.) *Soviet ethnology and anthropology today*, The Hague: Mouton.

Asad, Talal (1972) 'Market model, class structure and consent. A reconsideration of Swat political organisation', *Man* 7: 74–94.

Asad, Talal (ed.) (1973) *Anthropology and the colonial encounter*, London: Ithaca Press.

Aurora, Gurdip Singh (1967) *New frontiersmen: a sociological study of Indian immigrants in the U.K.*, Bombay: Popular Prakashan.

Ballard, Roger (1994) 'What should we mean by ethnicity?', Unpublished paper presented at OPCS/ESRC Conference on The Ethnic Census volumes, Leeds, 5–6 Septemper 1994.

Ballard, Roger and Christine Ballard (1977) 'The Sikhs: the development of South Asian settlements in Britain', in James Watson (ed.) *Between two cultures*, Oxford: Basil Blackwell.

Ballard, Roger and Virinder Singh Kalra (1994) *The ethnic dimensions of the 1991 Census: a preliminary report*, Manchester: University of Manchester Census Dissemination Unit.

Banton, Michael (1955) *The coloured quarter: Negro immigrants in an English city*, London: Jonathan Cape.

Banton, Michael (1957) *West African city: a study of tribal life in Freetown*, London: Oxford University Press for the International African Institute.

Banton, Michael (1959) *White and coloured: the behaviour of British people towards coloured immigrants*, London: Jonathan Cape.

Banton, Michael (1977) *The idea of race*, London: Tavistock Publications.

Banton, Michael (1979) 'Analytical and folk concepts of race and ethnicity', *Ethnic and racial studies* 2.2: 127–38.

Banton, Michael (1983) *Racial and ethnic competition*, Cambridge: Cambridge University Press.

Banton, Michael (1987) *Racial theories*, Cambridge: Cambridge University Press.

Barnes, R. H. (1991) Review of: Bruce Kapferer, *Legends of people, myths of state: violence, intolerance, and political culture in Sri Lanka and Australia* (Smithsonian Institution Press 1988), *JASO* 22.1: 91–3.

Barot, Rohit (1973) 'A Swaminarayan sect as a community', *New community* 2: 34–7.

Barth, Frederik (1959) *Political leadership among the Swat Pathans*, London: Athlone.

Barth, Frederik (ed.) (1969a) *Ethnic groups and boundaries: the social organisation of culture difference*, Bergen/London: Universitets Forlaget/ George Allen and Unwin.

Barth, Frederik (1969b) 'Introduction', in Frederik Barth (ed.) *Ethnic groups and boundaries: the social organisation of culture difference*, Bergen/ London: Universitets Forlaget/George Allen and Unwin.

Barth, Frederik (1969c) 'Pathan identity and its maintenance', in Frederik Barth (ed.) *Ethnic groups and boundaries: the social organisation of culture difference*, Bergen/London: Universitets Forlaget/George Allen and Unwin.

Baxter, Sue and Geoff Raw (1988) 'Fast food, fettered work: Chinese women in the ethnic catering industry', in Sallie Westwood and Parminder Bhachu (eds) *Enterprising women: ethnicity, economy, and gender relations*, London: Routledge.

Bell, Daniel (1975) 'Ethnicity and social change', in Nathan Glazer and Daniel Moynihan (eds) *Ethnicity: theory and experience*, Cambridge, Mass.: Harvard University Press.

Benson, Susan (1981) *Ambiguous ethnicity: interracial families in London*, Cambridge: Cambridge University Press.

Benson, Susan (in press) 'Asians have culture, West Indians have problems: discourses of race and ethnicity in and out of anthropology', in Ossie Stuart, Yunis Samad and Terence Ranger (eds) *The politicization of ethnicity*, Aldershot: Avebury.

Bentley, G. Carter (1987) 'Ethnicity and practice', *Comparative studies in society and history* 29.1: 24–55.

Bhachu, Parminder (1985) *Twice migrants: East African Sikh settlers in Britain*, London: Tavistock.

Bhachu, Parminder (1988) *'Apni marzi kardhi.* Home and work: Sikh women in Britain', in Sallie Westwood and Parminder Bhachu (eds) *Enterprising women: ethnicity, economy, and gender relations*, London: Routledge.

Blu, Karen L. (1980) *The Lumbee problem: the making of an American Indian people*, Cambridge: Cambridge University Press.

Boissevain, Jeremy (1984) 'Small entrepreneurs in contemporary Europe', in Robin Ward and Richard Jenkins (eds) *Ethnic communities in business: strategies for economic survival*, Cambridge: Cambridge University Press.

Bott, Elizabeth (1971 [1957]) *Family and social network: roles, norms and external relationships in ordinary urban families* [Second Edition], London: Tavistock.

Bouquet, Mary (1986) '"You cannot be a Brahmin in the English countryside." The partitioning of status, and its representation within the farm family in Devon', in Anthony P. Cohen (ed.) *Symbolising boundaries: identity and diversity in British cultures*, Manchester: Manchester University Press.

Bourdieu, Pierre (1977 [1972]) *Outline of a theory of practice*, Cambridge: Cambridge University Press.

Bourdieu, Pierre (1984 [1979]) *Distinction: a social critique of the judgement of taste*, London: Routledge and Kegan Paul.

Bradley, Tony and Philip Lowe (1984) 'Introduction: locality, rurality and social theory', in Tony Bradley and Philip Lowe (eds) *Locality and rurality: economy and society in rural regions*, Norwich: Geo Books.

Braham, Peter, Ali Rattansi and Richard Skellington (eds) (1992) *Racism and antiracism: inequalities, opportunities and policies*, London: Sage, in association with The Open University.

Brass, Paul R. (1974) *Language, religion and politics in north India*, London and New York: Cambridge University Press.

Breuilly, John (1993 [1982]) *Nationalism and the state*, Manchester: Manchester University Press.

Bromley, Yulian (1974) 'The term *ethnos* and its definition', in Yulian Bromley (ed.) *Soviet ethnology and anthropology today*, The Hague: Mouton.

Bromley, Yulian (ed.) (1975) *Contemporary ethnic processes in the USSR* [in Russian], Moscow: USSR Academy of Science.

Bromley, Yulian (1980) 'The object and the subject-matter of ethnography', in Ernest Gellner (ed.) *Soviet and Western anthropology*, London: Duckworth.

Bromley, Yulian and Viktor Kozlov (1989) 'The theory of ethnos and ethnic processes in Soviet social science', *Comparative studies in society and history* 31.3: 425–38.

Brown, R. (1973) 'Anthropology and colonial rule: Godfrey Wilson and the Rhodes-Livingstone Institute, Northern Rhodesia', in Talal Asad (ed.) *Anthropology and the colonial encounter*, London: Ithaca.

Caplan, Pat (1994) Review of: *Bloody Bosnia: a European tragedy* (Channel Four Television and the *Guardian* publication), *Anthropology in action* 1.1: 38–9.

Cashmore, Ernest (1979) *Rastaman*, London: Allen and Unwin.

Cashmore, E. Ellis and Barry Troyna (1983) *Introduction to race relations*, London: Routledge and Kegan Paul.

Castles, Stephen and Godula Kosack (1973) *Immigrant workers and class structure in western Europe*, London: Oxford University Press for the Institute of Race Relations.

Chapman, Malcolm (1978) *The Gaelic vision in Scottish culture*, London: Croom Helm.

Chapman, Malcolm (1992) *The Celts: the construction of a myth*, Basingstoke/New York: Macmillan Press/St Martin's Press.

Chapman, Malcolm (ed.) (1993a) *Social and biological aspects of ethnicity*, Oxford: Oxford University Press for the Biosocial Society.

Chapman, Malcolm (1993b) 'Social and biological aspects of ethnicity', in Malcolm Chapman (ed.) *Social and biological aspects of ethnicity*, Oxford: Oxford University Press for the Biosocial Society.

Chapman, Malcolm, Maryon McDonald and Elizabeth Tonkin (1989) 'Introduction', in Elizabeth Tonkin, Maryon McDonald and Malcolm Chapman (eds) *History and ethnicity*, London: Routledge.

Charsley, Simon (1986) '"Glasgow's miles better": the symbolism of community and identity in the city', in Anthony P. Cohen (ed.) *Symbolising boundaries: identity and diversity in British cultures*, Manchester: Manchester University Press.

Charsley, Simon (1987) 'Interpretation and custom: the case of the wedding cake', *Man* 22.1: 93–110.

Charsley, Simon (1992) *Wedding cakes and cultural history*, London: Routledge.

Clarke, Colin, David Ley and Ceri Peach (eds) (1984) *Geography and ethnic pluralism*, London: George Allen and Unwin.

Cohen, Abner (1969) *Custom and politics in urban Africa: a study of Hausa migrants in Yoruba towns*, London: Routledge and Kegan Paul.

Cohen, Abner (ed.) (1974a) *Urban ethnicity*, London: Tavistock Publications.

Cohen, Abner (1974b) 'Introduction. The lesson of ethnicity', in Abner Cohen (ed.) *Urban ethnicity*, London: Tavistock Publications.

Cohen, Anthony P. (ed.) (1982a) *Belonging: identity and social organization in British rural cultures*, Manchester: Manchester University Press.

Cohen, Anthony P. (1982b) 'Belonging: the experience of culture', in Anthony P. Cohen (ed.) *Belonging: identity and social organization in British rural cultures*, Manchester: Manchester University Press.

Cohen, Anthony P. (1982c) 'Blockade: a case study of local consciousness in an extra-local event', in Anthony P. Cohen (ed.) *Belonging: identity and social organization in British rural cultures*, Manchester: Manchester University Press.

Cohen, Anthony P. (1985) *The symbolic construction of community*, London: Tavistock.

Cohen, Anthony P. (ed.) (1986a) *Symbolising boundaries: identity and diversity in British cultures*, Manchester: Manchester University Press.

Cohen, Anthony P. (1986b) 'Of symbols and boundaries, or, does Ertie's greatcoat hold the key?', in Anthony P. Cohen (ed.) *Symbolising boundaries: identity and diversity in British cultures*, Manchester: Manchester University Press.

Cohen, Anthony P. (1987) *Whalsay. Symbol, segment and boundary in a Shetland island community*, Manchester: Manchester University Press.

Cohen, Ronald (1978) 'Ethnicity: problem and focus in anthropology', in Bernard Siegal, Alan Beals and Stephen Tyler (eds) *Annual review of anthropology 7*, Palo Alto: Annual Reviews Inc.

Collins, S. F. (1957) *Coloured minorities in Britain*, London: Lutterworth Press.

Cox, Oliver Cromwell (1948) *Caste, class and race: a study in social dynamics*, New York: Monthly Review Press.

Davis, Allison, Burleigh Gardner and Mary Gardner (1941) *Deep South: a social anthropological study of caste and class*, Chicago: University of Chicago Press.

de Waal, Alex (1994a) Editorial: 'Genocide in Rwanda', *Anthropology today* 10.3: 1–2.

de Waal, Alex (1994b) 'The genocidal state: Hutu extremism and the origins of the "final solution" in Rwanda', *Times literary supplement* 1 July 4761: 3–4.

de Waal, Alex (1994c) Letter: 'Genocide in Rwanda', *Anthropology today* 10.4: 28–9.

Degler, Carl (1986 [1971]) *Neither black nor white: slavery and race relations in Brazil and the United States*, Wisconsin: University of Wisconsin Press.

Dench, Geoff (1975) *Maltese in London: a case-study in the erosion of ethnic consciousness*, London: Routledge and Kegan Paul.

Desai, Rashmi (1963) *Indian immigrants in Britain*, London: Oxford University Press for the Institute of Race Relations.

Douglas, Mary (1966) *Purity and danger*, London: Routledge and Kegan Paul.

Douglas, Mary (1970) *Natural symbols: explorations in cosmology*, London: Barrie and Rockliffe.

Dragadze, Tamara (1975) 'Comment on Gellner, "The Soviet and the savage"', *Current anthropology* 16.4: 604.

Dragadze, Tamara (1980) 'The place of "ethnos" theory in Soviet anthropology', in Ernest Gellner (ed.) *Soviet and Western anthropology*, London: Duckworth.

Drake, St Clair (1956) 'The "colour problem" in Britain: a study in social definitions', *Sociological review (NS)* 3: 197–217.

Drake, St Clair and Horace R. Cayton (1945) *Black Metropolis: a study of Negro life in a northern city*, New York: Harcourt, Brace and Company.

Dumont, Louis (1980 [1966]) *Homo Hierarchicus: the caste system and its implications* [Complete revised English edition], Chicago: University of Chicago Press.

Edwards, John (1985) *Language, society and identity*, Oxford: Basil Blackwell.

Eidheim, Harald (1969) 'When ethnic identity is a social stigma', in Frederik Barth (ed.) *Ethnic groups and boundaries: the social organisation of culture difference*, Bergen/London: Universitets Forlaget/George Allen and Unwin.

Epstein, A. L. (1958) *Politics in an urban African community*, Manchester: Manchester University Press.

Epstein, A. L. (1978) *Ethos and identity: three studies in ethnicity*, London: Tavistock.

Eriksen, Thomas Hylland (1991) 'The cultural contexts of ethnic differences', *Man* 26.1: 127–44.

Eriksen, Thomas Hylland (1992) *Us and them in modern societies: ethnicity and nationalism in Mauritius, Trinidad and beyond*, London: Scandinavian University Press.

Eriksen, Thomas Hylland (1993) *Ethnicity and nationalism: anthropological perspectives*, London: Pluto Press.

Evans, Arthur J. (1877) *Through Bosnia and Herzegovina on foot, during the insurrection, August and September 1875, and a glimpse at the Croats, Slavonians, and the ancient republic of Ragusa*, London: Longmans, Green, and Co.

Foner, Nancy (1979) *Jamaica farewell*, London: Routledge and Kegan Paul.

Forsythe, Diana (1989) 'German identity and the problems of history', in Elizabeth Tonkin, Maryon McDonald and Malcolm Chapman (eds) *History and ethnicity*, London: Routledge.

Furnival, J. S. (1939) *Netherlands India: a study of plural economy*, Cambridge: Cambridge University Press.

Garbett, G. Kingsley (1980) 'Graph theory and the analysis of multiplex and manifold relationships', in J. Clyde Mitchell (ed.) *Numerical techniques in social anthropology*, Philadelphia: Institute for the Study of Human Issues.

Geertz, Clifford (1975) 'Thick description: toward an interpretive theory of culture', in Clifford Geertz (ed.) *The interpretation of cultures*, London: Hutchinson.

Gellner, Ernest (1964) *Thought and change*, London: Weidenfeld and Nicolson.

Gellner, Ernest (1975) 'The Soviet and the savage', *Current anthropology* 16.4: 595–601.

Gellner, Ernest (1982) 'Nationalism and the two forms of cohesion in complex society', Radcliffe-Brown Lecture in Social Anthropology, *Proceedings of the British Academy* 68: 165–87.

Gellner, Ernest (1983) *Nations and nationalism*, Oxford: Basil Blackwell.

Gellner, Ernest (1988 [1977]) 'Modern ethnicity', in Ernest Gellner (ed.) *State and society in Soviet thought*, Oxford: Basil Blackwell.

Glazer, Nathan and Daniel P. Moynihan (1970 [1963]) *Beyond the melting pot: the Negroes, Puerto Ricans, Jews, Italians and Irish of New York City*, Cambridge, Mass.: The MIT Press.

Glazer, Nathan and Daniel P. Moynihan (eds) (1975a) *Ethnicity: theory and experience*, Cambridge, Mass.: Harvard University Press.

Glazer, Nathan and Daniel P. Moynihan (1975b) 'Introduction', in Nathan Glazer and Daniel P. Moynihan (eds) *Ethnicity: theory and experience*, Cambridge, Mass.: Harvard University Press.

Glenny, Misha (1992) *The fall of Yugoslavia: the third Balkan war*, London: Penguin.

Gluckman, Max (1958) *Analysis of a social situation in modern Zululand*, Manchester: Manchester University Press for the Rhodes-Livingstone Institute.

Gluckman, Max (n. d.) *History of the Manchester 'School' of social anthropology and sociology*, Unpublished ms.: Manchester University.

Gordon, Milton M. (1964) *Assimilation in American life*, New York: Oxford University Press.

Gordon, Milton M. (1975) 'Toward a general theory of racial and ethnic group relations', in Nathan Glazer and Daniel P. Moynihan (eds) *Ethnicity: theory and experience*, Cambridge, Mass.: Harvard University Press.

Greeley, Andrew and William McCready (1975) 'The transmission of cultural heritages: the case of the Irish and the Italians', in Nathan Glazer and Daniel P. Moynihan (eds) *Ethnicity: theory and experience*, Cambridge, Mass.: Harvard University Press.

Gregory, Chris (1982) *Gifts and commodities*, London: Academic Press.

Haaland, Gunnar (1969) 'Economic determinants in ethnic processes', in Frederik Barth (ed.) *Ethnic groups and boundaries: the social organisation of culture difference*, Bergen/London: Universitets Forlaget/ George Allen and Unwin.

Hall, Stuart *et al.* (1978) *Policing the crisis: mugging, the state, and law and order*, London: Macmillan.

Hannerz, Ulf (1969) *Soulside: inquiries into Ghetto culture and community*, New York: Columbia University Press.

Hechter, Michael (1986) 'Rational choice theory and the study of race and ethnic relations', in John Rex and David Mason (eds) *Theories of race and ethnic relations*, Cambridge: Cambridge University Press.

Hobsbawm, Eric and Terence Ranger (eds) (1983) *The invention of tradition*, Cambridge: Cambridge University Press.

Hoover, Dwight W. (1990) *Middletown revisited*, Muncie, Indiana: Ball State University.

Humphrey, Caroline (1983) *Karl Marx Collective: economy, society and religion in a Siberian collective farm*, Cambridge/Paris: Cambridge University Press/Editions de la Maison des Sciences de l'Homme.

Isaacs, Harold R. (1975) 'Basic group identity: the idols of the tribe', in Nathan Glazer and Daniel P. Moynihan (eds) *Ethnicity: theory and experience*, Cambridge, Mass.: Harvard University Press.

Izikowitz, Karl G. (1969) 'Neighbours in Laos', in Frederik Barth (ed.) *Ethnic groups and boundaries: the social organisation of culture difference*, Bergen/London: Universitets Forlaget/George Allen and Unwin.

Jackson, Anthony (ed.) (1986) *Anthropology at home*, London: Routledge.

Jackson, P. and S. Smith (eds) (1981) *Social interaction and ethnic segregation*, London: Academic Press.

Jenkins, Richard (1986) 'Social anthropological models of inter-ethnic relations', in John Rex and David Mason (eds) *Theories of race and ethnic relations*, Cambridge: Cambridge University Press.

Jenkins, Richard (1992) *Pierre Bourdieu*, London: Routledge.

Jenkins, Richard (1994) 'Rethinking ethnicity: identity, categorization and power', *Ethnic and racial studies* 17.2: 197–223.

Just, Roger (1989) 'Triumph of the ethnos', in Elizabeth Tonkin, Maryon McDonald and Malcolm Chapman (eds) *History and ethnicity*, London: Routledge.

Kapferer, Bruce (ed.) (1976) *Transaction and meaning: directions in the anthropology of exchange and symbolic behaviour*, Philadelphia: Institute for the Study of Human Issues.

Kapferer, Bruce (1988) *Legends of people, myths of state: violence, intolerance, and political culture in Sri Lanka and Australia*, Washington: Smithsonian Institution Press.

Kedourie, Elie (1960) *Nationalism*, London: Hutchinson.

Kedourie, Elie (ed.) (1970) *Nationalism in Asia and Africa*, London: Weidenfeld and Nicolson.

Keyes, Charles (1976) 'Towards a new formulation of the concept of ethnic group', *Ethnicity* 3.3: 202–13.

Kilson, Martin (1975) 'Blacks and neo-ethnicity in American political life', in Nathan Glazer and Daniel P. Moynihan (eds) *Ethnicity: theory and experience*, Cambridge, Mass.: Harvard University Press.

Kirkwood, Kenneth, M. A. Herbertson and Alan S. Parkes (eds) (1983) *Biosocial aspects of ethnic minorities: proceedings of a Galton Foundation and Biosocial Society conference held in London 31 March – 2 April 1982*, Cambridge: Galton Foundation.

Kohn, Hans (1944) *The idea of nationalism: a study of its origins and background*, New York: Macmillan.

Kuper, Adam (1983) *Anthropology and anthropologists: the modern British school*, London: Routledge and Kegan Paul.

Lal, Barbara Ballis (1990) *The romance of culture in an urban civilization. Robert E. Park on race and ethnic relations in cities*, London: Routledge.

Larsen, Sidsel Saugestad (1982a) 'The two sides of the house: identity and social organisation in Kilbrony, Northern Ireland', in Anthony P. Cohen (ed.) *Belonging: identity and social organization in British rural cultures*, Manchester: Manchester University Press.

Larsen, Sidsel Saugestad (1982b) 'The Glorious Twelfth: the politics of legitimation in Kilbrony', in Anthony P. Cohen (ed.) *Belonging: identity and social organization in British rural cultures*, Manchester: Manchester University Press.

Leach, Edmund R. (1976) *Culture and communication. The logic by which symbols are connected. An introduction to the use of structuralist analysis in social anthropology*, Cambridge: Cambridge University Press.

Leary, James P. and Richard Marsh (1991) 'Dutchman bands: genre, ethnicity, and pluralism in the Upper Midwest', in Stephen Stern and John Allan Cicala (eds) *Creative ethnicity: symbols and strategies of contemporary ethnic life*, Logan, Utah: Utah State University Press.

Lee, Reba (1956) *I passed for white (as told to Mary Hastings Bradley)*, London: Peter Davies.

Lewis, Oscar (1964) *The children of Sanchez: autobiography of a Mexican family*, London: Penguin.

Lieberson, Stanley (1985a) 'Stereotypes: their consequences for race and ethnic interaction', in C. Marrett and C. Leggon (eds) *Research in race and ethnic relations: a research annual (Volume 4)*, Greenwich, CT: JAI Press.

Lieberson, Stanley (1985b) 'Unhyphenated whites in the United States', in Richard D. Alba (ed.) *Ethnicity and race in the U.S.A.: toward the twenty-first century*, London: Routledge and Kegan Paul.

Liebow, Elliot (1967) *Tally's corner: a study of negro street-corner men*, Boston, Mass.: Little, Brown and Company.

Little, Kenneth (1947) *Negroes in Britain: a study of racial relations in English society*, London: Kegan Paul, Trench, Trubner and Co.

Little, Kenneth (1965) *West African urbanization: a study of voluntary associations in social change*, Cambridge: Cambridge University Press.

Little, Kenneth (1973) *African women in towns: an aspect of Africa's social revolution*, Cambridge: Cambridge University Press.

Little, Kenneth (1974) *Urbanization as a social process. An essay on movement and change in contemporary Africa*, London: Routledge and Kegan Paul.

Lodge, Olive (1941) *Peasant life in Jugoslavia*, London: Seeley, Service and Co.

Lynd, Robert S. and Helen M. Lynd (1929) *Middletown: a study in American culture*, New York: Harcourt, Brace.

MacClancy, Jeremy (1993) 'Biological Basques, sociologically speaking', in Malcolm Chapman (ed.) *Social and biological aspects of ethnicity*, Oxford: Oxford University Press for the Biosocial Society.

McDonald, Maryon (1989) *'We are not French!' Language, culture and identity in Brittany*, London: Routledge.

McDonald, Maryon (1993) 'The construction of difference: an anthropological approach to stereotypes', in Sharon Macdonald (ed.) *Inside European identities: ethnography in Western Europe*, Providence/Oxford: Berg.

Macdonald, Sharon (ed.) (1993a) *Inside European identities: ethnography in Western Europe*, Providence/Oxford: Berg.

Macdonald, Sharon (1993b) 'Identity complexes in Western Europe: social anthropological perspectives', in Sharon Macdonald (ed.) *Inside European identities: ethnography in Western Europe*, Providence/Oxford: Berg.

McFarlane, Graham (1986) '"It's not as simple as that": the expression of the Catholic and Protestant boundary in Northern Irish rural communities', in Anthony P. Cohen (ed.) *Symbolising boundaries: identity and diversity in British cultures*, Manchester: Manchester University Press.

McKechnie, Rosemary (1993) 'Becoming Celtic in Corsica', in Sharon Macdonald (ed.) *Inside European identities: ethnography in Western Europe*, Providence/Oxford: Berg.

Marable, Manning (1994) 'Beyond racial identity politics: towards a liberation theory for multicultural democracy', *Race and class* 35: 113–30.

Mayer, Philip (1971) *Townsmen or tribesmen: conservatism and the process of urbanization in a South African city*, Cape Town: Oxford University Press.

Meeker, Michael (1980) 'The twilight of a South Asian heroic age', *Man* 15.4: 682–701.

Mewett, Peter (1986) 'Boundaries and discourse in a Lewis crofting community', in Anthony P. Cohen (ed.) *Symbolising boundaries: identity and diversity in British cultures*, Manchester: Manchester University Press.

Miles, Robert (1982) *Racism and migrant labour*, London: Routledge and Kegan Paul.

Miles, Robert (1989) *Racism*, London: Routledge.

Miles, Robert (1993) *Racism after 'race relations'*, London: Routledge.

Mitchell, J. Clyde (1956) *The Kalela dance: aspects of social relationships among urban Africans in Northern Rhodesia*, Manchester: Manchester University Press for the Rhodes-Livingstone Institute.

Mitchell, J. Clyde (ed.) (1969) *Social networks in urban situations: analysis of personal relationships in Central African towns*, Manchester: Manchester University Press for the Institute of Social Research, University of Zambia.

Mitchell, J. Clyde (1974) 'Perceptions of ethnicity and ethnic behaviour: an empirical exploration', in Abner Cohen (ed.) *Urban ethnicity*, London: Tavistock Publications.

Mitchell, J. Clyde (ed.) (1980) *Numerical techniques in social anthropology*, Philadelphia: Institute for the Study of Human Issues.

Moerman, Michael (1974 [1968]) 'Accomplishing ethnicity', in Roy Turner (ed.) *Ethnomethodology*, Harmondsworth: Penguin.

Morgan, Lewis Henry (1851) *League of the Ho-de-no-sau-nee, or Iroquois*, Rochester, NY: Sage and Bros.

Morris, H. Stephen (1968) *The Indians in Uganda*, London: Weidenfeld and Nicolson.

Nagata, Judith (1974) 'What is a Malay? Situational selection of ethnic identity in a plural society', *American ethnologist* 1.2: 331–50.

Nairn, Tom (1977) *The break-up of Britain: crisis and neo-nationalism*, London: New Left Books.

Naylor, Fred (1989) *Dewsbury: the school above the pub. A case-study in multicultural education*, London: The Claridge Press in association with The Educational Research Trust.

Needham, Rodney (1971) 'Introduction', in Rodney Needham (ed.) *Rethinking kinship and marriage*, London: Tavistock.

Obeyasekere, Gananath (1975) 'Sinhalese Buddhist identity in Ceylon', in

George De Vos and Lola Romanucci-Ros (eds) *Ethnic identity*, Palo Alto, CA: Mayfield.

Okamura, Jonathan (1981) 'Situational ethnicity', *Ethnic and racial studies* 4: 452–63.

Ortner, Sherry B. (1984) 'Theory in anthropology since the sixties', *Comparative studies in society and history* 26.1: 126–66.

Park, Robert (1950) *Race and culture*, Glencoe, IL: The Free Press.

Park, Robert, Ernest Burgess and Roderick McKenzie (1967 [1925]) *The city*, Chicago: University of Chicago Press.

Parsons, Talcott (1975) 'Some theoretical considerations on the nature and trends of change of ethnicity', in Nathan Glazer and Daniel P. Moynihan (eds) *Ethnicity: theory and experience*, Cambridge, Mass.: Harvard University Press.

Patterson, Sheila (1963) *Dark strangers: a study of West Indians in London*, London: Tavistock.

Patterson, Sheila (1977) 'The Poles: an exile community in Britain', in James Watson (ed.) *Between two cultures*, Oxford: Basil Blackwell.

Peach, Ceri, Vaughan Robinson and S. Smith (eds) (1981) *Ethnic segregation in cities*, London: Croom Helm.

Pehrson, R. (1966) *The social organization of the Marri Baluch (compiled and analysed from his notes by Frederik Barth)*, Chicago/New York: Wenner-Gren Foundation for Anthropological Research, Inc.

Petersen, William, Michael Novak and Philip Gleason (1980) 'Concepts of ethnicity', in William Petersen, Michael Novak and Philip Gleason (eds) *Concepts of ethnicity*, Cambridge, Mass.: Belknap Press, Harvard University Press.

Phizacklea, Annie (1988) 'Entrepreneurship, ethnicity, and gender', in Sallie Westwood and Parminder Bhachu (eds) *Enterprising women: ethnicity, economy, and gender relations*, London: Routledge.

Pottier, Johan (1994) Letter: 'Genocide in Rwanda', *Anthropology today* 10.4: 28.

Powdermaker, Hortense (1993 [1939]) *After freedom: a cultural study in the deep South* [with a new introduction by Brackette F. Williams and Drexel G. Woodson], Madison: University of Wisconsin Press.

Reed, Ishmael, Shawn Wong, Bob Callahan and Andrew Hope (1989) '"Is ethnicity obsolete?"', in Werner Sollors (ed.) *The invention of ethnicity*, New York: Oxford University Press.

Reeves, Frank (1983) *British racial discourse: a study of British political discourse about race and race-related matters*, Cambridge: Cambridge University Press.

Rex, John (1970) *Race relations in sociological theory*, London: Weidenfeld and Nicolson.

Rex, John (1986) *Race and ethnicity*, Milton Keynes: Open University Press.

Rex, John and David Mason (eds) (1986) *Theories of race and ethnic relations*, Cambridge: Cambridge University Press.

Richmond, Anthony H. (1954) *Colour prejudice in Britain*, London: Routledge and Kegan Paul.

Said, Edward W. (1985 [1978]) *Orientalism*, Harmondsworth: Peregrine.

Sanjek, Roger (1971) 'Brazilian racial terms: some aspects of meaning and learning', *American anthropologist* 73: 1126–44.

Shanin, Teodir (1989) 'Ethnicity in the Soviet Union: analytical perceptions and political strategies', *Comparative studies in society and history* 31.3: 409–24.

Shaw, Alison (1988) *A Pakistani community in Britain*, Oxford: Basil Blackwell.

Sheehy, Ann and Bohdan Nahaylo (1980) *The Crimean Tatars, Volga Germans and Meskhetians: Soviet treatment of some national minorities* [Third Edition], London: Minority Rights Group.

Siverts, Henning (1969) 'Ethnic stability and boundary dynamics in Southern Mexico', in Frederik Barth (ed.) *Ethnic groups and boundaries: the social organisation of culture difference*, Bergen/London: Universitets Forlaget/George Allen and Unwin.

Smith, Anthony D. (1981) *The ethnic revival*, Cambridge: Cambridge University Press.

Smith, Anthony D. (1986) *The ethnic origins of nations*, Oxford: Basil Blackwell.

Smith, M. G. (1986) 'Pluralism, race and ethnicity in selected African countries', in John Rex and David Mason (eds) *Theories of race and ethnic relations*, Cambridge: Cambridge University Press.

Smith, Raymond T. (1963) 'Culture and social structure in the Caribbean: some recent work on family and kinship studies', *Comparative studies in society and history* 6: 24–45.

Sollors, Werner (ed.) (1989a) *The invention of ethnicity*, New York: Oxford University Press.

Sollors, Werner (1989b) 'Introduction: the invention of ethnicity', in Werner Sollors (ed.) *The invention of ethnicity*, New York: Oxford University Press.

Steinberg, Stephen (1981) *The ethnic myth: race, ethnicity, and class in America*, New York: Atheneum.

Stern, Stephen and John Allan Cicala (eds) (1991a) *Creative ethnicity: symbols and strategies of contemporary ethnic life*, Logan, Utah: Utah State University Press.

Stern, Stephen and John Allan Cicala (1991b) 'Preface', in Stephen Stern and John Allan Cicala (eds) *Creative ethnicity: symbols and strategies of contemporary ethnic life*, Logan, Utah: Utah State University Press.

Stocking, George W. (1968) *Race, culture, and evolution: essays in the history of anthropology*, New York: Free Press.

Street, Brian (1975) *The savage in literature: representations of 'primitive' society in English fiction 1858–1920*, London: Routledge and Kegan Paul.

Szynkiewicz, Slawoj (1990) 'Mythologized representations in Soviet thinking on the nationalities problem', *Anthropology today* 6.2: 2–5.

Tambs-Lyche, Harald (1980) *London Patidars: a case study in urban ethnicity*, London: Routledge and Kegan Paul.

Thomas, William I. and Florian Znaniecki (1984 [1918–1922]) *The Polish peasant in Europe and America*, Urbana: University of Chicago Press.

Turton, David (1994) 'Mursi political identity and warfare: the survival of an idea', in Katsuyoshi Fukui and John Markakis (eds) *Ethnicity and conflict in the Horn of Africa*, London/Athens, Ohio: James Currey/Ohio University Press.

van den Berghe, Pierre (1981) *The ethnic phenomenon*, New York: Elsevier Press.

van den Berghe, Pierre (1986) 'Ethnicity and the sociobiology debate', in John Rex and David Mason (eds) *Theories of race and ethnic relations*, Cambridge: Cambridge University Press.

van der Veer, Peter (1994) *Religious nationalism: Hindus and Muslims in India*, Berkeley: University of California Press.

Van Teeffelen, T. (1978) 'The Manchester School in Africa and Israel: a critique', *Dialectical anthropology* 3: 67–83.

Vasiljeva, E., V. Pimenov and L. Khristoljubova (1974) 'Contemporary ethno-cultural processes in Udmurtia (program and method of investigation)', in Yulian Bromley (ed.) *Soviet ethnology and anthropology today*, The Hague: Mouton.

Volkman, Toby Alice (1984) 'Great performances: Toraja cultural identity in the 1970s', *American ethnologist* 11.1: 152–69.

Vulliamy, Ed (1994) *Seasons in hell: understanding Bosnia's war*, London: Simon and Schuster.

Wade, Peter (1993) *Blackness and race mixture: the dynamics of racial identity in Colombia*, Baltimore: Johns Hopkins University Press.

Wallman, Sandra (1978) 'The boundaries of race: processes of ethnicity in England', *Man* 13.2: 200–17.

Wallman, Sandra (1979) 'Introduction: the scope for ethnicity', in Sandra Wallman (ed.) *Ethnicity at work*, London: Macmillan.

Wallman, Sandra (1986) 'Ethnicity and the boundary process in context', in John Rex and David Mason (eds) *Theories of race and ethnic relations*, Cambridge: Cambridge University Press.

Ward, Robin and Richard Jenkins (eds) (1984) *Ethnic communities in business: strategies for economic survival*, Cambridge: Cambridge University Press.

Warner, W. Lloyd (1936) 'American caste and class', *American journal of sociology* 42: 234–7.

Warner, W. Lloyd and Paul S. Lunt (1942) *The status system of a modern community*, New Haven: Yale University Press.

Warner, W. Lloyd and Leo Srole (1945) *The social systems of American ethnic groups*, New Haven: Yale University Press.

Waters, M. C. (1990) *Ethnic options: choosing identities in America*, Berkeley: University of California Press.

Watson, James (1975) *Emigration and the Chinese lineage: the Mans in Hong Kong and London*, Berkeley: University of California Press.

Watson, James (ed.) (1977a) *Between two cultures*, Oxford: Basil Blackwell.

Watson, James (1977b) 'Introduction: immigration, ethnicity, and class in Britain', in James Watson (ed.) *Between two cultures*, Oxford: Basil Blackwell.

Watson, James (1977c) 'The Chinese: Hong Kong villagers in the British catering trade', in James Watson (ed.) *Between two cultures*, Oxford: Basil Blackwell.

Werbner, Pnina (1988) 'Taking and giving: working women and female bonds in a Pakistani immigrant neighbourhood', in Sallie Westwood and Parminder Bhachu (eds) *Enterprising women: ethnicity, economy, and gender relations*, London: Routledge.

Werbner, Pnina (1990) *The migration process: capital, gifts and offerings among British Pakistanis*, New York and Oxford: Berg.

Werbner, Pnina (forthcoming) 'Fun spaces: on identity and social empowerment among British Muslims', in Jeremy MacClancy (ed.) *Sport and identity: comparative perspectives*, Providence and Oxford: Berg.

Werbner, Pnina and Muhammad Anwar (eds) (1991) *Black and ethnic leaderships in Britain: the cultural dimensions of political action*, London: Routledge.

Werbner, Richard P. (1984) 'The Manchester School in South-Central Africa', in Bernard Siegal, Alan Beals and Stephen Tyler (eds) *Annual review of anthropology 13*, Palo Alto: Annual Reviews Inc.

Westwood, Sallie (1988) 'Workers and wives: discontinuities in the lives of Gujarati women', in Sallie Westwood and Parminder Bhachu (eds) *Enterprising women: ethnicity, economy, and gender relations*, London: Routledge.

Westwood, Sallie and Parminder Bhachu (eds) (1988a) *Enterprising women: ethnicity, economy, and gender relations*, London: Routledge.

Westwood, Sallie and Parminder Bhachu (1988b) 'Introduction', in Sallie Westwood and Parminder Bhachu (eds) *Enterprising women: ethnicity, economy, and gender relations*, London: Routledge.

Wetherell, Margaret and Jonathan Potter (1992) *Mapping the language of racism: discourse and the legitimation of exploitation*, New York/London: Harvester Wheatsheaf.

Whyte, William Foote (1981 [1943]) *Street corner society: the social structure of an Italian slum*, Chicago: University of Chicago Press.

Williams, Brackette F. (1989) 'A class act: anthropology and the race to nation across ethnic terrain', in Bernard Siegal, Alan Beals and Stephen Tyler (eds) *Annual review of anthropology 18*, Palo Alto: Annual Reviews Inc.

Williams, Robin M. *et al.* (1964) *Strangers next door: ethnic relations in American communities*, Englewood Cliffs, New Jersey: Prentice-Hall, Inc.

Wilson, Richard (1945) 'Introduction' to St Clair Drake and Horace R. Cayton *Black Metropolis: a study of Negro life in a northern city*, New York: Harcourt, Brace and Company.

Wilson, William Julius (1978) *The declining significance of race: blacks and changing American institutions*, Chicago: University of Chicago Press.

Winters, Christopher (ed.) (1991) *International dictionary of anthropologists*, New York: Garland Publishing.

Yelvington, Kevin A. (1991) 'Ethnicity as practice? A comment on Bentley', *Comparative studies in society and history* 33.1: 158–68.

Yinger, J. Milton (1986) 'Intersecting strands in the theorisation of race and ethnic relations', in John Rex and David Mason (eds) *Theories of race and ethnic relations*, Cambridge: Cambridge University Press.

Zaretsky, Eli (1984) 'Editor's introduction' to William I. Thomas and Florian Znaniecki *The Polish peasant in Europe and America*, Urbana: University of Chicago Press.

Zenner, Walter P. (1985) 'Jewishness in America: ascription and choice', in Richard D. Alba (ed.) *Ethnicity and race in the U.S.A.: toward the twenty-first century*, London: Routledge and Kegan Paul.

Index

DATE DUE